Computational Methods in Economic Dynamics

For other titles published in this series, go to
www.springer.com/series/5859

Dynamic Modeling and Econometrics in Economics and Finance

Volume 13

Aims and Scope

The series will place particular focus on monographs, surveys, edited volumes, conference proceedings and handbooks on:

- Nonlinear dynamic phenomena in economics and finance, including equilibrium, disequilibrium, optimizing and adaptive evolutionary points of view; nonlinear and complex dynamics in microeconomics, finance, macroeconomics and applied fields of economics.
- Econometric and statistical methods for analysis of nonlinear processes in economics and finance, including computational methods, numerical tools and software to study nonlinear dependence, asymmetries, persistence of fluctuations, multiple equilibria, chaotic and bifurcation phenomena.
- Applications linking theory and empirical analysis in areas such as macrodynamics, microdynamics, asset pricing, financial analysis and portfolio analysis, international economics, resource dynamics and environment, industrial organization and dynamics of technical change, labor economics, demographics, population dynamics, and game theory.

The target audience of this series includes researchers at universities and research and policy institutions, students at graduate institutions, and practitioners in economics, finance and international economics in private or government institutions.

Computational Methods in Economic Dynamics

by editors

Herbert Dawid

University of Bielefeld, Germany

and

Willi Semmler

New School for Social Research, USA

Springer

Editors
Professor Herbert Dawid
Department of Economics
and Business Administration
University of Bielefeld
Universitätsstr. 25
33501 Bielefeld
Germany
hdawid@wiwi.uni-bielefeld.de

Professor Willi Semmler
Department of Economics
New School for Social Research
79 Fifth Ave.
New York, NY 10003
USA
semmlerw@newschool.edu

ISSN 1566-0419
ISBN 978-3-642-16942-7 e-ISBN 978-3-642-16943-4
DOI 10.1007/978-3-642-16943-4
Springer Heidelberg Dordrecht London New York

Library of Congress Control Number: 2011923539

Cover design: eStudio Calamar S.L.

Printed on acid-free paper

Springer is part of Springer Science+Business Media (www.springer.com)

Contents

Contributors

Bolanle Abudu Centre for Computational Finance and Economic Agents, University of Essex, Colchester, UK

Herbert Dawid Department of Business Administration and Economics and Institute of Mathematical Economics, Bielefeld University, Universitätsstraße 25, 33615 Bielefeld, Germany, hdawid@wiwi.uni-bielefeld.de

Christophe Deissenberg GREQAM, Universitée de la Méditerranée II, Château Lafarge, Route des Milles, 13290 Les Milles, France, christophe.deissenberg@univmed.fr

Xue-Zhong He School of Finance and Economics, University of Technology, Sydney, Australia, Tony.He1@uts.edu.au

Philipp Hungerländer Department of Economics, Klagenfurt University, Universitaetsstrasse 65-67, 9020 Klagenfurt, Austria, philipp.hungerlaender@uni-klu.ac.at

Hongyan Li ABB Inc., Raleigh, NC, USA, lihy@iastate.edu

Marco LiCalzi Dept. of Applied Mathematics and Advanced School of Economics, University of Venice, Dorsoduro 3825/E, 30123 Venice, Italy, licalzi@unive.it

Luca Marchiori CREA, Université du Luxembourg, Luxembourg City, Luxembourg, luca.marchiori@uni.lu

Serafín Martínez Dirección General de Análisis del Sistema Financiero, Banco de México, Mexico City, Mexico

Stan Miles Department of Economics, School of Business and Economics, Thompson Rivers University, 900 McGill Road, P.O. Box 3010, Kamloops, BC, Canada V2C 5N3, stanmiles@tru.ca

Lucia Milone Dept. of Applied Mathematics and Advanced School of Economics, University of Venice, Dorsoduro 3825/E, 30123 Venice, Italy, lucia.milone@unive.it

Timothy D. Mount Department of Applied Economics and Management, Cornell University, 215 Warren Hall, Ithaca, NY 14853-7801, USA, TDM2@cornell.edu

Reinhard Neck Department of Economics, Klagenfurt University, Universitaetsstrasse 65-67, 9020 Klagenfurt, Austria, reinhard.neck@uni-klu.ac.at

Hyungna Oh Department of Economics, West Virginia University, 411 B&E, Morgantown, WV 26506, USA, Hyungna.Oh@mail.wvu.edu

Tonatiuh Peña Dirección General de Investigación Económica, Banco de México, Mexico City, Mexico, tpena@banxico.org.mx

Paolo Pellizzari Dept. of Applied Mathematics and Advanced School of Economics, University of Venice, Dorsoduro 3825/E, 30123 Venice, Italy, paolop@unive.it

Patrice Pieretti CREA, Université du Luxembourg, Luxembourg City, Luxembourg, patrice.pieretti@uni.lu

Willi Semmler Department of Economics, New School for Social Research, 79 Fifth Ave., New York, NY 10003, USA, semmlerw@newschool.edu

Lei Shi School of Finance and Economics, University of Technology, Sydney, Australia, Lei.Shi@uts.edu.au

Barry Smith Department of Economics, York University, Toronto, Canada, jbsmith@yorku.ca

Junjie Sun Office of the Comptroller of the Currency, U.S. Treasury, Washington, DC 20219, USA, junjie.sun@occ.treas.gov

Leigh Tesfatsion Economics Department, Iowa State University, Ames, IA 50011-1070, USA, tesfatsi@iastate.edu

Sander van der Hoog Dept. of Business Administration and Economics, Bielefeld University, Universitätsstrasse 25, 33615 Bielefeld, Germany, svdhoog@gmail.com

Benteng Zou CREA, Université du Luxembourg, Luxembourg City, Luxembourg, benteng.zou@uni.lu

Editorial: Computational Methods in Economic Dynamics

Herbert Dawid and Willi Semmler

This book contains selected papers presented at the 14th International conference on Computing in Economics and Finance (CEF 2008), organized by the Society of Computational Economics as well as some additional invited papers. A main topic in this volume is the issue of market design and resulting market dynamics. The economic crisis of 2007–2009 has once again highlighted the importance of a proper design of market protocols and institutional details for economic dynamics and macroeconomics. In particular, it became clear that the failure of many traditional models to capture behavioral details of agents' decision making, contagion effects, spillovers between markets and effects to the macroeconomy made it difficult to understand the mechanisms driving the economic meltdown. Also apart from the treatment of economic crises it has been recognized in several important areas of economic policy, like regulation of energy markets, that a proper study of implications of different institutional setups is crucial for an understanding of the evolution of markets as well as policy effects.

Most of the articles in this volume build on the representation of the heterogeneity of economic agents with respect to behavior and expectations and stress the interconnectedness of the decisions and actions of the different agents in the market. Furthermore, explicit representation of interaction protocols plays an important role. As is demonstrated in several papers of this volume the interplay of agents' behavior and interaction protocols gives rise to emergent properties on the market level that often would not be anticipated based on the consideration of the single parts of the model. Agent-based simulation techniques have become an important tool to provide insights into such kind of emergent properties. On the one hand, computational methods are used to replicate and understand market dynamics emerging from interaction of heterogeneous agents, on the other hand, computational intelligence provides useful tools to develop models that have predictive power for complex market

H. Dawid (✉)
Department of Business Administration and Economics and Institute of Mathematical Economics, Bielefeld University, Universitätsstraße 25, 33615 Bielefeld, Germany
e-mail: hdawid@wiwi.uni-bielefeld.de

H. Dawid, W. Semmler (eds.), *Computational Methods in Economic Dynamics*,
Dynamic Modeling and Econometrics in Economics and Finance 13,
DOI 10.1007/978-3-642-16943-4_1,

dynamics. Whereas the papers by LiCalzi et al., Oh & Mount, He & Shi, Li et al. and van der Hoog and Deissenberg in this volume belong to the first of these categories, the papers by Miles & Smith and Pena et al. contribute to the second stream of literature. Also in the framework of intertemporally optimizing, rather than boundedly rational, individuals the explicit consideration of agents' heterogeneity is important for the evaluation of dynamic effects of policy measures. Again, computational techniques are demonstrated to be crucial to expand the tractability and applicability of such models. The papers by Marchiori et al. and Hungerländer & Neck provide examples in this respect by considering overlapping generations models and differential games with heterogeneous actors.

Overall, the work in this volume gives strong evidence of the advancement of research in the area of computational economics and highlights the potential of this approach for a proper understanding of economic dynamics and related policy issues.

Part I
Market Dynamics with Heterogeneous Agents

Allocative Efficiency and Traders' Protection Under Zero Intelligence Behavior

Marco LiCalzi, Lucia Milone, and Paolo Pellizzari

Abstract This paper studies the continuous double auction from the point of view of market engineering: we tweak a resampling rule often used for this exchange protocol and search for an improved design. We assume zero intelligence trading as a lower bound for more robust behavioral rules and look at allocative efficiency, as well as three subordinate performance criteria: mean spread, cancellation rate, and traders' protection. This latter notion measures the ability of a protocol to help traders capture their share of the competitive equilibrium profits.

We consider two families of resampling rules and obtain the following results. Full resampling is not necessary to attain high allocative efficiency, but fine-tuning the resampling rate is important. The best allocative performances are similar across the two families. However, if the market designer adds any of the other three criteria as a subordinate goal, then a resampling rule based on a price band around the best quotes is superior.

1 Introduction

In a seminal paper, Gode and Sunder (1993a) define a *zero intelligence* (ZI) trader as an agent that "has no intelligence, does not seek or maximize profits, and does not observe, remember or learn." (p. 121) Such zero intelligence assumption is not meant to provide a descriptive model of individual behavior: on the contrary, it is used to instantiate severe cognitive limitations that should impede the overall performance of the market.

A ZI agent is usually modeled as a robot player that submits random offers in an exchange market, under a minimal assumption of *individual rationality*: he never takes actions that can lead him to trade at prices below his cost or above his valuation. To the best of our knowledge, the first (unnamed) use of individually rational zero intelligence behavior in economic theory goes back to the B-process studied in Hurwicz et al. (1975); they prove that, if the market protocol allows unlimited

M. LiCalzi (✉)
Dept. of Applied Mathematics and Advanced School of Economics, University of Venice, Dorsoduro 3825/E, 30123 Venice, Italy
e-mail: licalzi@unive.it

H. Dawid, W. Semmler (eds.), *Computational Methods in Economic Dynamics*, Dynamic Modeling and Econometrics in Economics and Finance 13,
DOI 10.1007/978-3-642-16943-4_2, © Springer-Verlag Berlin Heidelberg 2011

retrading, an economy without externalities must converge to a Pareto optimal allocation. Throughout this paper, we take the postulate of individual rationality for granted and speak simply of zero intelligence behavior.

By simulating the actions of (individually rational) ZI traders in a continuous double auction, Gode and Sunder (1993a) achieved levels of allocative efficiency similar to the outcomes generated by human subjects in laboratory experiments. This was used to argue that the main feature leading to a high allocative efficiency is the market protocol rather than the trading strategies used by the agents. More boldly put, the market can substitute for the cognitive limitations of the individuals. This conclusion has spawned a large literature venturing in different directions, including experimental economics and computer science; see Duffy (2006) for a thorough survey.

In general, it is widely acknowledged that the interpretation of Gode and Sunder's results is controversial. Gjerstad and Shachat (2007) emphasize the role of individual rationality as the key crucial assumption for allocative efficiency. A recurrent theme is the robustness of Gode and Sunder's conclusion: it is not difficult to produce environments where the allocative efficiency reached by ZI agents badly underperforms humans' results; see e.g. Brewer et al. (2002). On the other hand, the literature has shown that even minor improvements to the basic ZI trading rules suffice to achieve convergence to the competitive equilibrium; see Cliff and Bruten (1997) or Crockett et al. (2008).

Clearly, humans' cognitive abilities provide more leverage than zero intelligence. Therefore, we do not expect that the performance of a market protocol in an environment populated with ZI agents would be the same as with human traders. On the other hand, it is not unreasonable to postulate that the performance of a market protocol under a ZI behavioral assumption provides a plausible benchmark for its evaluation in view of use by human subjects. In his recent discussion of the "market-centered theory of computational economics", Mirowski (2007) attributes to the zero intelligence literature the computational insight that human cognitive abilities can be ignored under controlled circumstances to focus on the causal capacities of the market protocols. In a similar vein, Sunder (2004, p. 521) states that "[w]hen seen as human artifacts, a science of markets need not be built from the science of individual behavior." The implicit claim is that we may learn about the properties of markets regardless of the agents operating in them.

Our viewpoint is the following. Market protocols are complex artifacts; see Subrahmanian and Talukdar (2004). Their design requires a special attention to details and minutiæ that partakes of the engineering attitude advocated in Roth (2002): we need to complement theory with experiments and computational simulations. In order to make fine-grained comparisons among different protocols, it is necessary to pin down agents' behavior to a simple standard. The ZI assumption provides a rough simplification under which it is possible to evaluate markets protocols *in silico* in order to select more promising designs.

The purpose of this paper is to exemplify this approach with regard to the continuous double auction. We replicate the results produced in Gode and Sunder (1993a) and show that they depend crucially on a subtle assumption about the market protocol that has gone unnoticed in the literature. They write: "There are several variations of the double auction. We made three choices to simplify our implementation of the double auction. Each bid, ask, and transaction was valid for a single unit. *A transaction canceled any unaccepted bids and offers*. Finally, when a bid and a ask crossed, the transaction price was equal to the earlier of the two." (p. 122, emphasis added). As discussed below, the second emphasized assumption forces a frequent resampling of agents' quotes that is crucial (under zero intelligence) for allocative efficiency. We call this assumption *full resampling*: speaking figuratively, it mandates to toss away the book after each transaction. This seems both unrealistic and unpalatable for practical market design.

We are thus left to ask whether Gode and Sunder's implementation of the continuous double auction is a promising design. Taking the viewpoint of a market designer who is interested in allocative efficiency, we evaluate alternative market protocols that enforce different degrees of resampling. As it turns out, the assumption of full resampling is not necessary to achieve very high allocative efficiency under zero intelligence. There is a continuum of protocols, ordered by the strength of their resampling properties, that attain comparable levels of efficiency. This makes it possible to search for more effective protocols than Gode and Sunder's (1993a) without renouncing the objective of allocative efficiency.

To refine our selection, we introduce a subordinate criterion. While allocative efficiency is desirable from an aggregate point of view, a single trader in an exchange market is likely to be more interested in getting a fair deal. Let the *competitive share* of a trader be the profit he would make by transacting at the (competitive) equilibrium price. A market protocol that is more effective in helping traders realize their competitive share offers a superior *traders' protection*. Therefore, we study the traders' protection offered by comparably efficient market protocols to devise a practical and simple implementation of the continuous double auction.

We study two families of resampling rules and identify a design that delivers a significant improvement over Gode and Sunder's (1993a). However, barring an experimental validation with human subjects, we can only claim that the lower bounds on its performance with regard to both allocative efficiency and traders' protection are higher under zero intelligence.

The organization of the paper is the following. Section 2 describes the model used in our computational experiments and clarifies some technical details in the implementation of Gode and Sunder's (1993a) continuous double auction. The zero intelligence assumption is maintained throughout the paper. Section 3 proves that some (possibly not full) resampling is a necessary condition for allocative efficiency in the continuous double auction; see also LiCalzi and Pellizzari (2008). Section 4 shows that partial resampling may be sufficient for allocative efficiency. Based on this result, we study a family of resampling rules for the implementation of the continuous double auction protocol that modulates the probability of clearing the book after a transaction. Several rules within this family attain comparable levels of allocative efficiencies. Section 5 introduces an alternative way to effect resampling that is based on the use of a price band. Section 6 compares the alternatives and argues that the second method delivers a better protocol. Section 7 recapitulates our conclusions.

2 The Model

We use a setup very similar[1] to Gode and Sunder (1993a), who consider a simple exchange economy. Following Smith (1982), we identify three distinct components for our (simulated) exchange markets. The environment in Sect. 2.1 describes the general characteristics of our simulated economy, including agents' preferences and endowments. Section 2.2 specifies how agents make decisions and take actions under the zero intelligence assumption. This behavioral rule is kept fixed throughout this paper to let us concentrate on the effects of tweaking the market design. Finally, Sect. 2.3 gives a detailed description of the institutional details that form the protocol of a continuous double auction (and its variants) which regulate the exchange.

2.1 The Environment

There is an economy with a number n of traders, who can exchange single units of a generic good. (We set $n = 40, 200, 1000$ to look at size effects.) Each agent is initialized to be a seller or a buyer with equal probability. Each seller i is endowed with one unit of the good for which he has a private cost c_i that is independently drawn from the uniform distribution on [0, 1]. Each buyer j holds no units and has a private valuation v_j for one unit of the good that is independently drawn from the uniform distribution on [0, 1]. Without loss of generality, prices are assumed to lie in [0, 1].

2.2 Zero Intelligence Behavior

Zero intelligence reduces behavior to a very simple rule: when requested a quote for an order, a trader draws a price from a random distribution (usually taken to be uniform). We assume that traders' behavior abides by *individual rationality*: each seller i is willing to sell his unit at a price $p \geq c_i$ and each buyer j is willing to buy one unit at a price $p \leq v_j$. Therefore, throughout this paper, the zero intelligence assumption pins down behavior as follows: when requested a quote for an order, a seller i provides an ask price that is an independent draw from the uniform distribution on $[c_i, 1]$; similarly, a buyer j makes a bid that is an independent draw from the uniform distribution on $[0, v_j]$. This behavioral rule is called ZI-C in Gode and Sunder (1993a).

Note that the only action requested by an agent is to issue a quote: it is left to the market to process traders' quotes and execute transactions on their behalf.

---

[1]There are negligible differences. We consider n agents who can trade at most one unit, while they have 12 traders who can exchange several units but must trade them one by one. Our setup is simpler to describe because it associates with each trader a single unit and a one-dimensional type (his cost/valuation).

This is consistent with an approach of market engineering: we are not interested in the performance of more sophisticated behavioral rules, but rather in the design of protocols that take decent care even of simple-minded agents.

In particular, this paper studies protocols that implement variants of the continuous double auction, where agents sequentially place quotes on the selling and buying books. Orders are immediately executed at the outstanding price if they are marketable; otherwise, they are recorded on the books with the usual price-time priority and remain valid unless a cancellation occurs. When a transaction takes place, the orders are removed from the market and the traders leave the market and become inactive.

The zero intelligence assumption places a second restriction on agents' behavior. In a sequential protocol like the continuous double auction, an agent can choose both his action and the time at which to take it; see Gul and Lundholm (1995). Zero intelligence robs agents of the opportunity to make decisions about the timing at which to issue a quote. Agents are exogenously arranged in a queue and reach the market one at a time, until the queue is exhausted or some exogenous event triggers the formation of a new queue.

The standard implementation is the following. At the beginning of a simulation, all agents are active and placed in the queue. If an agent reaches the market and trades his unit, he becomes inactive for the rest of the simulation. Otherwise, he is in one of two states: either he has an order on the book (because he is active and the queue has already reached him), or he is still queueing for a chance to act. An important detail in the design of an experiment is the set of events that triggers the formation of a new queue, reshuffling the state of active agents. For instance, the full resampling assumption in Gode and Sunder (1993a) makes each transaction a trigger event that sends all traders with an order on the book back to the end of the queue.

2.3 The Protocol

The implementation of the continuous double auction in Gode and Sunder (1993a) is based on several rules. Some of them are not stated explicitly in the paper, but may be gathered by a joint reading of other related papers; see in particular Gode and Sunder (1993b, 2004). For completeness and ease of reference, we collect here all the ingredients we found necessary to replicate their results.

The first three rules correspond to the assumptions cited above. We begin with the first and the third. The *single unit* rule states that all quotes and prices refer to one unit of the good. A standard rule of *precedence* decides the transaction price: when two quotes cross, the price is set by the earlier quote. We maintain both the single unit and the precedence rules, because they entail no loss of generality.

The second of the three assumptions put forth in Gode and Sunder (1993a) as "simplifications" states that the book is cleared after each transaction. By itself, this rule is surprising because tossing away the book at any opportunity seems to run contrary to the obvious purpose of storing past orders and make them available to future traders. In Gode and Sunder's design, moreover, this rule triggers a refreshing of the queue: after each transaction, all recorded orders are deleted and their owners are given a new chance to act. When a ZI agent goes back to the queue and comes up again, he randomly issues a new quote. Hence, the real consequence of tossing away the book is to free up the agents' past quotes and force them to issue novel ones. That is, after each trade, all active agents who have placed an order since the former transaction are resampled. This is the reason for calling their assumption *full resampling*. Section 3 shows that full resampling is crucial for Gode and Sunder's results and hence cannot be dismissed as a mere "simplification". In fact, one of the motivations for this paper is to study the import of this neglected assumption.

There are other rules that need to be made explicit. *No retrading* states that buyers and sellers can never exchange roles: a buyer (seller) who acquires (transfers) a unit is not allowed to sell (buy) it later to other traders. The intuition that, given sufficient retrading, a market populated with ZI agents should reach full allocative efficiency is proven in Hurwicz et al. (1975). Therefore, no retrading is necessary to avoid trivialities. Gode and Sunder (2004) provide further comments on the role and plausibility of this assumption.

The *uniform sequencing* of agents within a simulation arranges them in a queue according to an exogenously given order, which is independently drawn from the uniform distribution over all permutations of agents. As explained in Gode and Sunder (2004), in their simulations the queue of traders is sampled *without replacement*. That is, when the execution of a transaction triggers a refreshing of the queue, the agents who have a quote stored on the book re-enter it behind the traders still waiting in the original queue. The no replacement assumption is a sensible simplification that allows for faster and more efficient coding. However, since this rule violates anonymity, its practical implementation requires either additional information processing (when control is centralized) or some traders' coordination (under decentralization). Therefore, in the interest of simplicity and realism, we maintain the uniform sequencing rule but we switch to sampling with replacement: when an event triggers the formation of a queue, we simply apply uniform sequencing over all active agents.

Finally, the *halting* rule mandates when a trading session is over. In Gode and Sunder (1993a) a trading session is a period of fixed duration that lasts 30 seconds for each computational simulation. Traders are put in a queue and asked to provide a quote. If all the queued agents have issued a quote and no transaction has occurred, the books are cleared and a new queue is started until time is over. Given that robot players are remarkably fast, this implies that an agent is likely to be asked to issue a quote several times. (We have been unable to determine how often queues are restarted in Gode and Sunder (1993a) only because the time limit has not been reached.) Unfortunately, given that hardware (and software) vary in processing power (and efficiency), a halting rule based on a fixed duration is not sufficient to ensure comparable results when simulations are run on different machines. Therefore, we choose a different halting rule that allows for full comparability: a trading session is over when the queue of traders waiting to place an order is exhausted.

An additional advantage of this assumption is that it biases our simulations in the proper direction: *ceteris paribus*, we resample traders less often because our halting rule is more stringent. This makes allocative efficiency harder to attain.

For the reader's convenience, we recap here the rules of the continuous double auction protocol used in all the simulations discussed in this paper. We use single unit trading, set the transaction price by precedence, exclude retrading, and apply uniform sequencing. Differently from Gode and Sunder (1993a), we put traders back in the queue with replacement and use a more restrictive halting rule.

3 The Resampling Assumption

We test the import of the resampling assumption for the allocative efficiency of the continuous double auction (as implemented by our protocol). As usual, we define allocative efficiency as the ratio between the realized gains from the trade and the maximum feasible gains from trade, which can be formally defined as done in Zhan et al. (2002, p. 678). This measure is adimensional, facilitating comparisons throughout the paper.

3.1 Resampling Is Necessary for Allocative Efficiency

We contrast full resampling against no resampling under zero intelligence trading. *Full resampling* mandates that after each transaction the book is cleared and active traders with an order on the book are sent back to the waiting queue. *No resampling* postulates that submitted orders stay on the book until the end of the trading session (unless they are used up for a transaction); e.g. see Maslov (2000).

The difference between full and no resampling is stark. A ZI agent acts only when its turn in the waiting queue comes up. Under no resampling, each agent is given only one chance to act by sending a random quote to the book. Under full resampling, on the other hand, until an agent completes a trade and becomes inactive, any refresh of the waiting queue following a transaction may give him a new chance to act and generate another random quote. Therefore, the number of opportunities for actions is much greater under full resampling, and this should increase allocative efficiency.

The datapoints on the left-hand side of Fig. 1 represent the allocative efficiencies under *full resampling* for 500 different runs with $n = 200$ agents. The data match Gode and Sunder's (1993a) results, confirming that the impact of our (more stringent) halting rule on allocative efficiency is negligible. The right-hand side provides analogous information for the case of *no resampling*. The y-axes use the same scale, so that a direct comparison by visual inspection is immediate: the higher the level, the higher the allocative efficiency.

The difference in performance under full or no resampling is remarkably substantial. The mean (median) allocative efficiency is 0.910 (0.916) with full resampling and 0.497 (0.498) with no resampling. (All statistics reported in this paper

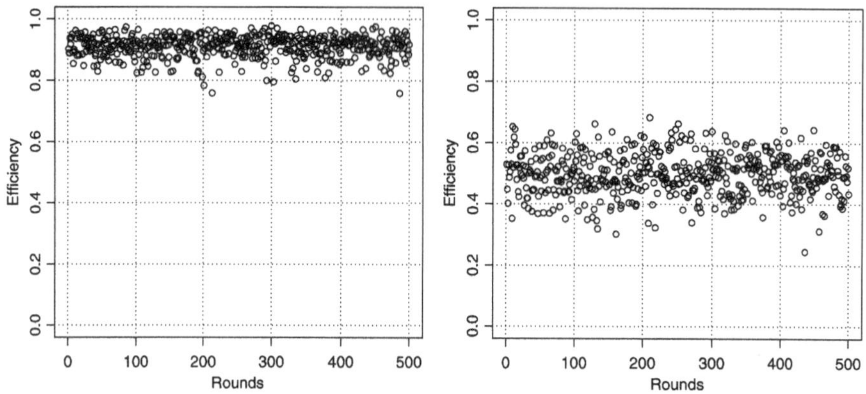

Fig. 1 Allocative efficiency under full (*left*) or no resampling (*right*)

are rounded to the closest third decimal digit.) The min–max range (standard deviation) for the allocative efficiency is $[0.759, 0.978]$ (0.036) with full resampling and $[0.246, 0.684]$ (0.070) with no resampling. Within our sample, the worst allocative efficiency with $n = 200$ agents under full resampling (0.759) is much higher than the best allocative efficiency under no resampling (0.684). Visual inspection strongly suggests that the distribution of the allocative efficiency under full resampling stochastically dominates the distribution under no resampling.[2] More modestly, we claim that the expected value of the allocative efficiency under full resampling is higher. In fact, the Wilcoxon signed-rank test rejects the hypothesis that the means are equal at a level of significance of 10^{-3}. (Throughout the rest of the paper, unless otherwise noted, we use the Wilcoxon signed-rank test to compare means and we require a p-value lower than 10^{-3} to claim statistical significance.)

Similar effects occur for different values of n, but a larger number of agents tends to improve allocative efficiency. Thus, when comparing data for a different number of agents, we should take into account a fixed size effect. We believe that $n = 200$ is a representative case, but for comparability Table 1 lists the main statistics for $n = 200/5 = 40$ and $n = 200 \times 5 = 1000$.

Based on the relative size of the agents' pool, we say that the market is *thin* ($n = 40$), *thick* ($n = 200$), or *crowded* ($n = 1000$). Each column summarizes 500 distinct simulation rounds.

It is apparent that no resampling may be calamitous in a thin market, because an agent who happens to issue a "wrong" quote is given no later chance to remedy. Analogously, a few "lucky" trades may shoot allocative efficiency up. Hence, the dispersion of the allocative efficiency is much higher in a thin market. Such effects are washed out in a crowded market. Overall, an increase in n has a positive effect on allocative efficiency under either resampling assumption. But the effect is sharper under full resampling, because this rule gives traders more chances to trade.

---

[2] LiCalzi and Pellizzari (2008) document a similar effect over four different trading protocols.

Table 1 Summary statistics for the allocative efficiency

	Full resampling			No resampling		
	$n = 40$	$n = 200$	$n = 1000$	$n = 40$	$n = 200$	$n = 1000$
Mean	0.735	0.910	0.949	0.441	0.497	0.517
Median	0.765	0.916	0.951	0.456	0.498	0.518
Minimum	0.053	0.759	0.911	0.000	0.246	0.405
Maximum	1.000	0.978	0.971	0.933	0.684	0.609
Std. dev.	0.169	0.036	0.009	0.157	0.070	0.032

Our experiment shows that, *ceteris paribus*, full resampling yields a much higher allocative efficiency than no resampling. Speaking figuratively, no resampling switches off the ability of a protocol to help ZI agents capture most of the available gains from trade. We conclude that (at least some) resampling is a necessary condition for allocative efficiency. This reduces the scope of Gode and Sunder's (1993a) results about the ability of a market to substitute for agents' lack of rationality: an effective protocol for ZI agents must include rules that ensure an adequate amount of resampling.

On the other hand, our results do not invalidate their claim that it is possible to design markets that may overcome agents' cognitive limitations. To the contrary, they suggest that the use of a (partial) resampling rule may be a particularly clever design choice for fostering allocative efficiency in exchange markets. Section 4 sets out to examine a continuum of alternative rules that enforce different degrees of resampling in this respect. We find that less than full resampling is sufficient to reach high levels of efficiency.

3.2 *Efficiency and Full Resampling*

Before moving to issues of market engineering, there are two hanging questions to address. First: why does full resampling lead to higher allocative efficiency than no resampling? Second: where does the efficiency loss go?

We begin with the second question, whose answer leads naturally to the first one. Gode and Sunder (1997, p. 605) point out that in general there are "three causes of inefficiency: (1) traders participate in unprofitable trades; (2) traders fail to negotiate profitable trades' and (3) extramarginal traders displace intramarginal traders." Since individual rationality rules out the first source of inefficiency, we need being concerned only with the other two. They can be measured; e.g., see Zhan and Friedman (2007) who also provide formal definitions.

Let p^* be the market-clearing price. (There may be an interval of market-clearing prices. We assume that p^* is the midpoint.) Individually rational traders who would transact at p^* are called *intramarginal*; all other traders are *extramarginal*. If at the end of a trading session an intramarginal trader i has failed to trade, this creates a

Table 2 A breakdown of the efficiency loss

	Full resampling			No resampling		
	$n = 40$	$n = 200$	$n = 1000$	$n = 40$	$n = 200$	$n = 1000$
AE	0.735	0.910	0.950	0.441	0.497	0.517
MT	0.241	0.055	0.012	0.548	0.495	0.477
EM	0.025	0.035	0.037	0.011	0.008	0.006

loss of total surplus equal to $v_i - p^*$ if he is a buyer and $p^* - c_i$ if he is a seller. The sum of these losses corresponds to (2) above: we call it *MT*, as a mnemonic for the inefficiency caused by *missed trades*. The third case comes about when a transaction involves an extramarginal trader, causing a loss equal to his profit at p^*. The sum of such losses corresponds to (3) above: we call it *EM*, as a mnemonic for the inefficiency due to *extramarginal* trades. As discussed in Zhan and Friedman (2007), the allocative efficiency decomposes as $AE = 1 - MT - EM$; or, equivalently, $MT + EM = 1 - AE$ measures the allocative inefficiency. Table 2 provides a breakdown of the efficiency loss for thin, thick and crowded markets by listing mean values over 500 distinct simulation rounds. Values may not add up to 1 because of rounding effects.

There are two observations to be made. The first one is that the efficiency loss (*MT*) attributable to missed trades is decreasing in the thickness of the market, because thicker markets facilitate the search for a matching quote. Moreover, trading under no resampling terminates too soon: most of the efficiency loss comes from missed trades. (The difference between the mean values for *MT* under full or no resampling is statistically significant.) The reason for a high allocative efficiency under full resampling is elementary: this rule is of course more effective in prolonging the trading session, and hence gives traders enough chances to find their right match. This suggests that an effective market protocol should offer agents an adequate number of matching opportunities to keep the *MT* component of the efficiency loss under control.

The second observation points out a shortcoming of full resampling. The average value of *EM* is higher under such rule. (The difference between the means is once again statistically significant.) This is not difficult to explain: by the precedence rule, the best outstanding bid and ask in the book bound the price of the next transaction. The narrower the spread, the more difficult is to steal a deal for an extramarginal trader. Storing earlier quotes in the book provides (intramarginal) traders with some price protection and makes them less exploitable by extramarginal agents. As the full resampling rule tosses away the book after each transaction, it renounces such protection all too frequently (compared to no resampling). This is apparent by a straightforward comparison: the average spread (sampled before a trader places an order) is 0.152 with no resampling and 0.327 with full resampling when $n = 200$. (Corresponding values are 0.267 and 0.398 for $n = 40$; 0.113 and 0.268 for $n = 1000$.) The differences between the mean values are statistically significant. Since the zero intelligence assumption prevents traders from adjusting their quotes

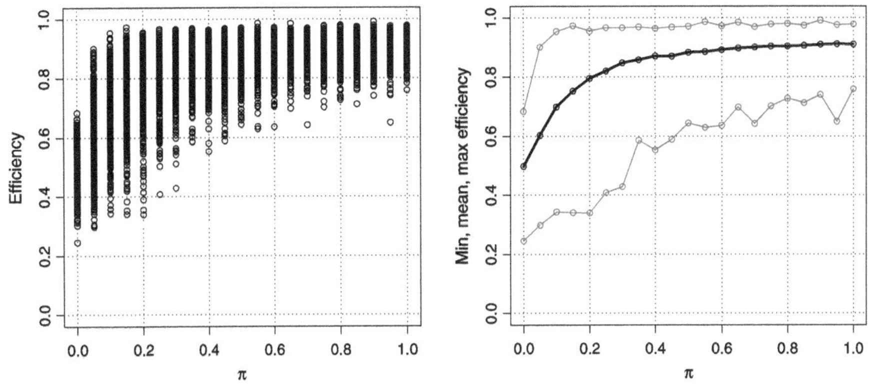

Fig. 2 Allocative efficiency under π-resampling

based on the state of the book, full resampling is a rule more favorable to extra-marginal traders than no resampling. This suggests that an effective market protocol should incorporate some form of price protection to keep the *EM* component of the efficiency loss under control.

4 Randomized Resampling

Section 3.1 established that the resampling rule is crucial to reach allocative efficiency under zero intelligence. To evaluate its impact, this section begins by looking at a continuum of resampling rules that generalize the simple dichotomy between no and full resampling. We emphasize that these rules are chosen to compare and understand how resampling affects the trading protocol. Like engineers, we are searching for improvements and tweaks over a basic design.

4.1 Full Resampling Is Not Necessary for Allocative Efficiency

A simple way to conceptualize the distinction between no and full resampling is to note that these two rules react differently to the same event; namely, the occurrence of a transaction. When two orders cross, full resampling clears the book with probability one whereas no resampling does so with probability zero. This naturally suggests to consider a family of randomized resampling rules that clear the book with probability π in $[0, 1]$ whenever there is a transaction. This set embeds full resampling for $\pi = 1$ and no resampling for $\pi = 0$.

The right-hand side of Fig. 2 shows the allocative efficiency under π*-resampling* with $n = 200$ agents. The graph is obtained as follows. We choose the 21 equispaced points $\{0, 0.05, 0.10, \ldots, 0.90, 0.95, 1\}$ in the $[0, 1]$ interval. For each of these π-values, we run 500 distinct simulations. The allocative efficiencies obtained over these $21 \times 500 = 10500$ simulations are plotted as datapoints on the left-hand side of Fig. 2. We summarize these data by the mean allocative efficiency for each π. (The difference between a mean and the corresponding median is never greater than 0.022.) The 21 sample averages are joined using segments to obtain the thicker central piecewise linear representation.[3] The two external thin graphs are similarly obtained by joining respectively the minimum and maximum values obtained for the allocative efficiency at a given value of the resampling probability π. We emphasize that the resulting band is not a confidence interval but the actual range of efficiencies obtained under our simulations: its main purpose is to provide a simple visual diagnostic for the dispersion of the data around their central tendency. We adopt the usual [0, 1]-scale for the y-axis.

The graph on the right of Fig. 2 is easily interpreted. As expected, allocative efficiency is on average increasing in the probability π that a transaction triggers a clearing of the book. Under zero intelligence, the frequency with which resampling takes place has a direct effect on the ability of the protocol to reap high levels of efficiency. On the other hand, the graph shows also that full resampling ($\pi = 1$) is not necessary: the (average) allocative efficiency in our simulations is more than 90% for $\pi \geq 0.7$ with a (statistically insignificant) peak of 91.08% at $\pi = 0.95$; the standard deviations are never greater than 0.132. There is an upper bound on the allocative efficiency that can be attained but a sufficiently large π is enough to approach it.

Similar results hold for thin and crowded markets: when $n = 40$, $AE \geq 67\%$ for $\pi \geq 0.7$ with a peak of 73.48% at $\pi = 1$ and standard deviations never greater than 0.209; when $n = 1000$, $AE \geq 93\%$ for $\pi \geq 0.2$ with a (statistically insignificant) peak of 95.12% at $\pi = 0.85$ and standard deviations never greater than 0.080. The thickness of the market affects the upper bound on the allocative efficiency but, in general, there is a whole range of resampling probabilities that achieve comparably high levels of allocative efficiency under zero intelligence.

Our conclusion is that full resampling is not necessary for allocative efficiency. Full resampling sets $\pi = 1$ and tosses the book away after each transaction: this yields a high allocative efficiency under zero intelligence, but it is also an extreme assumption that is likely to be unpalatable for human traders in real markets. As it turns out, we can temper the strength of full resampling at the mere cost of a tiny reduction (if any) in allocative efficiency.

This leads naturally to frame the choice of a resampling rule as a tradeoff between its allocative benefits and its implementation costs. On the part of the market designer, there are obvious costs to continuously monitor and update the state of the book. Similarly, traders who are forced to check whether their past orders have been voided are likely to resist frequent cancellations. Intuitively, when the costs of full resampling are not trivial, we expect partial resampling ($0 < \pi < 1$) to be preferable. The rest of this section fleshes up this argument. Section 5 takes up a related

[3] We consistently apply this approach to construct the graphs for this paper: a broken line joins 21 points, each of which represents a statistic over 500 distinct simulations for a fixed value of a parameter such as π.

question and examines a different family of resampling rules to find out whether they perform better than π-resampling.

4.2 Where Is the Best π?

Let us take stock of the starting point we have reached so far. First, given the thickness of the market, there is an upper bound on the (mean) allocative efficiency that can be attained using π-resampling. Second, the set of π-values for which the protocol reaches comparably high levels of efficiency is an interval. Thus, we need to look at additional performance criteria in order to pinpoint a smaller interval for the choice for π.

We do not claim that it is possible to find the *best* π and reduce such interval to a singleton, because the zero intelligence assumption provides at best a lower bound for the evaluation of a protocol. More modestly, we can define plausible performance criteria and measure them for different values of π under zero intelligence trading. Clearly, this procedure cannot provide a final verdict for the performance of the protocol with human subjects. Hence, the aim of this section is to carry out an engineering exercise and derive a robust choice: what is the range of π for which performance under zero intelligence is better, and why?

We consider two simple criteria. (Others are of course possible, and we take up a third major one in Sect. 4.3.) The first criterion deals with the basic requirement that an effective market protocol should offer some guidance to traders' choice in the form of a price signal. The closer the outstanding bid and ask straddle the (competitive) equilibrium price, the stronger the information that they provide. It is obvious that zero intelligence makes no use of this information: therefore, the object of our investigation is the ability of the protocol to provide an effective price signal *independently* of traders' behavior.

We measure it by the (mean) spread on the market: the closer the spread, the stronger the signal. The average is taken by sampling data when a trader arrives and places an order (as opposed to just before a transaction occurs), because we are interested in the state of the book found by a generic agent reaching the market. As it turns out, our environment is sufficiently regular that the best bid and the best ask are (on average) symmetric around the equilibrium price p^*. Hence, the outstanding spread is a sufficient statistic for such purpose. The left-hand side of Fig. 3 shows the (mean) outstanding bid and ask under π-resampling. The y-axis is truncated to [0.3, 0.7] to enhance readability.

Unsurprisingly, the spread is on average increasing in π. When resampling is more frequent, the book is cleared more often and hence is more likely to have both fewer quotes and a larger spread. For $n = 200$, the average (median) spread in our simulations increases monotonically from 0.152 (0.124) at $\pi = 0$ to a peak of 0.327 (0.232) at $\pi = 1$; the standard deviations are never greater than 0.033. Qualitatively similar results hold for $n = 40$ and $n = 1000$, and spreads are smaller in thicker markets. This leads to the following general piece of advice. Suppose

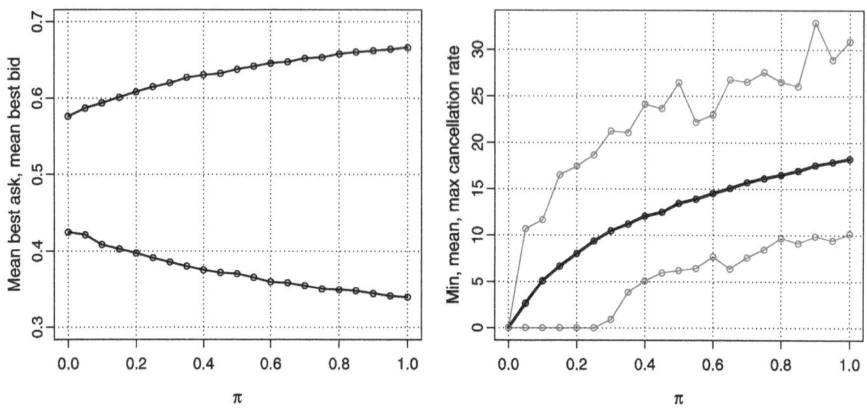

Fig. 3 Mean spreads and cancellation rates under π-resampling

that, conditional on achieving comparable levels of allocative efficiency, a market designer prefers narrower spreads. Then he should aim towards choosing a level of π that is bounded away from zero (to achieve efficiency) as well as from one (to obtain smaller spreads). The thicker the market, the weaker the need to stay away from one.

A second simple criterion has to do with the number of cancellations imposed on traders. (Recall that traders cannot cancel their orders.) The benefit of a cancellation is to offer a new chance for action to the trader. On the other hand, in general there are costs associated with the inconvenience of monitoring the state of an order or placing a new one. Therefore, when the allocative efficiency of two protocols are similar, it is reasonable to expect that the one leading to fewer cancellations should be preferred. We measure the cancellation rate as the average of the ratio between the number of orders canceled over the number of transactions completed over each of our 500 simulated trading sessions. Clearly, allocative efficiency is strongly correlated with volume; hence, the higher the ratio, the higher the cost of redundant cancellations. The right-hand side of Fig. 3 depicts the (mean) cancellation ratio with $n = 200$ agents. As usual, we report the mean values as a thick black line surrounded by thinner red lines that correspond to the minima and maxima.

Similarly to the spread, the cancellation rate is on average increasing in π because the amount of resampling directly correlates with the number of canceled orders. For $n = 200$, the mean (and standard deviation) of the cancellation rate go up[4] from 2.643 (2.498) at $\pi = 0.05$ to a peak of 18.22 (3.002) at $\pi = 1$; the standard deviations are never greater than 3.124. Similar results hold for $n = 40$ and $n = 1000$, and mean cancellation rates are higher in thicker markets. The conclusion we draw is similar to the earlier one. Suppose that, conditional on achieving comparable levels of allocative efficiency, a market designer prefers a lower cancellation rate. Then an optimal π should be bounded away from zero (for efficiency)

[4] We start from $\pi = 0.05$ because the cancellation rate at $\pi = 0$ is zero by assumption.

as well as from one (for a lower rate). The thicker the market, the stronger the need to stay away from one.

4.3 Traders' Protection

The last performance criterion that we consider in this paper is directly inspired by Stigler (1964), who pioneered the use of simulations to address issues of market engineering. He put down a clear statement: "The paramount goal of the regulations in the security markets is to protect the innocent (but avaricious) investor" (p. 120). While his paper is concerned with security markets, the conditions for achieving this goal should also be investigated for exchange markets. Curiously, the literature on zero intelligence has so far neglected this issue to the point that there is not even an agreed convention on the exact meaning of protection.

This section provides a measurable criterion for traders' protection in an exchange market, and then applies it to the evaluation of the π-resampling rule. Ideally, in a competitive equilibrium, all[5] the intramarginal traders exchange the good at the same equilibrium price p^*: nobody pays (or is paid) differently from the others. On the other hand, a continuous double auction offers neither of these guarantees: first, an intramarginal trader may fail to close a deal; second, the price at which a trade occurs may be different from the price agreed for another trade. Both of these events deny the competitive outcome to the intramarginal trader. When a market protocol hold such events under control, it manages to offer *traders' protection*.

Clearly, allocative efficiency does not measure traders' protection: since it focuses on the gains from trade that are realized, it fails to register at what terms these gains materialize. We need a more sophisticated measure that takes into account the price at which a transaction is carried out, and hence touches on the distribution of gains. To this purpose, we define the *competitive share* of a trader as the (positive part of the) profit he would make by transacting at the competitive equilibrium price. Given an equilibrium price p^*, the competitive share of a buyer with valuation v is $(v - p^*)^+$ and that of a seller with cost c is $(p^* - c)^+$. Clearly, the competitive share of any extramarginal trader is zero.

The *realized competitive share* is the portion of his competitive share realized by an agent. (Extramarginal traders are entitled to no competitive share.) If an agent fails to trade, this portion is zero. If a trade occurs at price p, the realized competitive share is $v - \max\{p, p^*\}$ for an (intramarginal) buyer and $\min\{p, p^*\} - c$ for an (intramarginal) seller.

The realized competitive share is concerned only with measuring whether a trader gets its due, and ignores any additional gains that he may be able to reap. The profit realized by an intramarginal trader may be greater than his realized competitive share if he manages to secure terms of trade more favorable than p^*; similarly,

[5]When the number of intramarginal traders is odd, one of them will not trade for lack of a partner.

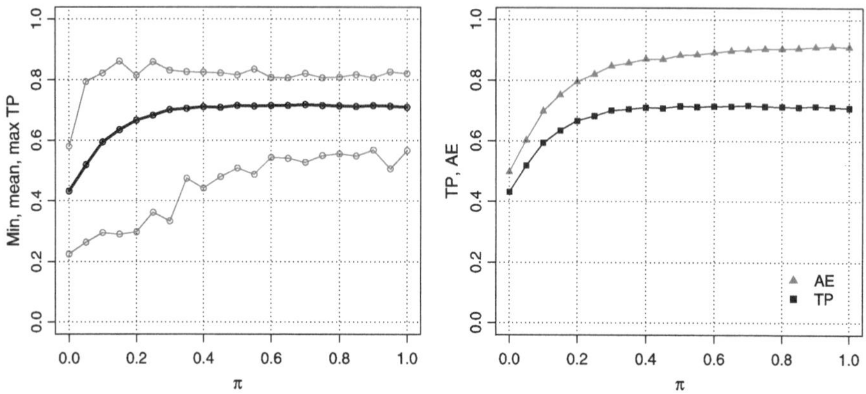

Fig. 4 Traders' protection (*left*), superimposed to allocative efficiency (*right*)

any extramarginal agent who completes a trade makes positive profits by individual rationality, but his realized competitive share remains zero.

Note that the sum of all the competitive shares equals the maximum feasible gains from trade. In analogy with allocative efficiency (*AE*), we define the traders' protection (for short, *TP*) offered by a market protocol as the ratio of the realized competitive shares and the sum of all the competitive shares. This measure is adimensional and takes values in [0, 1].

The left-hand side of Fig. 4 shows the traders' protection under π-resampling with $n = 200$ agents. As usual, we report the mean values surrounded by minima and maxima. The right-hand side superimposes *AE* and *TP* to allow for a direct comparison: the black line corresponding to *TP* is the same visible on the left, while the red line depicting *AE* corresponds to the inner black line from the right-hand side of Fig. 2.

In general, traders' protection is not increasing in π. For $n = 200$, the mean protection starts at 0.431 in $\pi = 0$, peaks at 0.718 in $\pi = 0.7$ and then declines to 0.709 in $\pi = 1$ (with two local maxima of 0.711 at $\pi = 0.4$ and 0.715 at $\pi = 0.9$); the standard deviations are never greater than 0.111. Qualitatively similar results hold for crowded and thin markets. When $n = 1000$, *TP* is 0.461 in $\pi = 0$, peaks at 0.791 in $\pi = 0.2$ and then declines to 0.744 in $\pi = 1$ with no other local maxima and standard deviations never greater than 0.070. For $n = 40$, *TP* is 0.355 in $\pi = 0$ and peaks at 0.563 in $\pi = 1$, with four more local maxima in between and standard deviations never greater than 0.172.

Here, the thickness of the market has a very strong effect on the range of the best value for π: the more crowded the market, the smaller the resampling rate that provides the best protection. The overall conclusion is similar to the above, with a strong word of caution as regards the thickness of the market. Suppose that, conditional on achieving comparable levels of allocative efficiency, a market designer prefers to offer a higher traders' protection. Then an optimal π should be bounded away from zero (for efficiency) as well as from one (for protection). When the market gets thicker, however, the need to stay away from one is remarkably higher.

To sum it up, we have considered three criteria based respectively on spread, cancellation rate, and traders' protection. To a different extent, they all support a choice of π from the interior of the interval $[0, 1]$: at the cost of a nominal reduction in allocative efficiency, it is possible to have lower spreads, fewer cancellations, and higher traders' protection. It is clear that both the relative importance of these criteria to the market designer as well as the thickness of the market matter for the exact choice of π. However, generally speaking, all of our performance criteria strongly suggest that full resampling is unlikely to be a defensible choice.

5 Resampling Outside of a Price Band

Section 4 has studied randomized resampling, but it is obvious that there exist many other rules. It may be impossible to pick a best one, but we can compare the performance of different resampling techniques. This section considers a different rule that shares a few basic properties with π-resampling. First, it depends on a single parameter γ in $[0, 1]$. Second, it implies an average resampling rate that is increasing in the parameter. Third, it embeds the two extreme cases of full and no resampling for $\gamma = 1$ and $\gamma = 0$. Fourth, it requires minimal information and thus imposes very little burden on the market protocol or the cognitive abilities of the traders.

The γ-resampling rule is the following. After a trade carries out at price p, the protocol cancels all outstanding orders that fall outside the *price band* $[\gamma p, \gamma p + (1-\gamma)]$; moreover, in the special case $\gamma = 1$, we require the protocol to erase even the outstanding orders at price p so that it clears the book entirely. (This specification is necessary to embed full resampling, because the book might contain orders with price p but lower time priority.) It is useful to keep in mind that π is the probability with which the book is cleared after a transaction, while $(1-\gamma)$ is the width of the price band within which orders are *not* deleted after a transaction.

Like π-resampling, the γ-resampling rule is triggered whenever a transaction occurs. Differently from it, its application implies that traders whose orders are deleted may infer a one-sided bound for the last transaction price. For instance, given γ, when a buyer sees that his past order at price p has been canceled, he can deduce that the last transaction price must have been strictly greater than p/γ. We do not view this a significant limitation, since it is seems highly plausible that all agents would be given public access to such information. On the other hand, since it makes no use of the best outstanding bid and ask, the γ-resampling rule does not require to divulge this kind of information. This may be an additional advantage in view of the results in Arifovic and Ledyard (2007), who consider a sequence of call markets and show that the closed book design[6] brings about a higher allocative efficiency than an open book in environments populated with human subjects or (non ZI) simulated agents. If similar results should suggest adopting a closed book design for

[6]In a closed book, traders learn only the clearing price after each call; in an open book, they are also told the quotes processed in that call.

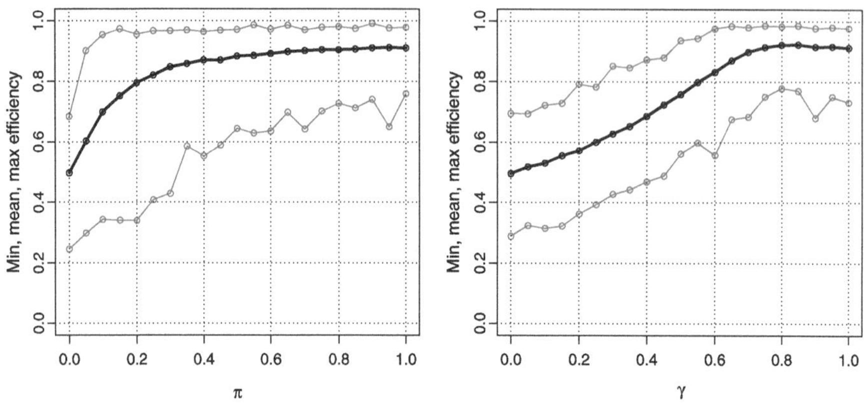

Fig. 5 Allocative efficiency under π- and γ-resampling

the continuous double auction, both π- and γ-resampling are compatible. For the current study, it suffices to say that the ZI assumption precludes a direct comparison between closed and open book design, because it prevents agents from making use of any disclosed information.

The γ-resampling rule may be easily adapted in other dimensions. For instance, our definition embeds a symmetry assumption that may be removed. We choose the endpoints of the price band at the same distance from the extremes of the price range: the left endpoint is a convex combination between the last transaction price p and the minimum possible price, while the right endpoint is a convex combination between p and the maximum possible price. Clearly, this choice requires the implicit assumption that we know that p lies in the interval $[0, 1]$. More generally, when no bounds for the price are known, it suffices to set the price band to be the interval $[\gamma p, (1/\gamma)p]$ for γ in $[0, 1]$ or other analogous formulations.

Figure 5 shows the allocative efficiency under π-resampling (on the left) and γ-resampling (on the right) with $n = 200$ agents.

The graph on the left is the same as in Fig. 2. The graph on the right is the analog for γ-resampling: a thick inner black line joins the mean values, and two thin outer red lines join the corresponding minima and maxima. The directionality of the graphs is aligned because they depict two resampling rules that coincide for $\pi = \gamma = 0$ and $\pi = \gamma = 1$.

Both resampling rules are on average increasing in the corresponding parameter. However, the qualitative behavior is different. Under π-resampling, allocative efficiency picks up fast and rapidly settles on a plateau: for $n = 200$, the sample average is greater than 0.90 for $\pi \geq 0.7$. As already discussed, even moderate levels of π suffice to attain an adequate level of efficiency. On the other hand, efficiency under γ-resampling grows up more slowly and, quite interestingly, peaks at $\gamma < 1$: for $n = 200$, the sample average is greater than 0.90 for $\pi \geq 0.75$ and peaks at 0.923 for $\gamma = 0.85$; the standard deviations are never greater than 0.073.

Similar results hold for the case of thin and crowded markets. For $n = 40$, the sample average is greater than 0.67 for $\gamma \geq 0.65$ and peaks at 0.743 for $\gamma = 0.9$,

Table 3 Maximum allocative efficiency under π- and γ-resampling

	π-resampling			γ-resampling		
	$n = 40$	$n = 200$	$n = 1000$	$n = 40$	$n = 200$	$n = 1000$
Maximum *AE*	0.735	0.911	0.951	0.743	0.923	0.960
Maximizer (π, γ)	1.000	0.950	0.850	0.900	0.850	0.800

with standard deviations never greater than 0.197; for $n = 1000$, the sample average is greater than 0.94 for $\gamma \geq 0.7$ and peaks at 0.96 for $\gamma = 0.8$ with standard deviations never greater than 0.033. Thicker markets exhibit a superior allocative performance for lower values of γ but the overall conclusion is the same: a narrow (but not empty) price band is a necessary condition to attain sufficiently high levels of efficiency.

6 A Comparison of Alternative Rules

This section compares the performance of the protocol when adopting π-resampling versus γ-resampling over four different criteria: allocative efficiency (*AE*), mean spread, cancellation rate, and traders' protection (*TP*).

Table 3 compares the allocative efficiency under π- and γ-resampling for thin, thick, and crowded markets.

For each combination of n and resampling rule, we list the highest mean values obtained. These are slightly higher under γ-resampling, but we would not stake big claims over tiny differences that are subject to sampling errors. (However, they are statistically significant for $n = 200$ and $n = 1000$.) We prefer to conclude that there is no clear winner over *AE*: both resampling rules can be tuned to attain comparably high levels of allocative efficiency .

The second performance criterion is the mean spread. Figure 6 shows the best bid and ask under both π-resampling (on the left) and γ-resampling (on the right) with $n = 200$ agents. The y-axes are truncated to $[0.3, 0.7]$ to enhance readability.

Predictably, as a mere visual inspection confirms, the clear winner is the γ-resampling rule that is based on an explicit form of price control. Table 4 validates this conjecture by listing the lowest mean spread obtained under π- and γ-resampling for thin, thick, and crowded markets. The difference between the mean values is statistically significant for each choice of n.

Conditional on choosing the right parameter, the mean spread with γ-resampling is remarkably smaller. However, note that the best performances of both π- and γ-resampling with regard to the mean spread require a choice of parameters that are far from being optimal for allocative efficiency. This is easily seen by comparing the second rows from Tables 3 and 4. Therefore, while it is clear that γ-resampling yields a lower mean spread than π-resampling under ideal conditions, we need a further test to find out whether it is still superior once we take into account both efficiency and mean spread.

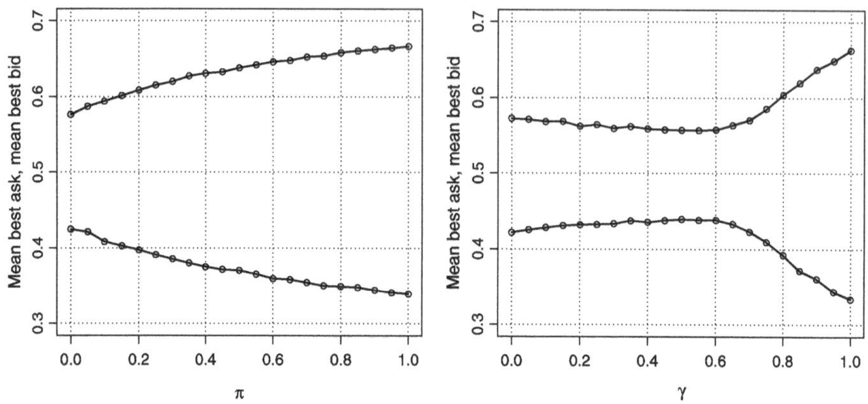

Fig. 6 Mean spread under π- and γ-resampling

Table 4 Mean spread under π- and γ-resampling

	π-resampling			γ-resampling		
	$n = 40$	$n = 200$	$n = 1000$	$n = 40$	$n = 200$	$n = 1000$
Minimum (mean) spread	0.267	0.152	0.113	0.228	0.118	0.086
Minimizer (π, γ)	0.000	0.000	0.000	0.450	0.500	0.600

This test is provided on the left-hand side of Fig. 7, where we plot the average outstanding bid and ask under both π-resampling (in red) and γ-resampling (in black) with $n = 200$ agents. This graph combines information about the two resampling rules. For each level of the (mean) allocative efficiency attained under either rule, we plot the corresponding average values of the best bid and ask and then join the datapoints using broken lines. Since the two rules attain different (mean) efficiencies, the datapoints are not vertically aligned. The left-hand picture shows clearly that, for comparable levels of allocative efficiency, γ-resampling leads to smaller (mean) spreads that π-resampling. In other words, a resampling rule based on a price band tends to produce a smaller spread than a rule based on a full clearing of the book, without sacrificing allocative efficiency.

Our third performance criterion is the cancellation rate. As is the case for π-resampling, this rate in on average increasing in γ because the width of the price band inversely correlates with the number of canceled orders. For $n = 200$, the mean (and standard deviation) of the cancellation rate go up from 1.868 (0.561) at $\gamma = 0.05$ (it is zero for $\gamma = 0$) to 18.16 (3.211) at $\gamma = 1$; the standard deviations are never greater than 3.212. A direct comparison shows that the range of attainable values for the cancellation rate is virtually identical under π- and γ-resampling. Similar results hold for $n = 40$ and $n = 1000$. Taken by itself, therefore, a criterion based on the cancellation rate is not conclusive.

As for the mean spread, however, we can compare the combined performance of either resampling rule with respect to allocative efficiency and cancellation rates.

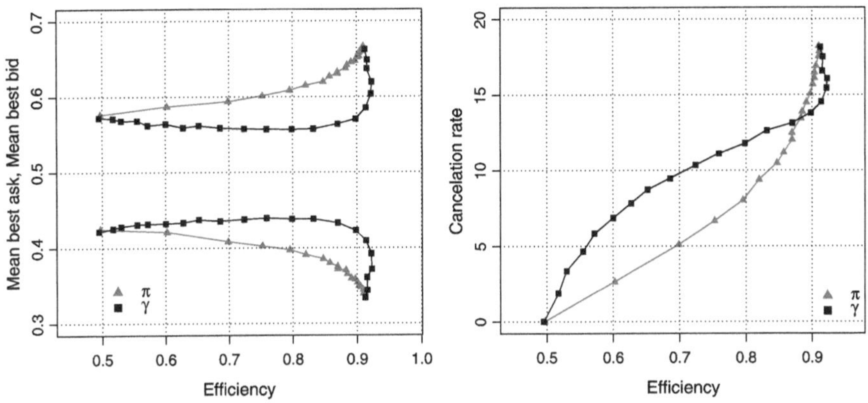

Fig. 7 Bid-ask spreads and cancellation rates versus allocative efficiency

Table 5 Maximum traders' protection under π- and γ-resampling

	π-resampling			γ-resampling		
	$n = 40$	$n = 200$	$n = 1000$	$n = 40$	$n = 200$	$n = 1000$
Maximum *TP*	0.563	0.718	0.791	0.589	0.774	0.833
Maximizer (π, γ)	1.000	0.700	0.200	0.800	0.750	0.700

The right-hand side of Fig. 7 plots the (average) cancellation rates for each level of the (mean) allocative efficiency attained under either rule. For a large range of (lower) allocative efficiencies, π-resampling has a substantially lower cancellation rate; for high values, γ-resampling comes out better by a thin margin. (We do not report the graphs for different values of n, but increasing n makes this conclusion sharper.) Hence, whenever the market designer views the cancellation rate as ancillary to the allocative performance, he should prefer a resampling rule based on the price band.

The last (and in our opinion, more important) criterion is traders' protection. Table 5 compares the performance of π- and γ-resampling in thin, thick, and crowded markets. Similarly to Table 3, we list the highest mean values obtained for each combination of n and resampling rule. For $n = 200$ or $n = 1000$, the differences between the mean values are statistically significant. (For $n = 40$, this holds at the 1% significance level.) Conditional on choosing the right parameter, traders' protection is higher using γ-resampling. Note also that the optimal values of π and γ are decreasing in the thickness of the market, but this effect is much stronger for π-resampling. Therefore, when the exact size of the market is not known, the choice of the parameter under γ-resampling is more robust.

This superiority carries over when traders' protection is ancillary to allocative efficiency. The left-hand side of Fig. 8 superimposes the usual graphs of the mean values for *AE* and *TP* under γ-resampling for $n = 200$. The equivalent representation for π-resampling is on the right-hand side of Fig. 4. In general, γ-resampling

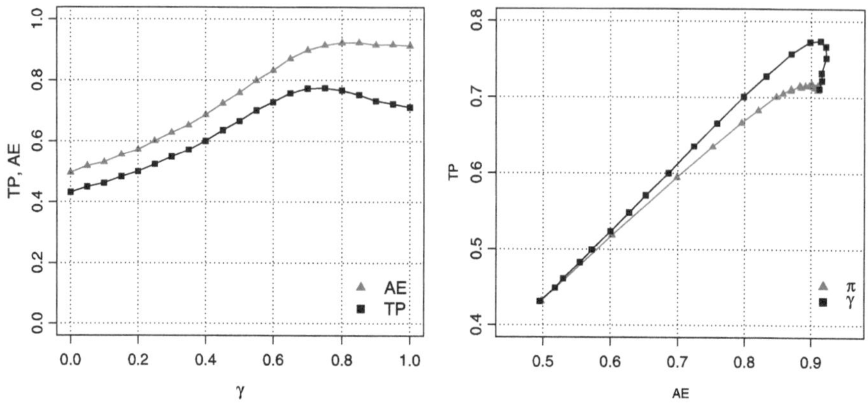

Fig. 8 Traders' protection and allocative efficiency for π- and γ-resampling

delivers a higher traders' protection than π-resampling for any given level of allocative efficiency. This is shown on the right-hand side of Fig. 8, where we report the (mean) traders' protection offered by the two resampling rules with respect to their (mean) allocative efficiency. The γ-resampling frontier on the *AE–TP* plane dominates the π-resampling frontier.

7 Conclusions

We have studied the continuous double auction from the point of view of market engineering, tweaking the trading protocol in search of improved designs. Our starting point has been the rules for exchange adopted by Gode and Sunder (1993a) for experiments with human agents and simulations with robot traders. We have disassembled their trading protocol into several component rules, and focused attention on resampling. We have assumed zero intelligence trading as a lower bound for more robust behavioral rules in order to elucidate the consequences of different resampling techniques.

Like Gode and Sunder (1993a) and most of the subsequent literature, we look first at allocative efficiency. Their trading protocol makes an extreme assumption that we call full resampling. We show that full resampling is especially favorable to allocative efficiency, biasing Gode and Sunder's results about the ability of the market to substitute for the lack of traders' intelligence. (A second negligible bias may come from their halting rule.) On the other hand, we demonstrate that partial resampling may be sufficient for the purpose of attaining a high allocative efficiency.

Based on this, we have devised a family of rules that includes as extreme cases both Gode and Sunder's full resampling and the opposite assumption of no resampling. This class of rules is parameterized by the probability π of clearing the book after a transaction occurs. We find that there is a large range of values for which π-resampling can attain a high allocative efficiency. In order to discriminate among such π's, we introduce three subordinate performance criteria: spread, cancellation rate, and traders' protection. The spread criterion measures the capacity of the protocol to provide a useful price signal. The cancellation rate looks at the inconvenience created by over-resampling. Finally, traders' protection measures the ability of a protocol to help agents capture their share of the competitive equilibrium profits. This latter criterion, patterned after the usual measure of allocative efficiency, is (to the best of our knowledge) new to the literature: we argue that ignoring it neglects one of the paramount goals of designing a market protocol.

We then introduce a different family of rules, based on the idea to delete only those quotes that fall outside of a price band parameterized by γ. We find that from the point of view of allocative efficiency, the optimized versions of either resampling rule are virtually indistinguishable. However, several differences emerge when we study their performance with respect to the other three criteria. In particular, when we consider a pair of criteria where the first one is allocative efficiency and the second one is any of the other three, we find that it is always the case that (at least for high efficiencies) γ-resampling dominates π-resampling. We then conclude that a resampling rule based on the price band is superior.

Acknowledgements This paper was written while the third author was visiting the School of Finance and Economics at the University of Technology of Sidney, whose financial assistance is gratefully acknowledged. We also received financial support from MIUR under grants 2007EE-NEAX and 2007TKLTSR.

References

Arifovic, J., & Ledyard, J. (2007). Call market book information and efficiency. *Journal of Economic Dynamics and Control*, *31*, 1971–2000.

Brewer, P. J., Huang, M., Nelson, B., & Plott, C. R. (2002). On the behavioral foundations of the law of supply and demand: human convergence and robot randomness. *Experimental Economics*, *5*, 179–208.

Cliff, D., & Bruten, J. (1997). *More than zero intelligence needed for continuous double-auction trading*. Hewlett Packard Laboratories Paper HPL-97-157, Bristol, England.

Crockett, S., Spear, S., & Sunder, S. (2008). Learning competitive equilibrium. *Journal of Mathematical Economics*, *44*, 651–671.

Duffy, J. (2006). Agent-based model and human subject experiments. In L. Tesfatsion & K. L. Judd (Eds.), *Handbook of computational economics* (pp. 950–1011). Amsterdam: Elsevier.

Gjerstad, S., & Shachat, J. M. (2007). Individual rationality and market efficiency, wp 1204, August. IRBEMS, Krannert School, Purdue University.

Gode, D. K., & Sunder, S. (1993a). Allocative efficiency of markets with zero intelligence traders: Market as a partial substitute for individual rationality. *Journal of Political Economy*, *101*, 119–137.

Gode, D. K., & Sunder, S. (1993b). Lower bounds for efficiency of surplus extraction in double auctions. In D. Friedman & J. Rust (Eds.), *The double auction market* (pp. 199–218). Reading: Addison–Wesley.

Gode, D. K., & Sunder, S. (1997). What makes markets allocationally efficient? *Quarterly Journal of Economics*, *112*, 603–630.

Gode, D. K., & Sunder, S. (2004). Double auction dynamics: structural effects of non-binding price controls. *Journal of Economic Dynamics and Control*, *28*, 1707–1731.

Gul, F., & Lundholm, R. (1995). Endogenous timing and the clustering of agents' decisions. *Journal of Political Economy*, *103*, 1039–1066.
Hurwicz, L., Radner, R., & Reiter, S. (1975). A stochastic decentralized resource allocation process: part I. *Econometrica*, *43*, 187–222.
LiCalzi, M., & Pellizzari, P. (2008). Zero-intelligence trading without resampling. In K. Schredelseker & F. Hauser (Eds.), *Complexity and artificial markets* (pp. 3–14). Berlin: Springer.
Maslov, S. (2000). Simple model of a limit order-driven market. *Physica A*, *278*, 571–578.
Mirowski, P. (2007). Markets come to bits: evolution, computation and markomata in economic science. *Journal of Economic Behavior and Organization*, *63*, 209–242.
Roth, A. E. (2002). The economist as engineer: game theory, experimentation, and computation as tools for design economics. *Econometrica*, *70*, 1341–1378.
Smith, V. L. (1982). Microeconomic systems as an experimental science. *American Economic Review*, *72*, 923–955.
Stigler, G. J. (1964). Public regulation of the securities markets. *Journal of Business*, *37*, 117–142.
Subrahmanian, E., & Talukdar, S. N. (2004). Engineering of markets and artifacts. *Electronic Commerce Research and Applications*, *3*, 369–380.
Sunder, S. (2004). Markets as artifacts. In M. Augier & J. March (Eds.), *Models of a man: essays in memory of Herbert A. Simon* (pp. 501–520). Cambridge: MIT Press.
Zhan, W., & Friedman, D. (2007). Markups in double auction markets. *Journal of Economic Dynamics and Control*, *31*, 2984–3005.
Zhan, W., Zhang, J., Yang, J., Wang, S., & Lai, K. K. (2002). *k*-ZI: A general zero-intelligence model in continuous double auction. *International Journal of Information Technology and Decision Making*, *1*, 673–691.

Using Software Agents to Supplement Tests Conducted by Human Subjects

Hyungna Oh and Timothy D. Mount

Abstract The objective of this paper is to test whether or not software agents can match the observed behavior of human subjects in laboratory tests of markets. For this purpose, one set of tests uses four software agents and two human subjects to represent six suppliers in three different market situations: no forward contracts, fixed price forward contracts, and renewable forward contracts. An identical set of tests is conducted using software agents to represent all of the suppliers. The results show that software agents were able to replicate the behavior of human subjects effectively in the experiments, and have the potential to be used effectively in testing electricity auctions, doing additional sensitivity tests, and supplementing results obtained using human subjects.

1 Introduction

Restructured electricity markets have exhibited unsatisfactory results, most notably in California. Since electricity is a central component of modern economies, market operators and regulatory agencies continually introduce new types of market structures to obtain a more reliable electricity market. Recent introductions include a micro-grid, a capacity market, long-term contracts, demand-side participation, financial transmission rights, and customers' choice of retail services. More recently, smart electricity meters and real-time pricing have also been considered to improve efficiency and mitigate wholesalers' market power. Furthermore, deregulation and the unbundling of generation, transmission, and distribution functions provide many choices for a supplier, such as vertical integration, merging with other firms, entering into the new market, or divesting from the market. This variety of choices for generating firms, customers, and market operators implies that electricity markets are not fixed, but continue to change.

This type of evolving market requires suitable modeling tools that can be used to test new market structures and new market rules before they are applied to real

---

H. Oh (✉)
Department of Economics, West Virginia University, 411 B&E, Morgantown, WV 26506, USA
e-mail: Hyungna.Oh@mail.wvu.edu

H. Dawid, W. Semmler (eds.), *Computational Methods in Economic Dynamics*, Dynamic Modeling and Econometrics in Economics and Finance 13,
DOI 10.1007/978-3-642-16943-4_3,

markets. Experimental economics has been used to test how wholesalers and consumers change their behavior when market conditions and rules are changed, and how spot prices are affected. However, there are some important restrictions on the design of an experiment. Viable results must be obtained using a relatively small number of suppliers and a relatively small number of trading periods. For example, the standard market test using *PowerWeb* (an interactive, distributed, Internet-based simulation platform developed by PSERC researchers at Cornell University)[1] at Cornell involves only six firms, and tests with more than 50 trading periods are rare. Agent-based simulation can be an alternative to laboratory tests using people. In an agent-based simulation, the role of human subjects in an experiment is taken on by software agents. One advantage of using software agents, rather than people, to test markets is that this makes running a much more extensive range of tests practical.

A software agent with computational intelligence is a computer program representing an economic decision, and it performs its assigned task in a virtual environment. In order to perform the task efficiently, an agent has at least a perception function and a decision function. The former receives new pieces of information and rearranges them to extract useful information, while the latter selects the best action to maximize its satisfaction. In this process, the algorithms rely on heuristic arguments and similarities to nature (Dawid 1999).

Agent-based Computational Economics (hereafter, ACE[2]) is a branch of economics utilizing artificial intelligence techniques in economic research. Advantages of these ACE approaches to electricity market research include the following: (1) an agent may generate different behaviors in the spot market even when market conditions are exactly the same as before. This time-variant strategy is the result of either learning effects or changes in market conditions; (2) the dynamic relation of suppliers' behavior to market price can be explained, since a software agent interacts with other agents, determines the market price and then reacts to the market price; (3) if new rules or market structures are specified, an ACE system can test how these alter the market price and the supplier's behavior; and (4) it can closely simulate real market conditions using diversified agents, with business goals, production conditions, risk attitudes and preferences, and accessibility to information different by agent.

There are various software agents designed for restructured electricity markets in the U.S. For example, the EMCAS (Electricity Market Complex Adaptive System) has been developed by Argonne National Laboratory and analyzes the technological and economical aspects of electrical power systems (see Argonne National Laboratory 2008). The learning used in EMCAS software agents is called "exploration-based learning." GenCo, a supplier agent in EMCAS, uses this learning and pursues its given goals (such as maximizing profits, maintaining the minimum market share, and avoiding regulatory intervention). Tesfatsion and her colleagues at ISU developed AMES (Agent-based Modeling of Electricity Systems),

---

[1]http://www.pserc.cornell.edu/powerweb.

[2]According to Tesfatsion's definition (2001), ACE is the computational study of economies modeled as evolving systems of autonomous interacting agents with learning capacities.

and tested the market power, efficiency and reliability issues in wholesale electricity markets (2007). Talukdar et al. at CMU simulated price spikes resulting from bidders' withholding behavior (2004) and showed how a cascading failure can occur, using autonomous adaptive software agents (2005). Finally, Cornell University combined autonomous software agents with human subjects in analyzing various market options and detecting market power (Oh and Thomas 2006; Oh et al. 2005; Mount and Oh 2004).

In the UK, Bower and Bunn (2000) applied agent-based techniques to the new two-settlement market (a Power Exchange and a Balancing Market), which included a discriminatory auction for the balancing market. The software agent in their simulation was designed to maximize profit conditional on maintaining a minimum market share. As Bunn and Oliveira (2001) recognized, they did not incorporate any learning effects. Bunn and Oliveira (2001) extended Bower and Bunn (2000) with reinforcement learning. Recently, Bunn and Day (2009) demonstrated that an ACE approach can be a very useful tool to explain continuously evolved strategies on a large scale and in a complex market.

The objective of this paper is to demonstrate that software agents can match the observed behavior of human subjects in laboratory tests of markets. For this purpose, one set of tests uses students to represent suppliers in an electricity auction with (1) no forward contracts (all dispatched capacity is paid at the spot price), (2) permanent forward contracts (i.e. two suppliers hold a permanent forward contract, the same contract is held for all trading periods, and the price of this contract is independent of the spot prices), and (3) renewable forward contracts (i.e. a forward contract is renewed periodically and spot prices influence the forward price). An identical set of tests is also conducted using software agents (i.e. artificial intelligence) to represent all of the suppliers.

The analysis is based on simulations of a wholesale market for electricity run by an Independent System Operator (ISO). Suppliers submit offers to a central auction, and the ISO determines the optimum pattern of dispatch to minimize the cost of meeting load. A uniform price auction is used to determine the market price.

Our software agents (see Mount and Oh 2004) have a backward looking function to learn about the current market from previous market outcomes. This adaptation involves updating an estimate of the residual demand curve faced by each firm, and this curve is used by the firm to determine the optimum set of offers to maximize expected profits in the next round of the auction. A noticeable result from our earlier work (Mount and Oh 2004) is that under the load uncertainty, agents replicate supply curves that are sharply kinked, like hockey sticks, for the last few units of the capacity offered. As Fig. 1 shows, this is exactly the type of behavior observed in deregulated electricity markets.

The results using software agents were encouraging. In the first set of tests, two students competed in each market with four software agents. By adjusting parameter values in the residual demand function, these four agents were designed as price-takers at the beginning. However, they can learn during the experiment, and evolve a Cournot strategy, a Bertrand strategy, or both. In almost all cases, the average earnings of the software agents were higher than the average earnings of the students. In

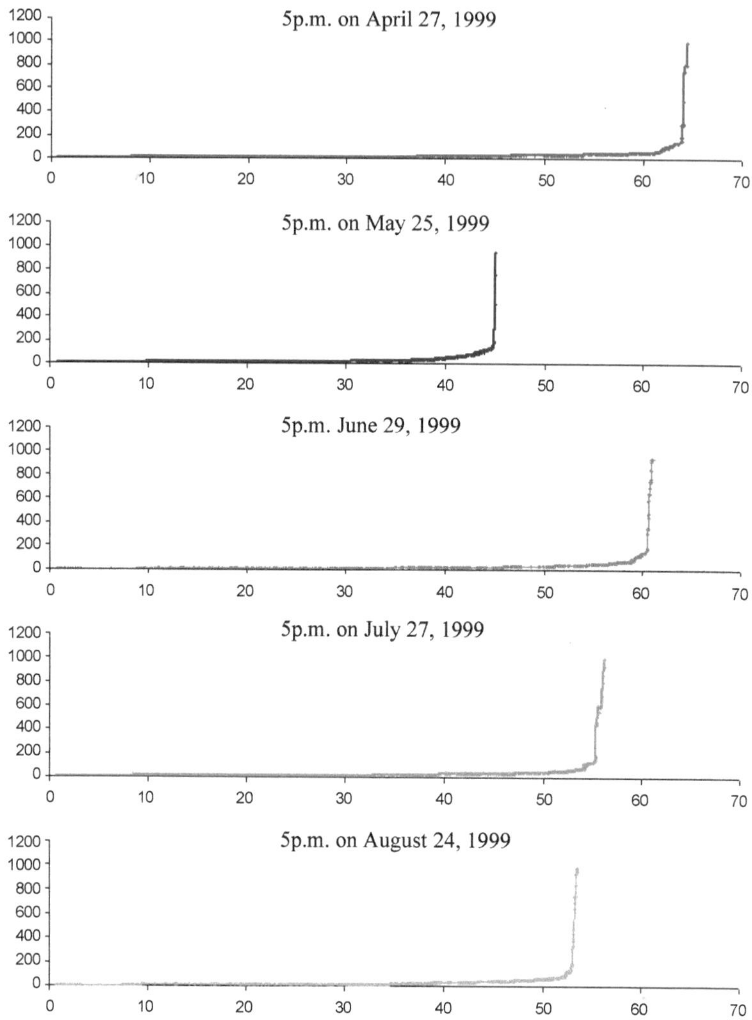

Fig. 1 Offer curves observed in the PJM wholesale market for electricity

the tests with all software agents, two software agents replaced the students. These two software agents were designed to test whether the electricity market can be imperfectly competitive. They were created by setting parameter values of their initial residual demand functions to give their shape a curvature. Average spot prices and earnings with all software agents corresponded closely to the highest values obtained by the students. Our outcomes demonstrate that software agents can be used effectively to test electricity auctions, conduct additional sensitivity tests, and supplement results obtained using humans.

The rest of this paper is organized as follows. Section 2 explains the experimental framework and design of software agents. Section 3 compares the performance of human subjects and software agents, and tests whether or not software agents can be used to replicate the behavior of actual suppliers and people in laboratory tests. In Sect. 4, we conclude the paper.

2 The Experimental Framework

2.1 An Experimental Design

All of the experiments are conducted using *PowerWeb* to test different electricity markets using human decision makers and/or computer agents. An Independent System Operator (ISO) determines the optimum dispatch of generators and the spot (nodal) prices paid to suppliers. The *PowerWeb* environment is designed to run unit commitment and optimal power flow routines to minimize the cost of meeting load subject to the physical constraints of an AC network. However, for our experiments, network constraints are not binding, and, in each trading period, the same spot price is paid to all suppliers, using a uniform price auction (last accepted offer).

After each trading period, the ISO announces a forecast of the load in the next trading period. Load is completely price inelastic but does vary from period to period. The forecasted load is generated randomly using a uniform distribution from 430 MW to 550 MW. The actual load is also generated randomly using a uniform distribution (Forecast $\pm$20 MW). The average load is 82% of the total installed capacity, which corresponds to realistic conditions in the summer when the load is relatively high.

For each trading period, each supplier submits offers to sell (or withhold) five blocks of capacity into the auction. A price cap (maximum offer allowed) of $100/MWh is enforced by the ISO (to keep the payments to participants in the test reasonably low). If the total capacity offered into the auction is less than the actual load, the ISO covers the shortfall by purchasing expensive imports from another market. However, when a shortfall occurs, the spot price is set by the highest offer and not by the price of imports.

Each supplier owns five blocks of generating capacity with capacities 50, 20, 10, 10, 10 (MW) and production costs 20, 40, 48, 50, 52 ($/MWh generated), respectively. In addition, there is a fixed standby cost of $5/MW to cover the opportunity cost of availability when a block is offered into the market. Withholding a block from the auction is the only way to avoid the standby cost for that block. There is also a fixed cost charged each period to cover capital costs ($1200/period, to make earnings roughly equal to profits in excess of competitive levels). These capacity and cost structures are the same for all six suppliers and remain the same in all markets tested.

As shown in Table 1, three different markets, (1) no forward contract (Test 1), (2) a permanent forward contract (Test 2), and (3) a renewable forward contract (Test 3), were tested during Fall semester, 2003 using 20 students majoring in applied economics or electrical engineering (the tests were part of a course on electricity markets). Each student represents a supplier in the market. In addition, some

Table 1 Experiment settings

Categories		Forward contracts	Number of students	Number of software agents		
				VIF	IPT	LS
I	Test 1	No forward contracts	2	2	2	0
	Test 2	Contract on first 50 MW at \$60/MW (permanent)	2[a]	2	2	0
	Test 3	Contract on first 50 MW, updated every 10 periods (renewable)	2[a]	2	2	0
II	Test 1	No forward contracts	0	2	2	2
	Test 2	Contract on first 50 MW at \$60/MW (permanent)	0	2	2	2[a]
	Test 3	Contract on first 50 MW, updated every 10 periods (renewable)	0	2	2	2[a]

Note: Category I—the first set of experiments with 4 agents and 2 students and Category II—the second set of experiment with all agents

[a]Indicates the holder of the forward contract

suppliers are represented by computer agents. In Test 1, none of the six suppliers holds a forward contract, but the two vertically integrated firms (agents) must meet one sixth of the load at a predetermined price. In Test 2, regulations require that each student must hold a forward contract for half of her capacity, and has already signed a contract for 50 MW (the first block of capacity) at a fixed price of \$60/MWh. These contracts are in place for all periods. Hence, the objective is to maximize profits from selling the remaining four blocks of capacity (the first block is submitted automatically). In all other respects, conditions are the same as in Test 1.

In Test 3, each student has to renew a 10-period forward contract for 50 MW every 10th period. The forward price is given in (2) with $\lambda = 0.25$ and a random residual added. The value of λ is not a priori information for the suppliers. The computer agents are designed to estimate λ based on the previous spot and forward prices. Simulation results show that the agents' estimates of λ are accurate after 3 periods. In Tests 2 and 3, the students are paid for the forward contracts as well as for earnings in the spot market. In Test 3, the first contract price is set at \$60/MWh for periods 1 to 10, and this contract is renewed in periods 10 and 20. The students' earnings are computed to reflect the forward prices in the two new contracts but not the initial contract (the actual revenue from the first two contracts is augmented by $50 \cdot 10 \cdot (P_{20}^F - 60)$). The reason for doing this is to provide the students with the same incentive to increase the forward price of a new contract throughout the test.

For each test, there are 10 sessions with six suppliers in each: two students, two vertically integrated firm agents (hereafter, VIF) and two initial price taking agents (hereafter, IPT) (believing that price spikes cannot occur). The lowest profit session in each test is excluded so that results correspond more closely to the behavior of professional traders in real markets.

The students in the tests represented experienced traders, and receive an initial briefing on how suppliers behave in the PJM market[3] (Instructions used for students are attached in Appendix). Hence, the students understand the rationale for speculating, and why offer curves shaped like hockey sticks cause price spikes. Test 1 (no contract) consists of 25 trading periods, and the next two tests, conducted a week later, consist of 20 trading periods each. Each student is paid in direct proportion to her cumulative earnings and told that the objective of the tests is to earn as much money as possible. Initial trading periods are treated as learning periods for developing an offer strategy, and the average results from the last 10 periods in each test are used in the analysis.

In the first set of experiments, two students compete with four agents. Two of these agents represent VIF that have to meet a fixed proportion of load and are paid a regulated price (=\$60/MWh) for this load. These firms have less incentive to speculate than the others. The other two agents are IPT. However, IPTs can learn to speculate if high prices do occur, and, in this sense, these two agents reinforce the behavior of the students. If the students do not speculate, none of the computer agents speculate, but if the students speculate, the agents learn to speculate and make the market easier to exploit.

An identical set of tests was also conducted using computer agents to represent all six suppliers, by replacing the students with two "latent speculators" (hereafter, LS) (believing price spikes can occur). These agents are more likely to speculate than initial price takers, and initial price takers evolve into latent speculators if there are high prices. The primary objective of the tests with all agents was to determine how well the computer agents can replicate the typical offer behavior of the students.

2.2 Design of Software Agents

In our experiment, the task of each software agent is to compete with other software agents and human subjects and maximize its own profit. Like human subjects, each software agent owns five generating blocks, submits offers to the uniform price auction, and observes market outcomes when the market is cleared. All software agents determine their offers synchronously and independently. This reflects market rules that prevent one firm from communicating with another on offer strategies. We assume that each software agent considers that the electricity auction is continuously operated in this way in order to exclude the possibility of atypical offers (i.e., terminal offers) that a software agent may make at the end of the simulation period.

Software agents in this study anticipate forthcoming market conditions using the residual demand function. In an earlier study (Oh 2003), we showed that an inverse

[3] PJM Interconnection LLC (PJM) is a regional transmission organization (RTO) which coordinates the flow of electricity from power plants to distribution companies over a network of transmission lines owned by its members in all or parts of Delaware, Illinois, Indiana, Kentucky, Maryland, Michigan, New Jersey, Ohio, Pennsylvania, Tennessee, Virginia, West Virginia, and the District of Columbia.

function (1) fits the total supply curve, shaped like a hockey stick, reasonably well. Hence we specify the residual demand function of individual firms based upon the following total supply curve.

$$P_t = 1/(a_t + b_t(TC_t - \hat{Q}_t)) \tag{1}$$

where

P_t is the market price at time t ($/MWh)
$\hat{Q}_t$ is the forecasted system load (MW/h), and
TC_t is the total offered capacity

From (1), we specify a residual demand curve as an inverse function of the "excess" capacity offered into the auction (i.e. the available capacity that is offered but is not dispatched) as follows:

$$\begin{aligned} P_t &= 1/(a_t + b_t(OC_t + q_t - \hat{Q}_t)) = 1/(a_t + b_t OC_t - b_t(\hat{Q}_t - q_t)) \\ &= 1/(\alpha_t - \beta_t(\hat{Q}_t - q_t)/IC) \end{aligned} \tag{2}$$

where

OC_t is the offered capacity from other firms,
IC is the installed capacity of other firms,
$q_t < q_{\max}$ is the own capacity dispatched, and
$a_t > 0$ and $b_t > 0$ are the subjective parameter values of the firm.

The re-parameterization to $\alpha_t = a_t + b_t OC_t$ is convenient because OC_t is unobserved, and this avoids the computational problems of getting $a_t < 0$ when updating (b_t is also used in the updating process, but β_t is specified here because the values are easier to interpret). $P_t^L = 1/\alpha_t$ corresponds to the low market price if the firm could undercut the offers of all other firms and cover all of the load (i.e. $q_t = \hat{Q}_t$). Clearly, the firm's own installed capacity, $q_{\max}$, is the maximum that can actually be offered in the auction by a firm. For the other parameter ($\beta_t = b_t IC$), $P_t^H = 1/(\alpha_t - \beta_t)$ corresponds to the highest possible price in the market when $q_t = \hat{Q}_t - IC$ (i.e. the price for the first unit of capacity dispatched in the market).

This form of residual demand allows for a wide range of market behavior from competitive to the type of speculation implied by "hockey stick" supply curves (see Oh 2003). In a truly competitive market, $P_t^L = P_t^H$ and $\beta_t = 0$. When $0 < \beta_t < \alpha_t$, $P_t^H > P_t^L$ and the firm believes that it has some market power. As $\beta_t \to \alpha_t$, P_t^H increases, and values greater than the price cap in the market can be interpreted as other firms withholding capacity from the auction. This type of withholding can be sufficiently large to make the firm "pivotal" (i.e. essential for meeting the load when $OC_t < \hat{Q}_t$). The restriction $0 < \beta_t \hat{Q}_t / IC < \alpha_t$ ensures that prices are positive and finite for $0 \le q_t \le q_{\max}$, which is the relevant range of quantity offers for the firm ($\beta_t \hat{Q}_t / IC > \alpha_t$ makes the firm pivotal).

This linkage between parameter values and suppliers' behavior provides information on the design of software agents. For example, we set initial values of α_0 and β_0 so that IPT agents' residual demand curve is almost flat and their expected market price is close to the competitive price for a given load: $\beta_0 = 0$ and

$1/\alpha_0 = [P_0^C|\text{load}]$. For LS agents, the initial value of α_0 is the same as IPT agent's but the initial value of β_0 is set to match $1/(\alpha_0 - \beta_0) = [P_0^H|\text{load}]$, where P_0^H is an IPT agent's expected market price for a given load. We can compute cost-based prices and determine the range of $P_0^C \in [45, 55]$. The range of P_0^H is selected, $P_0^H \in [65, 100]$, to cover 30 percent or above (up to price cap) mark-up pricing behavior. Then, a set of randomly drawn values is assigned for each software agent, and set initial values of α_0 and β_0 are used.

The parameter vector, $\boldsymbol{\delta}_t = [\alpha_t, \beta_t]$, in the residual demand function defined in (2) is time-varying and revised with Kalman adaptive learning whenever new information is available. New information is embodied in the price prediction error. In each round, software agents adjust their price prediction in the previous round by applying the actual load in (2), computing the price prediction error ($\boldsymbol{\eta}_{t|t-1}$). This error contains new information about $\boldsymbol{\delta}_t$ beyond that contained in $\boldsymbol{\delta}_{t|t-1}$. The updating equation, $\boldsymbol{\delta}_{t|t} = \boldsymbol{\delta}_{t|t-1} + K_t \cdot \boldsymbol{\eta}_{t|t-1}$, forms the new parameter vector as a weighted average of $\boldsymbol{\delta}_{t|t-1}$ and new information contained in the predictor error, $\boldsymbol{\eta}_{t|t-1}$. The Kalman gain ($K_t$) determines the weight assigned to new information included in the price prediction error. By applying load forecast for the current round and the new parameter vector $\boldsymbol{\delta}_{t|t}$, software agents update the new residual demand function. Based on the estimated residual demand function, they evaluate market conditions and investigate whether or not they can be better off using non-competitive strategies. This learning process can be termed a Kalman adaptive algorithm.

The main advantage of our approach is that the behavior of each firm agent can be evaluated directly using conventional economic criteria such as a supply function equilibrium (Klemperer and Meyer 1989). However, unlike human subjects, our software agents are incapable of learning about the structure of the market by employing complex counterfactual scenarios or deep introspection, and rely on simple adaptive learning using a Kalman filter.

Once the residual demand function is updated, the software agent determines the optimal offer for each block of capacity to maximize expected profits. A numerical search is used to determine the set of optimal offers. A numerical search consists of 6 steps: (1) generating a series of random numbers distributed around the load forecast, (2) drawing a level of load (L_j) from the distribution, and computing the residual demand function with it, (3) for a set of possible offer prices $P_i \in [0, 100]$, computing profits from the first block (base block) to the block currently considered for L_j, (4) considering load uncertainty, computing the expected profits for each offer price, (5) determining the optimal offer for each block to maximize expected profit, and (6) if the expected profit of the optimum offer cannot increase total expected profit, withholding the block from the market to avoid paying stand-by costs.

In our earlier study (Mount and Oh 2004), we demonstrated that, in the presence of load forecasting errors, our design of software agents can replicate observed supply curves, which are shaped like hockey sticks. Figure 2 shows the simulated offer curve with a price cap of $1,000/MWh in PJM. This is exactly the type of behavior observed in deregulated electricity markets, and also shown in Fig. 1.

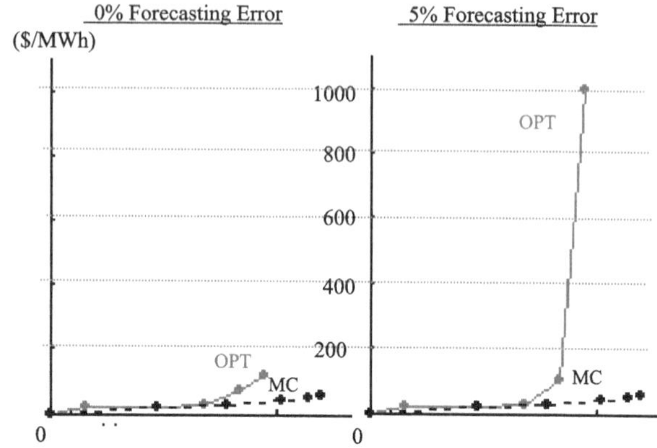

Fig. 2 The effect of different load forecasting errors (0% and 5%) on the optimum offers (OPT) of a firm (MC is the marginal cost) (Mount and Oh 2004)

3 Performance of Computer Agents

In the first part of this section, we will demonstrate that software agents can replicate the observed offer behavior of human subjects (students) and actual generating firms in the market. In the second part, the performance of the computer agents in the experiments is evaluated and compared to the performance of the two IPT agents and the two students, using average earnings in the three tests. Then, in the third part of this section, we will compare the results of experiments using all agents with those of experiments using four agents and two human subjects.

3.1 Replication of the Observed Behavior of Actual Suppliers and Human Subjects in Laboratory Tests

Figure 3 gives one example of how students and software agents behave in the auction. This example uses the session with the highest earnings for Test 1 (session 6). The 9th (top) and 24th (bottom) periods are selected to show the learning effects in offer behavior of software agents. Note that forecasted load and actual load are similar in these two periods. In earlier periods (including the 2nd and 3rd), students submitted the maximum offers ($100 MWh) for their 4th and 5th blocks and, as a result, students and software agents experienced very high market clearing prices ($100 MWh). In the 9th period, IPT agents submitted 80 percent of their installed capacity, similar to the proportion of forecasted load to the total installed capacity in the market (600 MWh), and their offer prices were above marginal costs. These offer behaviors were less competitive than their initial behaviors, but still more competitive than those of the students. However, as the auction was repeated, IPT agents evolved offer behaviors similar to students'. In the 24th period, IPT agents submitted the maximum offer prices ($100 MWh) and generated a supply curve shaped like a hockey stick, as the students did. This example demonstrates how IPT agents learned from market outcomes, developed their strategies and, finally, demonstrated offer behavior similar to that of students in the laboratory tests, and actual suppliers in the market.

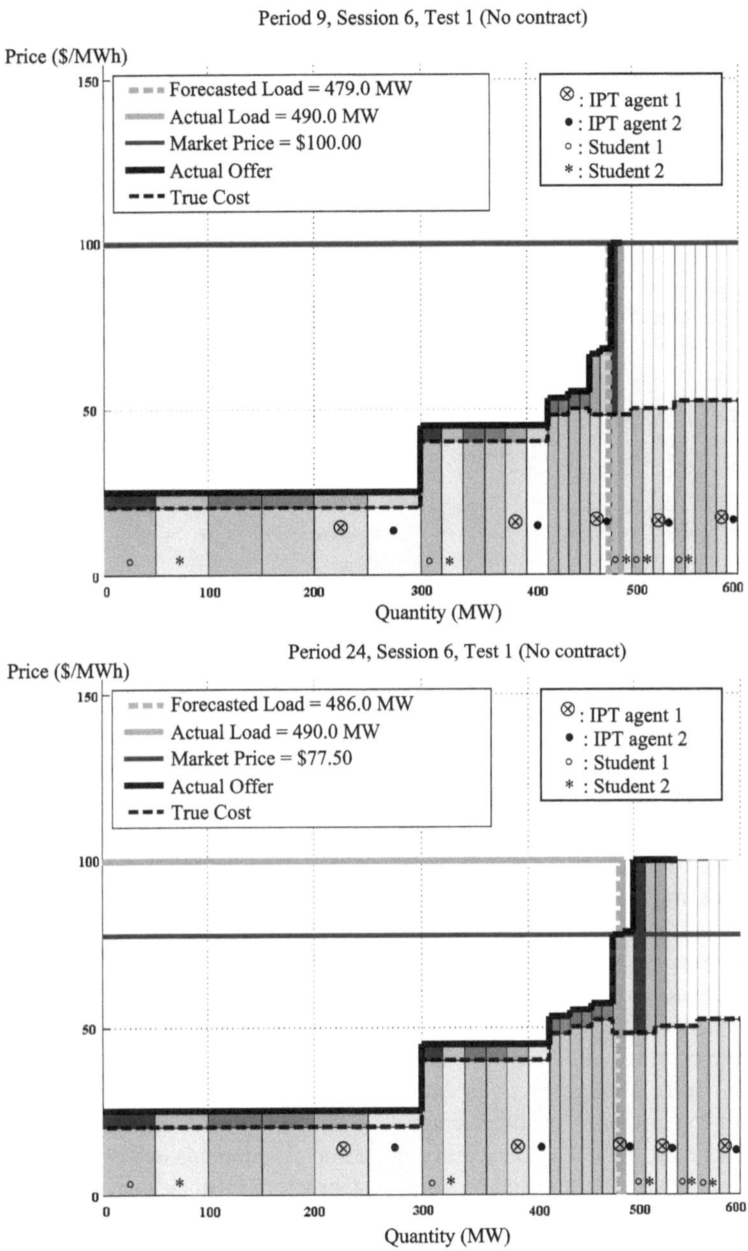

Fig. 3 Learning effects: offers submitted in the auction in periods of 4 and 24 (faded areas represent capacity blocks withheld from the market)

Table 2 Average earnings ($ in periods 11 to 20)

Tests	Students	VIF-agents	IPT-agents
Test 1	13,019	10,845	13,170
	(3,234)	(633)	(2,701)
Test 2	10,230	11,295	17,031
	(2,703)	(894)	(4,713)
Test 3	18,625	12,210	21,494
	(3,532)	(866)	(4,130)

Note: The standard deviation is given in parentheses

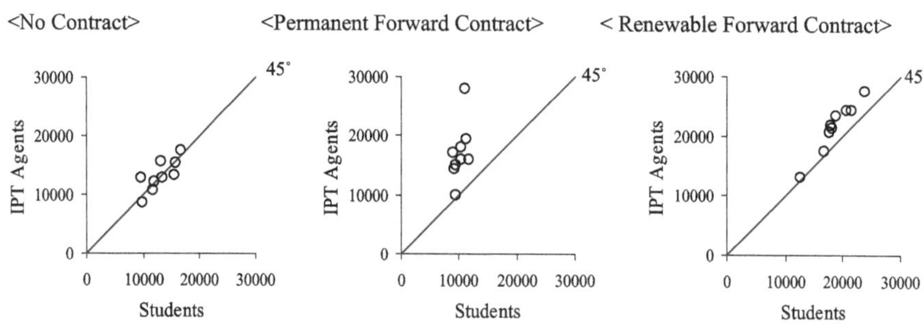

Fig. 4 Comparison of average earnings

3.2 *Human Subjects (Students) Versus IPT Agents*

Table 2 summarizes the main results of the first set of experiments in compact form. The average earnings of the IPT agents in different sessions were higher than the earnings of the students in all three tests, and significantly higher in Tests 2 and 3. The results for individual sessions are also depicted in Fig. 4. A circle above the 45 degree line implies that the two IPT agents in a specific session earned more than the two students. This was true for most sessions in all three tests. For the nine sessions in a test, earnings of the IPT agents were lower in 3 sessions for Test 1, but higher in every session for Tests 2 and 3.

The results for Test 1 are particularly important. In contrast to those in Tests 2 and 3, the earnings of the students and the IPT agents were similar in Test 1. Note that these were average earnings during 16–25 periods of Test 1, after a learning period of 15 periods. When the average earnings during the first 15 periods of Test 1 were compared, the IPT agents earned more than the students in 8 of the 9 sessions. Considering that all firms had the same cost structure for their generators, and that the students and IPT agents faced identical market conditions, the IPT agents did very well compared to the students.

In Test 2, the IPT agents had a distinct advantage because the students held a contract for 50 MW at a predetermined price. The objectives for the IPT agents and the students in Test 3 were different, but there was no clear advantage for the IPT agents. The results demonstrate that the IPT agents are (i) just as effective as the students in a simple market (Test 1), and (ii) are able to exploit market conditions effectively (Test 2 and Test 3) when given the opportunity. This provides some preliminary evidence that computer agents can be used effectively to test the performance of simple electricity markets.

It is also clear from Fig. 4 that the earnings of students and IPT agents are positively correlated. When one pair of students is successful in raising the market price, the IPT agents learn to speculate and reinforce the students' behavior. As a result, all firms obtain higher earnings. The IPT agents can also exploit unusual situations effectively. For example, in Session 2_9 of Test 2, one student sold only the contracted 50 MW and withheld everything else from the auction, and the other student submitted three of the four non-contracted blocks (40 MW in addition to the 50 MW contracted) at very high offer prices. As a result, the spot prices were high. These high prices persisted because the two students did not change their behavior. Under these circumstances, the IPT agents earned more than 2.5 times as much as the students. The IPT agents withheld less capacity than the first student and submitted lower price offers than the second student. It was not necessary for the IPT agents to speculate, because the students were speculating so aggressively. This is exactly the type of strategy that was followed by Eastern in the UK market during the 1990's, when high market prices were set on a predictable basis by two other firms.

Meanwhile, the earnings of the VIF agents were lower than those of the students in Tests 1 and 3, but not in Test 2, when the students had permanent contracts. This is expected, since a significant proportion of VIF agents' capacity is committed to be sold at a fixed price ($60/MWh), which is a lot lower than market clearing prices ($75/MWh or above).

3.3 Experiment with Human Subjects Versus Experiment with All Software Agents

When the three tests were repeated using computer agents to replace the two students, average earnings of firms and average market prices were higher than the corresponding values in all cases. For these tests, the students' firms were represented by Latent Speculators (LS). LS agents are more likely to speculate than IPT agents, but, when high prices occur, IPT agents adapt to the new market conditions and evolve into LS agents.

The average earnings by type of firm are summarized for the all-agent tests in Table 3. Percentage changes from the corresponding values in Table 2 are also shown, and, in eight out of the nine cases, these changes are positive. The small negative change for the VIF agents in Test 2 is the only exception. Positive changes for Test 1 (no contract) and Test 3 (renewable contract) are very large (ranging from 13% to 70%). It is only when the LS agents have a permanent contract in Test 2 that changes are relatively small (ranging from −1% to 21%). A comparison of the average earnings of the LS agents in Table 3 to corresponding session values for the students in Table 2 shows that the values for the LS agents fall in the ranges observed for

Table 3 Average earnings (\$/MWh)[a] for all-agent tests

Variable	LS-agents	VIF-agents	IPT-agents
Test 1	18,154	12,297	20,892
	(+39%)	(+13%)	(+59%)
Test 2	12,375	11,200	18,235
	(+21%)	(−1%)	(+7%)
Test 3	26,257	16,080	36,512
	(+41%)	(+32%)	(+70%)

[a]Percentage change from the corresponding value in Table 2 is given in parentheses

the students. For Tests 1 and 3, earnings of the LS agents are similar to the highest earnings of the students, but, for Test 2, they are only slightly above median value. The general conclusion is that the LS agents were able to exploit market power effectively when the opportunity arose in Tests 1 and 3. However, more students were able to get higher earnings than the LS agents in Test 2, when it was relatively difficult to exploit market power.

Using a Chow Type II test, it is possible to test whether or not the 18 new observations obtained from the all-agent tests deviated from the sample of 162 observations using students. A regression model is specified to make it easy to test the hypothesis as follows:

$$y_{ijk} = \mu + \sum_{i=2}^{3} \alpha_i M_i + \sum_{i=1}^{3}\sum_{j=2}^{3} \beta_{ij} F_{ij} + \sum_{i=1}^{3}\sum_{k=1}^{K-1} \gamma_{ik} S_{ik} + e_{ijk} \tag{3}$$

where y_{ijk} = log earnings for periods 11 to 20 for firm type j in session k of market i.

$M_i = 1$ for Test i, 0 otherwise
$F_{ij} = 1$ for Test i and Firm j, 0 otherwise
$j = 1$ for a student, 2 for a VIF agent and 3 for IPT agent
$S_{ik} = 1$ for Test i and Session k, -1 for Test i and the last session of each test, 0 otherwise

The parameters in model (3) were estimated using the pooled data set of 180 observations. Estimation outcomes from the first sample of 162 observations and the second sample of 180 observations are summarized in Appendix, Table 4.

The first null hypothesis assumed that the earnings of the all-agent firms were equal to the *average* earnings of the students (i.e. by setting the session effects for the all-agent tests to zero). The computed F statistic (3.82) is large and the null hypothesis is rejected (the critical value for an $F_{(18,130)}$ is 1.70 at the 5% level of significance). This implies that the earnings of the all-agent firms were statistically different from the average earnings in the tests using students.

The second null hypothesis assumed that the earnings of the all-agent firms were equal to the sessions with the *highest* earnings obtained by the students (i.e. by selecting the sessions with the largest positive session-coefficients for each market in Appendix, Table 4 (Sessions 6, 9 and 2 for Markets 1, 2 and 3, respectively)). In this case, the computed F statistic (0.95) is small and supports the null hypothesis (note that the critical value of 1.70 is still valid). In other words, the earnings for the all-agent firms were statistically equivalent to the sessions with the highest earnings obtained by the students.

Overall, the results from the all-agent tests are encouraging, and show that computer agents do provide a valid means of evaluating the performance of electricity markets. The computer agents were able to match the earnings of the best students. It will be interesting to find out in the future whether this also proves true for more complicated market structures, such as joint markets for energy and ancillary services.

4 Summary and Conclusions

The primary objective of this paper is to investigate how well computer agents can replicate the behavior of human subjects in tests of electricity auctions. Using *PowerWeb* to simulate the operation of a uniform price auction run by an ISO, four computer agents and two human subjects (graduate students) represent six supply firms in three different market situations. In each case, the patterns of load are exogenous and there are 20 trading periods (25 for Test 1). Three market structures are tested: (1) no forward contract (all dispatched capacity is paid the spot price), (2)'the two students hold a permanent forward contract (the contract price is fixed), and (3) the two students hold a renewable forward contract (the current spot price influences the forward price used to renew the contract). In a second experiment, the three tests are repeated with two additional computer agents replacing the students.

Results for the computer agents are reassuring. Using the maximization of expected profits as the objective criterion for submitting offers by an agent, it is possible to modify the general form of a computer agent to represent different types of firm, such as a vertically integrated firm, and to deal with different tests of forward contracts. In Test 1, with two students and four computer agents, the IPT agents and the students faced identical cost conditions. In 6 out of the 9 sessions in Test 1, the IPT agents had higher average earnings than the students. In the all-agent tests, earnings of the LS agents that replaced the students were higher than the corresponding average earnings of the students in all three tests. In Tests 1 and 3, earnings of the LS agents were similar to the highest earnings obtained by the students.

Our conclusion regarding the objective of the paper is that computer agents can replicate the behavior of students in an electricity auction effectively. In fact, the agents were also able to exploit unusual situations by, for example, behaving as free riders when the students in a session speculated aggressively. These results suggest that it is appropriate to do additional sensitivity tests using all computer agents. This is a promising line of research that is essential for developing realistic simulation models of deregulated electricity markets. Relying exclusively on human subjects to test different market structures will, due to the practical difficulty of recruiting enough people, limit the scope of the tests. Computer agents that can replicate realistic behavior can be used to extend the range and number of tests conducted with human subjects. This capability has tremendous potential for identifying potential flaws in market designs and finding effective ways to improve the performance of electricity markets before a specific market design is imposed on the public.

Acknowledgements We are grateful to students who participated in power experiments at Cornell University. This work was supported in part by the US Department of Energy through the Consortium for Electric Reliability Technology Solutions (CERTS) and in part by the National Science Foundation Power Systems Engineering Research Center (PSERC).

Appendix: General Instructions for Testing an Electricity Market Using Powerweb

A.1 Introduction

PowerWeb is a computer program that allows you to use your skills in economic decision-making to test an electricity market. You will have the opportunity to earn money through your actions in this test. Any money that you earn will be yours to keep, and you should try to make as much money as possible. Other people in the test will be competing directly against you in the market. Please do not communicate with any of the other participants. It is important to us that you understand these instructions. If you do, it will improve your chances of earning more money in the test and will improve the quality of the data we gather. If you have questions at any time, please raise your hand and an instructor will answer your question. When testing a market, it is essential that we have your full attention. Do NOT open other windows or check your email.

A.2 The Objective

For a standard test of an electricity market, you will be one of **six** different suppliers. (You do not need any prior knowledge of this type of market to participate in the test.) In each market, there is a single buyer of electricity who has the obligation to meet demand (load) at the least cost. As a supplier, you can generate a maximum of **100 megawatts (MW)** of electricity, and this production capacity is divided into five blocks (generators) with different operating costs. The size and operating cost of each of your generators will be revealed to you at the start of the test. The cost structures of all suppliers are very similar to each other.

Each test will last for a specified number of trading periods. In each period, **your goal is to maximize your own earnings**. The amount of money you keep at the end of the test will be proportional to your total earnings over all periods. In each period of the test, you will participate in an auction and submit offers to sell each of your generators. An offer represents the minimum price at which you are willing to sell each MW from that generator.

Table 4 Estimation results of (3): dependent variable = average earnings

Variable (Parameter)	Model 1			Model 2 (agents' earnings = average)			Model 3 (agents' earnings = the highest)		
	Est.	t-value	Pr > $\|t\|$	Est.	t-value	Pr > $\|t\|$	Est.	t-value	Pr > $\|t\|$
Intercept (μ)	9.441	252.33	<0.0001	9.477	230.57	<0.0001	9.451	265.12	<0.0001
Market2 (α_2)	−0.242	−4.57	<0.0001	−0.256	−4.40	<0.0001	−0.247	−4.90	<0.0001
Market3 (α_3)	0.374	7.07	<0.0001	0.373	6.42	<0.0001	0.370	7.34	<0.0001
Market1VIF (β_{12})	−0.151	−2.85	0.0051	−0.175	−3.01	0.0031	−0.175	−3.49	0.0006
Market1IPT(β_{13})	0.024	0.46	0.6445	0.036	0.62	0.5357	0.036	0.72	0.4717
Market2VIF (β_{22})	0.130	2.46	0.0151	0.107	1.85	0.0670	0.107	2.15	0.0336
Market2IPT (β_{23})	0.510	9.64	<0.0001	0.498	8.56	<0.0001	0.498	9.96	<0.0001
Market3VIF (β_{32})	−0.407	−7.69	<0.0001	−0.415	−7.15	<0.0001	−0.415	−8.31	<0.0001
Market3IPT (β_{33})	0.141	2.66	0.0088	0.160	2.75	0.0068	0.160	3.19	0.0017
Session1_2 ($\gamma_{1,2}$)	0.013	0.22	0.8289	0.013	0.19	0.8520	0.007	0.11	0.9136
Session1_3 ($\gamma_{1,3}$)	0.086	1.41	0.1597	0.086	1.22	0.2240	0.080	1.32	0.1905
Session1_4 ($\gamma_{1,4}$)	0.094	1.54	0.1253	0.094	1.33	0.1848	0.088	1.44	0.1506
Session1_5 ($\gamma_{1,5}$)	−0.096	−1.57	0.1183	−0.096	−1.36	0.1766	−0.103	−1.69	0.0925
Session1_6 ($\gamma_{1,6}$)[a]	0.206	3.36	0.0010	0.206	2.90	0.0042	0.259	5.70	<0.0001
Session1_7 ($\gamma_{1,7}$)	−0.050	−0.82	0.4149	−0.050	−0.71	0.4811	−0.057	−0.93	0.3521
Session1_8 ($\gamma_{1,8}$)	0.138	2.26	0.0256	0.138	1.95	0.0530	0.131	2.17	0.0319
Session1_9 ($\gamma_{1,9}$)	−0.130	−2.12	0.0358	−0.130	−1.83	0.0690	−0.136	−2.25	0.0262
Session2_2 ($\gamma_{2,2}$)	0.099	1.62	0.1068	0.099	1.40	0.1628	0.106	1.74	0.0838
Session2_3 ($\gamma_{2,3}$)	−0.232	−3.80	0.0002	−0.232	−3.28	0.0013	−0.226	−3.73	0.0003
Session2_4 ($\gamma_{2,4}$)	0.056	0.92	0.3596	0.056	0.79	0.4285	0.063	1.03	0.3044
Session2_5 ($\gamma_{2,5}$)	−0.034	−0.56	0.5798	−0.034	−0.48	0.6324	−0.028	−0.45	0.6501
Session2_6 ($\gamma_{2,6}$)	0.032	0.52	0.6069	0.032	0.45	0.6567	0.038	0.62	0.5335
Session2_7 ($\gamma_{2,7}$)	−0.064	−1.05	0.2964	−0.064	−0.91	0.3668	−0.058	−0.95	0.3429
Session2_8 ($\gamma_{2,8}$)	−0.077	−1.26	0.2086	−0.077	−1.09	0.2770	−0.071	−1.17	0.2445
Session2_9 ($\gamma_{2,9}$)[a]	0.221	3.62	0.0004	0.221	3.13	0.0021	0.170	3.76	0.0002
Session3_2 ($\gamma_{3,2}$)[a]	0.208	3.40	0.0009	0.207	2.93	0.0039	0.291	6.42	<0.0001
Session3_3 ($\gamma_{3,3}$)	0.055	0.91	0.3659	0.055	0.78	0.4346	0.045	0.74	0.4599
Session3_4 ($\gamma_{3,4}$)	−0.342	−5.59	<0.0001	−0.342	−4.83	<0.0001	−0.352	−5.80	<0.0001
Session3_5 ($\gamma_{3,5}$)	−0.023	−0.37	0.7091	−0.023	−0.32	0.7472	−0.033	−0.55	0.5834
Session3_6 ($\gamma_{3,6}$)	−0.105	−1.71	0.0891	−0.105	−1.48	0.1413	−0.115	−1.90	0.0596
Session3_7 ($\gamma_{3,7}$)	0.098	1.61	0.1098	0.098	1.39	0.1666	0.088	1.45	0.1495
Session3_8 ($\gamma_{3,8}$)	−0.012	−0.19	0.8492	−0.012	−0.16	0.8695	−0.022	−0.36	0.7157
Session3_9 ($\gamma_{3,9}$)	0.119	1.95	0.0537	0.119	1.68	0.0949	0.108	1.79	0.0758
Nobs	162 (=1st set of samples)			180 (=two sets of samples)			180(=two sets of samples)		
Sum of Squ. Errors	3.2503			4.9673			3.6759		

[a]Sessions with the highest earnings obtained by the students for each market

A.3 How the Auction Works

After all the offers have been collected from the suppliers, the buyer will rank them from the least expensive to the most expensive. The buyer will then accept offers in order from the lowest to highest offer price until sufficient capacity is purchased to meet the load. The buyer will pay all purchased generators the same price, and this price is equal to the offer for the most expensive generator purchased. This auction is called a **Uniform Price Auction** paying the **Last Accepted Offer**. (In some tests, a different auction rule may be used. However, additional information will be provided and you will always be told about the changes first.)

A.4 The Rules of the Market

(1) You may submit an offer for each of your five blocks of capacity in every period up to the maximum of 100 MW. If you choose to submit an offer on a block of capacity, you will have to pay a fixed **Standby Cost of $5/MWh** regardless of whether you actually sell any of that block. (The standby cost is a simple way to represent the opportunity cost of being available in the market. These costs could include postponing maintenance activities, not selling energy in another market and paying wages to part of the workforce.)

(2) You may choose not to sell a block of capacity by clicking the **shutdown** check-box, and in this case, the standby cost is automatically set to zero.

(3) The maximum price (**the price cap**) that the buyer is willing to pay for electricity is **$100/MWh**. If you offer a block of capacity above $100/MWh, the buyer will disregard your offer. You will receive an error message, and this will allow you to resubmit your offers.

(4) You will never receive less than your offer price for the capacity you sell. As a rule of thumb, if your offer price is less than the final clearing price then you will sell that block of capacity. If your offer is greater than the clearing price, you will not sell that block of capacity.

(5) There is a **fixed cost of $1200/period** that must be paid in every trading period to cover the finance cost of capital investments.

(6) At the start of each trading period, the buyer will post the forecasted load, but the actual load need not be the same as the forecasted level. You will be told the range of possible values for the actual load.

(7) Since there are incentives for suppliers to withhold some capacity from the auction, it is possible that the total capacity submitted into the auction is insufficient to meet the actual load. Hence, some scheme for dealing with capacity shortfalls is required. In this market, the following procedure is used:

> The market price is set to the highest offer submitted into the auction. The buyer meets the shortfall of capacity by contracting with suppliers in another power pool. The actual load reported does *not* include these imports, and consequently, it may be substantially below the forecasted load (i.e. outside the normal range of forecasting errors).

A.5 Submitting an Offer to the Auction

Each period of the auction begins with an **Offer Submission Page**. The screen shot for Seller 1 in Period 1 will help you understand the information presented and show you how to enter your offers into the auction. The parameters in this example are not necessarily the same as in the actual test. In this example, the seller has chosen to submit the first four blocks of capacity (Gen 1–4) and to withhold the last block (Gen 5). Every block submitted to the auction pays a standby cost of $5/MW, but the variable costs will only be paid on blocks that are purchased by the buyer.

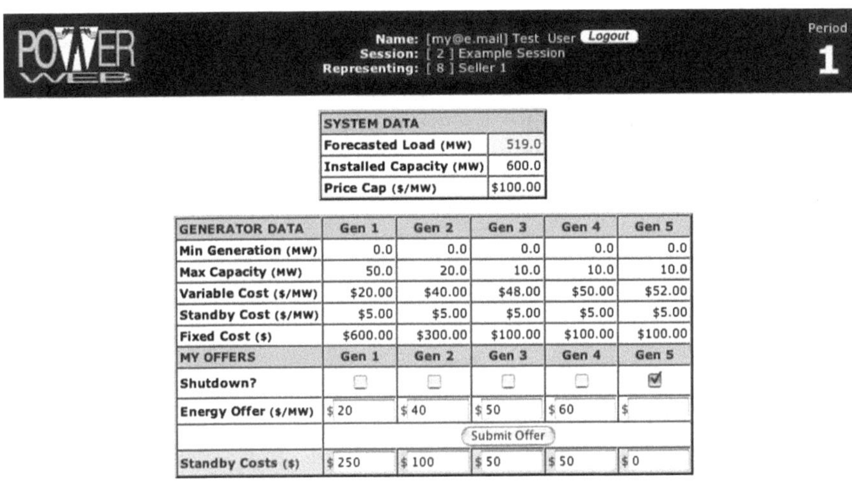

Name: [my@e.mail] Test User Logout
Session: [2] Example Session
Representing: [8] Seller 1
Period 1

SYSTEM DATA	
Forecasted Load (MW)	519.0
Installed Capacity (MW)	600.0
Price Cap ($/MW)	$100.00

GENERATOR DATA	Gen 1	Gen 2	Gen 3	Gen 4	Gen 5
Min Generation (MW)	0.0	0.0	0.0	0.0	0.0
Max Capacity (MW)	50.0	20.0	10.0	10.0	10.0
Variable Cost ($/MW)	$20.00	$40.00	$48.00	$50.00	$52.00
Standby Cost ($/MW)	$5.00	$5.00	$5.00	$5.00	$5.00
Fixed Cost ($)	$600.00	$300.00	$100.00	$100.00	$100.00
MY OFFERS	Gen 1	Gen 2	Gen 3	Gen 4	Gen 5
Shutdown?	☐	☐	☐	☐	☑
Energy Offer ($/MW)	$ 20	$ 40	$ 50	$ 60	$
			Submit Offer		
Standby Costs ($)	$ 250	$ 100	$ 50	$ 50	$ 0

The upper table of the **Offer Submission Page** gives the following information about the **SYSTEM DATA**:

(1) The **forecasted load** in MW will typically vary from period to period (the yellow background indicates that the forecasts may change).
(2) The **installed capacity** in MW gives the total of the maximum generating capacity of all suppliers in the market.
(3) The **price cap** in $/MWh is the maximum price paid in the auction, and offers above this price will not be accepted by the buyer.

The columns in the lower table on the **Offer Submission Page** correspond to the five different generators (**Gen 1–5**) that you control as a supplier. For each generator, the rows for the **GENERATOR DATA** are:

(1) The **minimum generation** in MW for the generator to operate.
(2) The **maximum capacity** in MW of output from the generator.
(3) The **variable cost** in $/MWh (for fuel etc.) of generating electricity.
(4) The **standby cost** in $/MW (the opportunity cost of being available for all capacity submitted to the auction).

(5) The **fixed cost** in $/trading period (the cost of financing capital investments, such as interest payments on bonds).

The corresponding rows for **MY OFFERS** are:

(1) A check box for **shutdown?** (i.e. withholding a generator from the auction), and if a generator is withheld, the offered price in the next row is disabled and the standby costs are set to zero.
(2) The **energy offer** in $/MW that you must specify for each generator that is not withheld (your offer is the minimum price that you are willing to accept for generating electricity).
(3) The actual **standby costs** in $/trading period that are paid whenever a generator is submitted into the auction (these cost are computed automatically and cannot be edited).

The **submit offer** button is used to submit a set of offers to the auction after you have specified an offer for (or decided to withhold) each of your five generators. NOTE: submitting a blank offer for a generator that is not explicitly withheld corresponds to submitting a zero offer—be careful.

A.6 Auction Results

After you have submitted your offers, PowerWeb will inform you to wait until all of the other suppliers have finished submitting their offers. The auction results will then be calculated by PowerWeb and presented to you in an **Auction Results Page**. The number of the trading period for these results is shown at the far right of the banner at the top of the screen. The top table gives information about the **SYSTEM DATA**. The first row repeats the **forecasted load** in MW from the **Offer Submission Page**, and the second row gives the **actual load** in MW.

The top section of the middle table under **GENERATOR DATA** repeats the **variable cost** in $/MW and the **standby cost** in $/MW for each one of your generators from the **Offer Submission Page**. The middle section under **MY OFFERS** summarizes the outcome of the auction for each one of your generators. The first pair of rows for **energy capacity** show the **offered** quantities in MW submitted to the auction, and the corresponding quantities **sold** in MW are shown underneath. The second pair of rows for **energy price** show the **offered** prices in $/MW for each generator, and the corresponding market prices **paid** in $/MW are shown underneath (market prices are also shown for generators that were withheld). If a generator was withheld, the capacity values and the offered price are blank and colored gray. A green background implies your offer was accepted (market price > the offer), a red background implies your offer was rejected (market price < the offer), and a yellow background implies your offer set the market price (market price = the offer). The last column of the table summarizes the total quantities and the average price paid for all five generators.

The bottom section of the middle table under **EARNINGS** summarizes the revenues and the costs for each generator. The five rows represent:

POWER WEB

Name: [my@e.mail] Test User Logout
Session: [2] Example Session
Representing: [8] Seller 1

Period **1**

SYSTEM DATA	
Forecasted Load (MW)	519.0
Actual Load (MW)	520.0

GENERATOR DATA		Gen 1	Gen 2	Gen 3	Gen 4	Gen 5	
Variable Cost ($/MW)		$20.00	$40.00	$48.00	$50.00	$52.00	
Standby Cost ($/MW)		$5.00	$5.00	$5.00	$5.00	$5.00	
MY OFFERS		Gen 1	Gen 2	Gen 3	Gen 4	Gen 5	Total (or Avg)
Energy Capacity (MW)	Offered	50.0	20.0	10.0	10.0		90.0
	Sold	50.0	20.0	10.0	10.0		90.0
Energy Price ($/MW)	Offered	$20.00	$40.00	$50.00	$60.00		
	Paid	$60.00	$60.00	$60.00	$60.00	$60.00	$60.00
EARNINGS		Gen 1	Gen 2	Gen 3	Gen 4	Gen 5	Total
Revenue from Energy Sales ($)		$3000.00	$1200.00	$600.00	$600.00		$5400.00
Variable Costs ($)		$1000.00	$800.00	$480.00	$500.00		$2780.00
Standby Costs ($)		$250.00	$100.00	$50.00	$50.00		$450.00
Fixed Costs ($)		$600.00	$300.00	$100.00	$100.00	$100.00	$1200.00
Total Earnings ($)		$1150.00	$0.00	($30.00)	($50.00)	($100.00)	$970.00

Continue >>

MARKET HISTORY																		
Period		Load (MW)		My Sales (MW)	Market Share	Capacity (MW)					Energy Price ($/MW)					Avg Price ($/MW)		Earnings ($)
		Forecast	Actual			Gen 1	Gen 2	Gen 3	Gen 4	Gen 5	Gen 1	Gen 2	Gen 3	Gen 4	Gen 5	Mine	Market	
1	In	519.0	520.0	90.0	17%	50.0	20.0	10.0	10.0		$20.00	$40.00	$50.00	$60.00		$60.00	$60.00	$970.00
	Out					50.0	20.0	10.0	10.0		$60.00	$60.00	$60.00	$60.00	$60.00			
																	Cumulative Earnings	$970.00
																	Cumulative Earnings * Exchange Rate(0.00025)	$0.24

(1) The **revenue from energy sales** in $/period is equal to the capacity sold times the market price paid.
(2) The **variable costs** in $/period are equal to the capacity sold times the variable cost/MW.
(3) The **standby costs** in $/period are equal to the capacity submitted into the auction times the standby cost/MW.
(4) The **fixed costs** in $/period are the same in every period and are not affected by the outcome of the auction.
(5) The **total earnings** in $/period are the difference between the revenue in row 1 and the sum of the costs in rows 2–4 (any value colored RED in parentheses is a LOSS).

The last column of the middle table under **EARNINGS** summarizes the revenues, costs and earnings for all five of your generators (if the value of **total earnings** is colored RED in parentheses, you lost money in this trading period). Clicking on **Continue >>** will send you to the **Offer Submission Page** for the next trading period.

The bottom table on the **Auction Results Page** gives a **MARKET HISTORY** of the previous auctions for up to five trading periods (in reverse order, with the results from the last trading period in the first row). There is also a link to the complete auction history. The columns display the following information:

(1) The number of the **period**.
(2) The **forecasted load** in MW.
(3) The **actual load** in MW.
(4) The amount of your capacity sold in MW (**my sales**).
(5) Your percentage **market share** (100xMy Sales/Actual Load).
(6) The **capacity** in MW offered (top row—**In**) and sold (bottom row—**Out**) for each one of your generators.
(7) The **price** in $/MW offered (top row—**In**) and paid (bottom row—**Out**) for each one of your generators (including generators that were withheld).
(8) The **average price** in $/MWh paid for your capacity (**mine**) and paid for all capacity purchased in the auction (**market**).
(9) The total **earnings** in $ for the trading period.

At the bottom of the **MARKET HISTORY**, the **cumulative earnings** over all trading periods are shown. The cumulative earnings are in "PowerWeb dollars", and these earnings are converted to real dollars using an explicit exchange rate. Once again, RED values of real dollars in parentheses mean that you are losing money and not earning enough to cover your fixed costs.

A.7 Test 1-A

A.7.1 Uniform Price Auction with Stochastic Load (No Price Response)

You are one of six suppliers in an electricity market. Each supplier owns 100 MW of capacity, divided into five blocks. Offers to sell these blocks are submitted into an auction. An ISO selects the least expensive combination of offers to meet the system load and determines the market clearing price (last accepted offer) paid to all successful offers. For each period, you will be given a forecast of the system load. The actual load is uncertain but it falls into the range of **Forecast ± 20 MW**. Market price does not affect actual load in any way. When actual load is above 500 MW, some of your capacity is essential to meet load. There is an equal chance that actual load is above or below the forecast.

There are two types of operating costs. The first is the operating cost/MWh for capacity that is dispatched. The second is a fixed standby cost of **$5/MWh** for submitting an offer. Hence, standby costs are paid when a block is offered into the market even if it is not dispatched. Withholding blocks from the auction is the only way to avoid standby costs for those blocks (the offer submission page for PowerWeb has check boxes for withholding blocks). There is also a fixed cost charged each period to cover capital costs. If the total capacity offered into the auction is less than the actual load, the ISO covers the shortfall by purchasing imports from outside of the market. Only the portion of the load served by suppliers in the market is reported as actual load. The portion served by imports is not included.

Name: [my@e.mail] Test User Logout
Session: [2] Example Session
Representing: [8] Seller 1
Period 1

SYSTEM DATA	
Forecasted Load (MW)	519.0
Installed Capacity (MW)	600.0
Price Cap ($/MW)	$100.00

GENERATOR DATA	Gen 1	Gen 2	Gen 3	Gen 4	Gen 5
Min Generation (MW)	0.0	0.0	0.0	0.0	0.0
Max Capacity (MW)	50.0	20.0	10.0	10.0	10.0
Variable Cost ($/MW)	$20.00	$40.00	$48.00	$50.00	$52.00
Standby Cost ($/MW)	$5.00	$5.00	$5.00	$5.00	$5.00
Fixed Cost ($)	$600.00	$300.00	$100.00	$100.00	$100.00
MY OFFERS	Gen 1	Gen 2	Gen 3	Gen 4	Gen 5
Shutdown?	☐	☐	☐	☐	☑
Energy Offer ($/MW)	$ 20	$ 40	$ 50	$ 60	$
	Submit Offer				
Standby Costs ($)	$ 250	$ 100	$ 50	$ 50	$ 0

Name: [my@e.mail] Test User Logout
Session: [2] Example Session
Representing: [8] Seller 1
Period 1

SYSTEM DATA	
Forecasted Load (MW)	519.0
Actual Load (MW)	520.0

GENERATOR DATA		Gen 1	Gen 2	Gen 3	Gen 4	Gen 5	
Variable Cost ($/MW)		$20.00	$40.00	$48.00	$50.00	$52.00	
Standby Cost ($/MW)		$5.00	$5.00	$5.00	$5.00	$5.00	
MY OFFERS		Gen 1	Gen 2	Gen 3	Gen 4	Gen 5	Total (or Avg)
Energy Capacity (MW)	Offered	50.0	20.0	10.0	10.0		90.0
	Sold	50.0	20.0	10.0	10.0		90.0
Energy Price ($/MW)	Offered	$20.00	$40.00	$50.00	$60.00		
	Paid	$60.00	$60.00	$60.00	$60.00	$60.00	$60.00
EARNINGS		Gen 1	Gen 2	Gen 3	Gen 4	Gen 5	Total
Revenue from Energy Sales ($)		$3000.00	$1200.00	$600.00	$600.00		$5400.00
Variable Costs ($)		$1000.00	$800.00	$480.00	$500.00		$2780.00
Standby Costs ($)		$250.00	$100.00	$50.00	$50.00		$450.00
Fixed Costs ($)		$600.00	$300.00	$100.00	$100.00	$100.00	$1200.00
Total Earnings ($)		$1150.00	$0.00	($30.00)	($50.00)	($100.00)	$970.00

Continue >>

MARKET HISTORY																			
Period		Load (MW)		My Sales (MW)	Market Share	Capacity (MW)					Energy Price ($/MW)					Avg Price ($/MW)		Earnings ($)
		Forecast	Actual			Gen 1	Gen 2	Gen 3	Gen 4	Gen 5	Gen 1	Gen 2	Gen 3	Gen 4	Gen 5	Mine	Market	
1	In	519.0	520.0	90.0	17%	50.0	20.0	10.0	10.0		$20.00	$40.00	$50.00	$60.00		$60.00	$60.00	$970.00
	Out					50.0	20.0	10.0	10.0		$60.00	$60.00	$60.00	$60.00	$60.00			
Cumulative Earnings																		$970.00
Cumulative Earnings * Exchange Rate(0.00025)																		$0.24

Your objective is to maximize your earnings over a series of 25 periods.

Summary

Auction: Uniform–Last Accepted Offer
Number of Suppliers: 6

Periods:	25
Load:	Forecast = 490 MW ± 60 MW, Actual = Forecast ± 20 MW
Price Response:	Load is price inelastic
Standby Costs:	\$5/MWh for each block
Shortfall Mechanism:	Unlimited imports available
Fixed Cost:	\$1200/period
Price Cap:	\$100/MWh
Exchange Rate:	1/4000

A.8 Test 1-B

A.8.1 Uniform Price Auction with Stochastic Load (No Price Response) (Suppliers Hold Forward Contracts for 50 MW of Capacity)

> Regulators are frustrated by the number of price spikes in electricity markets, which they attribute to unjustified speculation by suppliers. Consequently, regulations now require that all suppliers must hold forward contracts for selling some of their capacity each period. In this test, each supplier has already signed a contract for **50 MW** (the first block of capacity) at a fixed price of **\$60/MWh**, and this contract will be in place for all periods. Hence, your objective is to maximize the profits from selling the remaining four blocks of capacity (the first block will be submitted automatically). You will always be paid \$60 × 50 MW = \$3000 each period for the first block regardless of whether the market clearing price is above or below \$60/MWh. In all other respects, the rules of the auction are the same as TEST 1-A.

You are one of six suppliers in an electricity market. Each supplier owns 100 MW of capacity, divided into five blocks. Offers to sell these blocks are submitted into an auction. An ISO selects the least expensive combination of offers to meet the system load and determines the market clearing price (last accepted offer) paid to all successful offers. For each period, you will be given a forecast of the system load. The actual load is uncertain but it falls into the range of **Forecast ± 20 MW**. Market price does not affect actual load in any way. When actual load is above 500 MW, some of your capacity is essential to meet load. There is an equal chance that actual load is above or below the forecast.

There are two types of operating costs. The first is the operating cost/MWh for capacity that is dispatched. The second is a fixed standby cost of **\$5/MWh** for submitting an offer. Hence, standby costs are paid when a block is offered into the market even if it is not dispatched. Withholding blocks from the auction is the only way to avoid standby costs for those blocks (the offer submission page for PowerWeb has check boxes for withholding blocks). There is also a fixed cost charged each period to cover capital costs. If the total capacity offered into the auction is less than the actual load, the ISO covers the shortfall by purchasing imports from outside of the market. Only the portion of the load served by suppliers in the market is reported as actual load. The portion served by imports is not included.

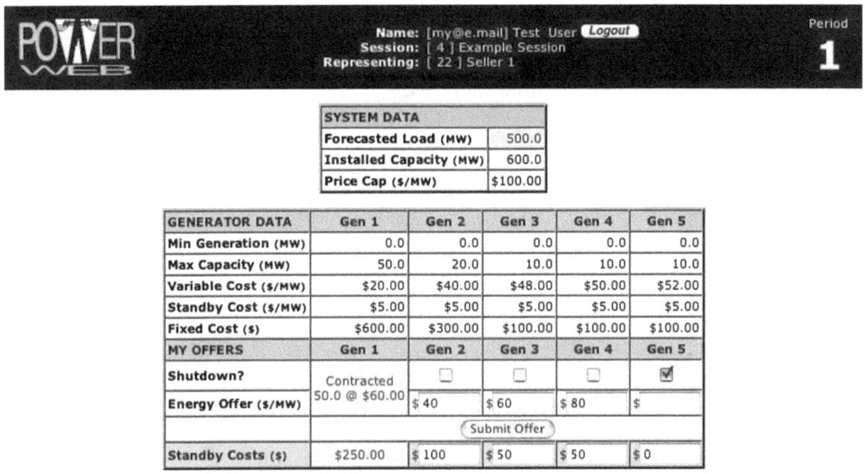

SYSTEM DATA	
Forecasted Load (MW)	500.0
Installed Capacity (MW)	600.0
Price Cap ($/MW)	$100.00

GENERATOR DATA	Gen 1	Gen 2	Gen 3	Gen 4	Gen 5
Min Generation (MW)	0.0	0.0	0.0	0.0	0.0
Max Capacity (MW)	50.0	20.0	10.0	10.0	10.0
Variable Cost ($/MW)	$20.00	$40.00	$48.00	$50.00	$52.00
Standby Cost ($/MW)	$5.00	$5.00	$5.00	$5.00	$5.00
Fixed Cost ($)	$600.00	$300.00	$100.00	$100.00	$100.00
MY OFFERS	**Gen 1**	**Gen 2**	**Gen 3**	**Gen 4**	**Gen 5**
Shutdown?	Contracted 50.0 @ $60.00	☐	☐	☐	☑
Energy Offer ($/MW)		$ 40	$ 60	$ 80	$
	Submit Offer				
Standby Costs ($)	$250.00	$ 100	$ 50	$ 50	$ 0

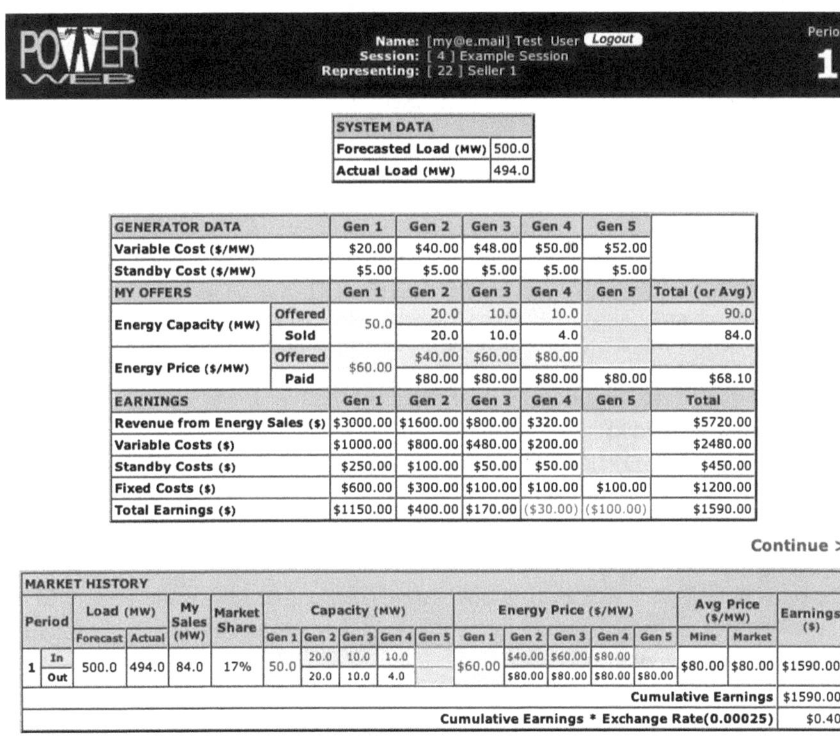

SYSTEM DATA	
Forecasted Load (MW)	500.0
Actual Load (MW)	494.0

GENERATOR DATA		Gen 1	Gen 2	Gen 3	Gen 4	Gen 5	
Variable Cost ($/MW)		$20.00	$40.00	$48.00	$50.00	$52.00	
Standby Cost ($/MW)		$5.00	$5.00	$5.00	$5.00	$5.00	
MY OFFERS		**Gen 1**	**Gen 2**	**Gen 3**	**Gen 4**	**Gen 5**	**Total (or Avg)**
Energy Capacity (MW)	Offered	50.0	20.0	10.0	10.0		90.0
	Sold		20.0	10.0	4.0		84.0
Energy Price ($/MW)	Offered	$60.00	$40.00	$60.00	$80.00		
	Paid		$80.00	$80.00	$80.00	$80.00	$68.10
EARNINGS		**Gen 1**	**Gen 2**	**Gen 3**	**Gen 4**	**Gen 5**	**Total**
Revenue from Energy Sales ($)		$3000.00	$1600.00	$800.00	$320.00		$5720.00
Variable Costs ($)		$1000.00	$800.00	$480.00	$200.00		$2480.00
Standby Costs ($)		$250.00	$100.00	$50.00	$50.00		$450.00
Fixed Costs ($)		$600.00	$300.00	$100.00	$100.00	$100.00	$1200.00
Total Earnings ($)		$1150.00	$400.00	$170.00	($30.00)	($100.00)	$1590.00

Continue >>

MARKET HISTORY																				
Period		Load (MW)		My Sales (MW)	Market Share	Capacity (MW)					Energy Price ($/MW)					Avg Price ($/MW)		Earnings ($)
		Forecast	Actual			Gen 1	Gen 2	Gen 3	Gen 4	Gen 5	Gen 1	Gen 2	Gen 3	Gen 4	Gen 5	Mine	Market	
1	In	500.0	494.0	84.0	17%	50.0	20.0	10.0	10.0		$60.00	$40.00	$60.00	$80.00		$80.00	$80.00	$1590.00
	Out						20.0	10.0	4.0			$80.00	$80.00	$80.00	$80.00			
Cumulative Earnings																		$1590.00
Cumulative Earnings * Exchange Rate(0.00025)																		$0.40

Your objective is to maximize your earnings over a series of 20 periods.

Summary

Auction: Uniform–Last Accepted Offer
Number of Suppliers: 6

Periods:	20
Load:	Forecast = 490 MW ± 60 MW, Actual = Forecast ± 20 MW
Price Response:	Load is price inelastic
Standby Costs:	$5/MWh for each block
Shortfall Mechanism:	Unlimited imports available
Fixed Cost:	$1200/period
Price Cap:	$100/MWh
Exchange Rate:	1/4000

A.9 Test 1-C

A.9.1 Uniform Price Auction with Stochastic Load (No Price Response) (Suppliers Renew Forward Contracts for 50 MW of Capacity)

This test is similar to Test 1-B with one modification. You will now have to renew the forward contract for the first block of 50 MW every 10th period during the test. (The first contract for periods 1 to 10 is set at $60/MWh.) You will be paid for the forward contracts as well as for the earnings on the other four blocks of capacity. A forward price will be reported with the auction results after each period, and it represents the current price of a new 10-period contract. This forward price is influenced by the market (spot) price in the auction. If your market prices are consistently above (below) the current forward price, then the forward price will gradually increase (decrease). The forward price in period 10 will determine the price for the new contract in periods 11–20. You will also be paid for renewing the contract in period 20 in the following way: [10 × 50 MW (forward price in period 20–$60)]. (This is equivalent to replacing the first contract with the final contract.)

You are one of six suppliers in an electricity market. Each supplier owns 100 MW of capacity, divided into five blocks. Offers to sell these blocks are submitted into an auction. An ISO selects the least expensive combination of offers to meet the system load and determines the market clearing price (last accepted offer) paid to all successful offers. For each period, you will be given a forecast of the system load. The actual load is uncertain but it falls into the range of **Forecast ± 20 MW**. Market price does not affect actual load in any way. When actual load is above 500 MW, some of your capacity is essential to meet load. There is an equal chance that actual load is above or below the forecast.

There are two types of operating costs. The first is the operating cost/MWh for capacity that is dispatched. The second is a fixed standby cost of **$5/MWh** for submitting an offer. Hence, standby costs are paid when a block is offered into the market even if it is not dispatched. Withholding blocks from the auction is the only way to avoid standby costs for those blocks (the offer submission page for PowerWeb has check boxes for withholding blocks). There is also a fixed cost charged each period to cover capital costs. If the total capacity offered into the auction is less than the actual load, the ISO covers the shortfall by purchasing imports from outside of the market. Only the portion of the load served by suppliers in the market is reported as actual load. The portion served by imports is not included.

Your objective is to maximize your earnings over a series of 20 periods.

Summary

Auction: Uniform–Last Accepted Offer
Number of Suppliers: 6
Periods: 20
Load: Forecast = 490 MW ± 60 MW, Actual = Forecast ± 20 MW
Price Response: Load is price inelastic
Standby Costs: $5/MWh for each block
Shortfall Mechanism: Unlimited imports available
Fixed Cost: $1200/period
Price Cap: $100/MWh
Exchange Rate: 1/4000

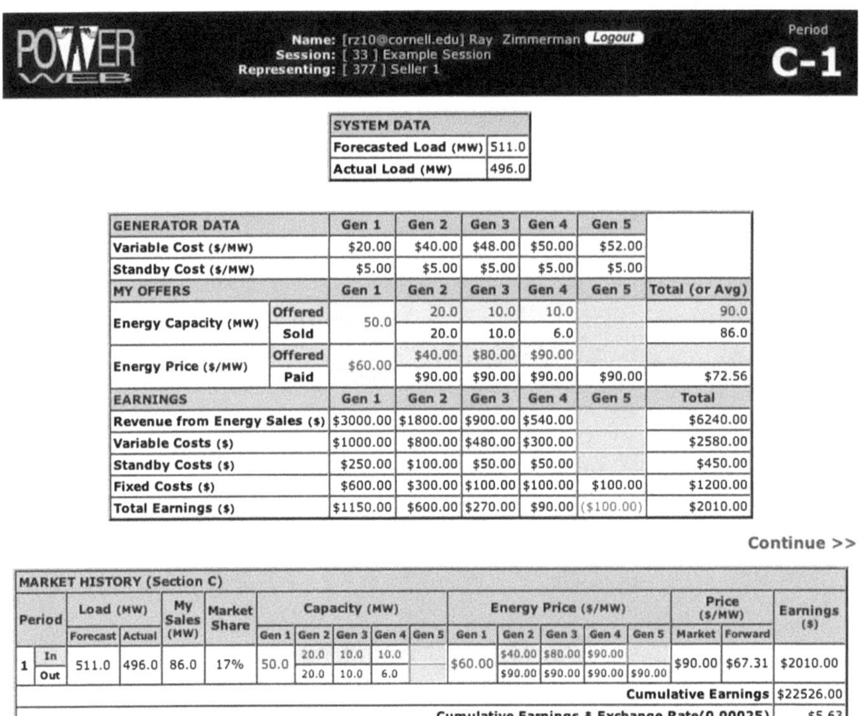
POWER WEB
Name: [rz10@cornell.edu] Ray Zimmerman Logout
Session: [33] Example Session
Representing: [377] Seller 1
Period C-1

SYSTEM DATA	
Forecasted Load (MW)	511.0
Actual Load (MW)	496.0

GENERATOR DATA		Gen 1	Gen 2	Gen 3	Gen 4	Gen 5	
Variable Cost ($/MW)		$20.00	$40.00	$48.00	$50.00	$52.00	
Standby Cost ($/MW)		$5.00	$5.00	$5.00	$5.00	$5.00	
MY OFFERS		Gen 1	Gen 2	Gen 3	Gen 4	Gen 5	Total (or Avg)
Energy Capacity (MW)	Offered	50.0	20.0	10.0	10.0		90.0
	Sold		20.0	10.0	6.0		86.0
Energy Price ($/MW)	Offered	$60.00	$40.00	$80.00	$90.00		
	Paid		$90.00	$90.00	$90.00	$90.00	$72.56
EARNINGS		Gen 1	Gen 2	Gen 3	Gen 4	Gen 5	Total
Revenue from Energy Sales ($)		$3000.00	$1800.00	$900.00	$540.00		$6240.00
Variable Costs ($)		$1000.00	$800.00	$480.00	$300.00		$2580.00
Standby Costs ($)		$250.00	$100.00	$50.00	$50.00		$450.00
Fixed Costs ($)		$600.00	$300.00	$100.00	$100.00	$100.00	$1200.00
Total Earnings ($)		$1150.00	$600.00	$270.00	$90.00	($100.00)	$2010.00

Continue >>

MARKET HISTORY (Section C)																			
Period		Load (MW)		My Sales (MW)	Market Share	Capacity (MW)					Energy Price ($/MW)					Price ($/MW)		Earnings ($)
		Forecast	Actual			Gen 1	Gen 2	Gen 3	Gen 4	Gen 5	Gen 1	Gen 2	Gen 3	Gen 4	Gen 5	Market	Forward	
1	In	511.0	496.0	86.0	17%	50.0	20.0	10.0	10.0		$60.00	$40.00	$80.00	$90.00		$90.00	$67.31	$2010.00
	Out						20.0	10.0	6.0			$90.00	$90.00	$90.00	$90.00			
Cumulative Earnings																		$22526.00
Cumulative Earnings * Exchange Rate(0.00025)																		$5.63

References

Argonne National Laboratory (2008). Electricity market complex adaptive system (EMCAS): model introduction. http://www.dis.anl.gov/pubs/61084.pdf.

Bower, J., & Bunn, D. (2000). A model-based comparison of pool and bilateral market mechanisms for electricity trading. *Energy Journal*, *21*(3), 1–29.

Bunn, D., & Oliveira, F. (2001). Agent-based simulation: an application to the new electricity trading arrangements of England and Wales. *IEEE Transactions on Evolutionary Computation*, *5*(5), 493–503.

Bunn, D., & Day, C. J. (2009). Computational modeling of price formation in the electricity pool of England and Wales. *Journal of Economic Dynamics and Control*, *30*(2), 363–376.

Dawid, H. (1999). *Adaptive learning by genetic algorithms* (2nd ed.). New York: Springer.

Klemperer, P. D., & Meyer, M. A. (1989). Supply function equilibria in oligopoly under uncertainty. *Econometrica*, *57*(6), 1243–1277.

Mount, T., & Oh, H. (2004). On the first price spike in summer. In *Proceedings of 37th annual Hawaiian international conference on system science*. http://doi.ieeecomputersociety.org/10.1109/HICSS.2005.583.

Oh, H. (2003). *Simulation methods for modeling offer behavior and spot prices in restructured markets for electricity*. Doctoral thesis. Cornell University, New York.

Oh, H., Thomas, R. J., Leiseutre, B. C., & Mount, T. (2005). A method for classifying offer strategies observed in an electricity market. *Journal of Decision Support Systems*, *40*, 449–460.

Oh, H., & Thomas, R. J. (2006). An agent-based optimal bidding function. In *Proceedings of 39th annual Hawaiian international conference on system science*. http://www.computer.org/portal/web/csdl/doi/10.1109/HICSS.2006.43.

Tesfatsion, L. (2001). Introduction to the special issue on agent-based computational economics. *Journal of Economic Dynamics and Control*, *25*(3–4), 281–293.

Diversification Effect of Heterogeneous Beliefs

Xue-Zhong He and Lei Shi

Abstract Through a mean-variance (MV) heterogeneous agent models with many risky assets, this paper examines the impact of behavioral heterogeneity on the market equilibrium and MV efficiency. We show that in market equilibrium, though the optimal portfolios of investors under their subjective beliefs are not MV efficient, they can be very close to the MV efficient frontier under the consensus belief. By imposing a mean-preserved spread distribution on the heterogeneous beliefs and conducting a statistical analysis based on Monte Carlo simulations, we show that diversity in the heterogeneous beliefs among investors can improve the Sharpe and Treynor ratios of the market portfolio and the optimal portfolios of investors, leading to a diversification effect of the heterogeneous beliefs.

1 Introduction

The Capital Asset Pricing Model (CAPM) developed by Sharpe (1964), Lintner (1965) and Mossin (1966) is perhaps the most influential equilibrium model in modern finance. It provides a theoretical foundation for relating risks linearly with expected return of assets. However, from a theoretical perspective, this paradigm has been criticized on a number of grounds, in particular concerning its extreme assumptions of homogeneous beliefs and the rational representative economic agent. Also, from a practical perspective this paradigm has faced difficulties in explaining many market anomalies, stylized facts, and market inefficiency in financial markets (see, for instance, Pagan 1996). As a result, heterogeneity and bounded rationality have been used as an alternative paradigm for asset price dynamics and this paradigm has been widely recognized in both academic and financial market practitioners. We refer to Hommes (2006), LeBaron (2006), Chiarella et al. (2009a) and Wenzelburger (2009) for surveys of recent literature on heterogeneous agent models (HAMs).

Literatures have made a significant contribution to the understanding of the impact of heterogeneous beliefs amongst investors on market equilibrium. Some have considered the problem in discrete time (for example, see Lintner 1969;

X.-Z. He (✉)
School of Finance and Economics, University of Technology, Sydney, Australia
e-mail: Tony.He1@uts.edu.au

H. Dawid, W. Semmler (eds.), *Computational Methods in Economic Dynamics*, Dynamic Modeling and Econometrics in Economics and Finance 13,
DOI 10.1007/978-3-642-16943-4_4,

Rubinstein 1974 and Sharpe 2007) and others in continuous time (for example, see Williams 1977; Detemple and Murthy 1994 and Zapatero 1998). Equilibrium models have been developed to consider the impact of heterogeneity under either mean-variance (MV) framework (see Lintner 1969 and Williams 1977) or in the Arrow-Debreu contingent claims economy (see Rubinstein 1976; Abel 2002). Heterogeneity may reflect differences either in information or in opinion. In the first case, investors may update their beliefs as new information become available, Bayesian updating rule is often used (see, for example, Williams 1977 and Zapatero 1998). In the second case, investor may revise their portfolio strategies as their views of the market change over time (see, for example Lintner 1969 and Rubinstein 1975).

Different from the above literature, the HAMs have been developed to characterize the dynamics of financial asset prices resulting from the interaction of heterogeneous agents with different attitudes towards risk and different expectations about the future evolution of asset prices. One of the key aspects of these models which distinguishes them from the previous literature is the expectations feedback mechanism—agents' decisions are based upon predictions of endogenous variables whose actual values are determined in equilibrium, see Brock and Hommes (1997, 1998). It is also interesting to find that adaptation, evolution, heterogeneity, and even learning can be incorporated into the Brock and Hommes type of framework, see, Gaunersdorfer (2000), Hommes (2001), Chiarella and He (2002, 2003) and Chiarella et al. (2002, 2006b). This broadened framework has successfully explained various market behaviour, such as the long-term swing of market prices from the fundamental price, asset bubbles and market crashes. It also shows a potential to characterize and explain the stylized facts (for example, Gaunersdorfer and Hommes 2007; LeBaron 2006) and various power law behavior (for instance Alfarano et al. 2005 and He and Li 2007) observed in financial markets.

Most of the HAMs analyzed in the literature involve financial market with only one risky asset. The main obstacle in dealing with heterogeneity is the complex and heavy notations involved when the number of assets and the dimension of heterogeneity (the so-called *wilderness* of heterogeneity) increase. Within the MV framework with one risk-free asset and many risky assets, Lintner (1969) is the first to consider the problem of market equilibrium by allowing for heterogeneity not only in the risky preferences and means of the risky assets but also in the variances/covariances of the risky assets across agents. Recent studies with many risky assets include Wenzelburger (2004), Westerhoff (2004), Böhm and Chiarella (2005), Böhm and Wenzelburger (2005), Chiarella et al. (2005, 2007), Westerhoff and Dieci (2006) and Horst and Wenzelburger (2008), showing that complex price dynamics may also result within a multi-asset market framework with heterogeneous beliefs. In a dynamic CAPM with heterogeneous expectations, Wenzelburger (2004) introduces a reference portfolio, which is MV efficient, to generalize the market portfolio. A simulation study in Böhm and Wenzelburger (2005) shows that the returns realized with an efficient portfolio does not necessarily outperform those non-efficient portfolios. By allowing social interaction among consumers, Horst and Wenzelburger (2008) show that asset price may behave in a non-ergodic manner.

By introducing a concept of *consensus belief*, Chiarella et al. (2006a, 2009b) show that the market equilibrium under heterogeneous beliefs can be characterized by the consensus belief, which can be constructed explicitly as a weighted average of the heterogeneous beliefs. They provide a simple explanation for Miller's hypothesis (Miller 1977) and the observed empirical relation between cross-sectional volatility and expected returns studied in Bart and Masse (1981), Diether et al. (2002), Johnson (2004) and Ang et al. (2006).

The above literature shows that in market equilibrium with boundedly rational heterogeneous investors, the optimal portfolios of investors under their subjective beliefs are MV inefficient in general. The question is how inefficient they can be. In general, what is the impact of heterogeneity on the market equilibrium, market MV frontier and the optimal portfolios of heterogeneous agents? Do the market and investors benefit from the diversity in beliefs? Within the framework of Chiarella et al. (2009b) on MV analysis under heterogeneous beliefs in asset return, this paper examines the above issues and questions. The heterogeneity is measured in terms of the risk preferences (the absolute risk aversion coefficients), the expected and the variances/covariances of the risky asset returns. We first illustrate that the subjectively optimal portfolios of investors are MV inefficient in general, but they can be located very close to the MV efficient consensus frontier and we refer this property to *quasi one fund theorem* under the heterogeneity and bounded rationality. To deal with the wilderness of heterogeneity and examine the impact of the heterogeneity on the market, motivated by Brock et al. (2005) and Diks and van der Weide (2005), we introduce a mean-preserved spread distribution for different aspects of heterogeneity. By conducting a statistical analysis based on Monte Carlo simulations, we show that dispersed beliefs in asset returns among investors can improve the Sharpe and Treynor ratios[1] of the optimal portfolios of investors and the market portfolio, implying that both the investors and market can benefit from the diversity in beliefs. In the spirt of the diversification effect in Markowitz portfolio theory, we call this phenomena as *diversification effect of the heterogeneous beliefs*.

The paper is structured as follows. In Sect. 2, we review the main results developed in Chiarella et al. (2009b). In Sect. 3, we examine the impact of the heterogeneity on the MV efficiency of the subjectively optimal portfolios. Based on Monte Carlo simulations, Sect. 4 presents a statistic analysis on the diversification effect of the heterogeneous beliefs. Section 5 concludes the paper.

2 Mean-Variance Asset Pricing with Heterogeneous Beliefs

In this section, we briefly review the main result in Chiarella et al. (2009b) in which the heterogeneous beliefs are formed in terms of asset returns. The result provides a foundation for our analysis in the following sections.

[1] Sharpe/Treynor ratio of a portfolio is a measure of expected excess return per unit of standard deviation/beta.

The set up follows the static MV analysis in Huang and Litzenberger (1988). Consider a market with one risk-free asset and $K(\geq 1)$ risky assets. Let r_f be the return of the riskless asset and $\tilde{r}_j$ $(j = 1, 2, \ldots, K)$ be the return of the risky asset j. Assume asset returns of the risky assets are multivariate normally distributed. There are I investors in the market indexed by $i = 1, 2, \ldots, I$ with heterogeneous (subjective) beliefs $\mathscr{B}_i = (E_i(\tilde{\mathbf{r}}), V_i)$ defined with respect to the means, variances and covariances of the returns of the risky assets

$$\mu_i = E_i(\tilde{\mathbf{r}}) = (\mu_{i,1}, \mu_{i,2}, \ldots, \mu_{i,K})^T, \qquad V_i = (\sigma_{i,kl})_{K\times K},$$

where $\mu_{i,k} = E_i[\tilde{r}_k]$ and $\sigma_{i,kl} = \mathrm{Cov}_i(\tilde{r}_k, \tilde{r}_l)$ for $i = 1, 2, \ldots, I$ and $k, l = 1, 2, \ldots, K$.

Assume investor i has a concave and strictly increasing utility function $u_i(w)$ such that $\theta_i := -E_i[u_i''(\tilde{W}_i)]/E_i[u_i'(\tilde{W}_i)]$ is a constant defining investor i's *global absolute risk aversion*, where $\tilde{W}_i = W_{i,o}(1 + r_f + \sum_{j=1}^K w_{ij}(\tilde{r}_j - r_f))$ is the end-of-period wealth of agent i, $W_{i,o}$ is the initial wealth of agent i, and w_{ij} is the fraction of wealth that agent i invests in the risky asset j. Let $\tau_i = 1/\theta_i$ be the risk tolerance.

A belief $\mathscr{B}_a = (E_a(\tilde{\mathbf{r}}), V_a)$ is called a *consensus belief* if and only if the equilibrium prices under the heterogeneous beliefs $\mathscr{B} = \{\mathscr{B}_i\}_{i=1}^I$ are also the equilibrium prices under the homogeneous belief $\mathscr{B}_a$. The following Proposition 2.1 obtained in Chiarella et al. (2009b) shows that the market equilibrium returns of the risky assets can be characterized by a CAPM-like relation under a consensus belief.

Proposition 2.1 *Let $\tau_a = \sum_{i=1}^I \tau_i$ and $\tilde{r}_m := r_f + \mathbf{w}_m^T(\tilde{\mathbf{r}} - r_f\mathbf{1})$ be the return of the market portfolio $\mathbf{w}_m$ of the risky assets. Define a consensus belief $\mathscr{B}_a = (E_a(\tilde{\mathbf{r}}), V_a)$ as follows:*

$$V_a = \left(\sum_{i=1}^I \frac{\tau_i}{\tau_a} V_i^{-1}\right)^{-1}, \qquad \mu_a = E_a(\tilde{\mathbf{r}}) = V_a\left(\sum_{i=1}^I \frac{\tau_i}{\tau_a} V_i^{-1} E_i(\tilde{\mathbf{r}})\right). \tag{1}$$

Then, in equilibrium, the asset return satisfies

$$E_a[\tilde{\mathbf{r}}] - r_f\mathbf{1} = \beta[E_a(\tilde{r}_m) - r_f] \tag{2}$$

and the market risk premium is given by

$$E_a(\tilde{r}_m) - r_f = \frac{1}{\tau_a} W_{m0}\sigma_{a,m}^2, \tag{3}$$

where $\beta = (\beta_1, \beta_2, \ldots, \beta_K)^T$, $\beta_k = \sigma_{a,jm}/\sigma_{a,m}^2$, and $\sigma_{a,m}^2 = \mathbf{w}_m^T\mathbf{V}_a\mathbf{w}_m$, $\mathbf{V}_a\mathbf{w}_m = [\sigma_{a,jm}]$.

The equilibrium relation (2) is the standard CAPM except that the mean and variance/covariance are calculated based on the consensus belief $\mathscr{B}_a$. The β coefficients of risky assets depend upon not only the covariance between the market returns and asset returns, but also the aggregation of the heterogeneous beliefs.

3 Mean-Variance Efficiency of the Optimal Portfolios

In the standard MV framework with homogeneous beliefs, it is well known that, in the presence of a risk-less asset, the one fund theorem holds. This means that the MV efficient frontier is the half line connecting the risk-free asset and the market portfolio and the optimal portfolio of investor, which is a linear combination of the risky market portfolio and the risk-less asset, is always located on the efficient frontier. When beliefs are heterogeneous, it is known that the standard one fund theorem does not hold in general, meaning that the subjectively optimal portfolios of the heterogeneous investors are MV inefficient. In the following, through some numerical examples, we show that, in market equilibrium, the optimal portfolios can be very close to the MV efficient frontier, though they are not efficient. The analysis is based on Proposition 2.1. We first examine the impact of a single source and then multiple sources of heterogeneity.

3.1 The Impact of Heterogeneous Expected Returns

To examine the impact of heterogeneous beliefs on the expected returns on the MV efficiency of the subjectively optimal portfolios, we consider the following example in which two investors have different beliefs about the expected returns of three risky assets.

Example 3.1 Consider a market with three risky assets with the expected returns and variance/covariances of their returns given by[2]

$$\mu_o = \begin{pmatrix} 0.3633 \\ 0.2686 \\ 0.7087 \end{pmatrix}, \qquad V_o = \begin{pmatrix} 0.0269 & 0.0044 & 0.0082 \\ 0.0044 & 0.0142 & 0.0035 \\ 0.0082 & 0.0035 & 0.0653 \end{pmatrix}. \tag{4}$$

Let the market endowment of risky assets be $\mathbf{z}_m = (1, 1, 1)^T$, risk-free rate $r_f = 5\%$ p.a. Assume that there are two investors who are homogeneous in their beliefs of the variance/covariance matrix $V_2 = V_1 = V_o$, but heterogeneous in their beliefs of the expected returns $\mu_1 = \mu_o$, $\mu_2 = \mu_1 + 0.2 \times \mathbf{1}$. To examine the role of the risk aversion, we consider three combinations of the absolute risk aversion (ARA) coefficients $(\theta_1, \theta_2) = (3, 3)$, $(4, 2)$ and $(2, 4)$. We also assume that the initial wealth is the same for the two investors, $W_{1,o} = W_{2,o} = \$10$.

In this case, we use Proposition 2.1 to construct the consensus belief, to calculate the market equilibrium returns and to plot the MV efficient frontiers under the two heterogeneous beliefs and the consensus belief, respectively. We also locate the

[2]The means and covariance matrix are generated from the annual payoffs of three stocks in the Australian market.

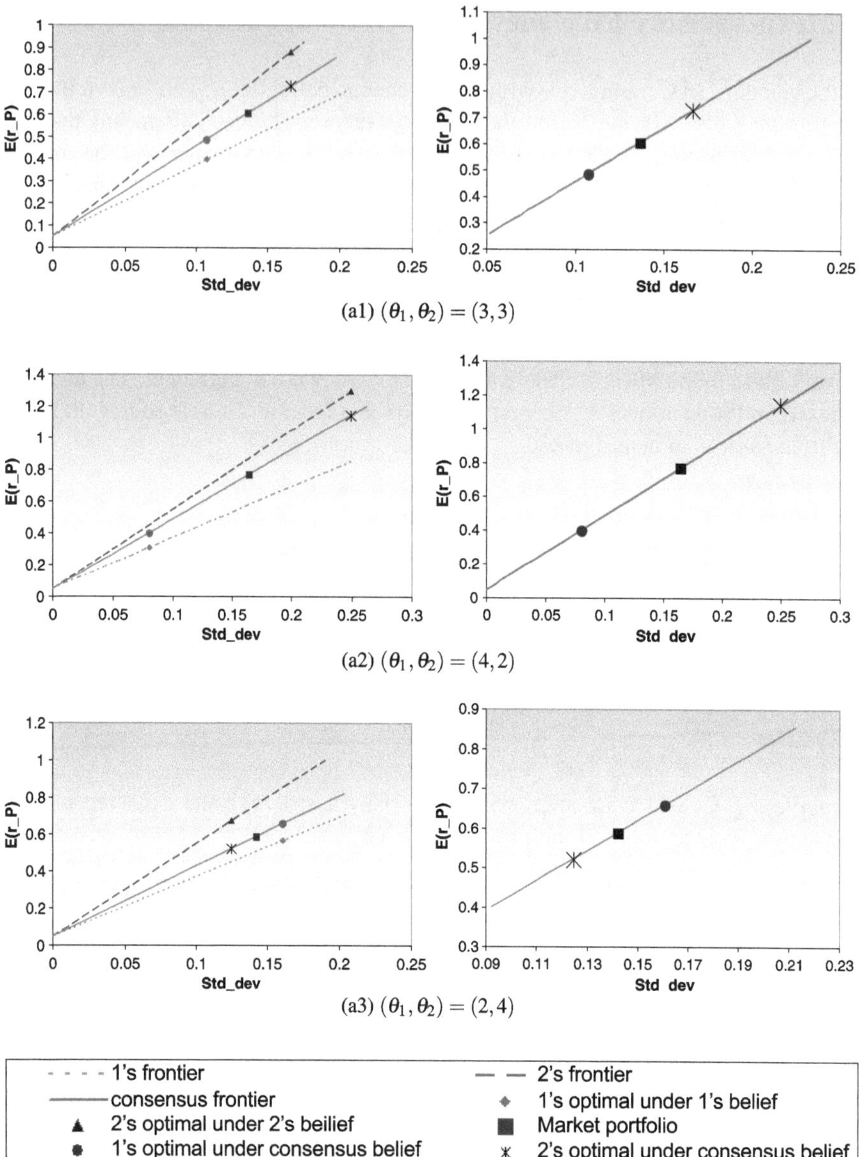

Fig. 1 Mean-Variance efficient frontiers, optimal portfolios and market portfolio under the heterogeneous and the consensus beliefs when $\mu_1 < \mu_2$ and $V_1 = V_2$ (*left panel*) and their close-ups (*right panel*)

optimal portfolios of the two investors under their beliefs and under the consensus belief, respectively. The results are plotted in Fig. 1 for three combinations of $(\theta_1, \theta_2) = (3, 3)$, $(4, 2)$ and $(2, 4)$, respectively. Based on Fig. 1, we have the following observations.

First, in market equilibrium, the standard one fund theorem does not hold in general and investors' optimal portfolios are located below the efficient frontier under the consensus belief (consensus frontier). However the optimal portfolios of both investors are located very close to the consensus frontier. In fact, they are too close to visualize the differences, even from the close-ups on the right panels. We refer to this phenomena as the *quasi-one fund theorem*. In fact, numerically it can be verified that the optimal portfolios are below the consensus frontier and the portfolio weights are significantly different between investors' optimal portfolios and portfolios actually located on the consensus frontier.[3] Although the differences are small, but significant enough to rule out the MV efficiency of the subjectively optimal portfolios.

Secondly, the consensus frontier is located between the efficient frontiers under investors' subjective beliefs, with the optimistic investor's frontier having the highest slope. This result is very intuitive, due to the homogeneous belief of the covariance matrix, the expected returns under the consensus belief is a risk tolerance weighted average of the subjective expected returns of the two investors. When investor 2 is less risk averse, the consensus frontier leans more towards the frontier of investor 2, see Fig. 1(a2). However, when investor 1 is less risk averse, the consensus frontier leans more towards the frontier of investor 1, see Fig. 1(a3).

Thirdly, the market portfolio is always located in the middle of the optimal portfolios under the consensus belief. The distance between each of the optimal portfolios from market portfolio is larger (smaller) when the optimistic (pessimistic) investor (in terms of expected returns) is less risk averse, see Fig. 1(a2) and (a3).

3.2 The Impact of Heterogeneous Variances/Covariances

In the next example, we examine the impact of the heterogeneous beliefs in variance/covariance on the MV efficiency of the subjectively optimal portfolios.

Example 3.2 Let $\mu_2 = \mu_1 = \mu_o$, the ARA coefficients and V_o be identical to their numerical value in Example 3.1. Assume that $V_2 = V_o$ and $V_1 = V_2 + 0.3 \times \mathbf{1}_3$, where $\mathbf{1}_3$ is a 3×3 unit matrix with all elements equal to 1.

[3]For example, in Fig. 1(a2), the optimal portfolio of investor 1 under the consensus belief has co-ordinates $(\sigma_{o_1}, \mu_{o_1}) = (0.0804, 0.398)$, the portfolio on the consensus frontier with the same standard deviation has co-ordinates $(0.0804, 0.402)$, about 40 basis points (bp) difference in the expected return. Also, the optimal portfolio weights of investor 1 are $(0.1815, 0.2764, 0.2146)$ while weights of the consensus frontier portfolio with the same standard deviation are $(0.1935, 0.3516, 0.1795)$. Similarly, the co-ordinates of the optimal portfolio for investor 2 and the one on the consensus frontier with same standard deviation are $(0.2494, 1.1414)$ and $(0.2494, 1.1427)$, respectively, only 13 bp in difference. Correspondingly, the optimal portfolio weights are $(0.6094, 1.1606, 0.5187)$, while the corresponding consensus frontier portfolio has weights $(0.6002, 1.0906, 0.5566)$.

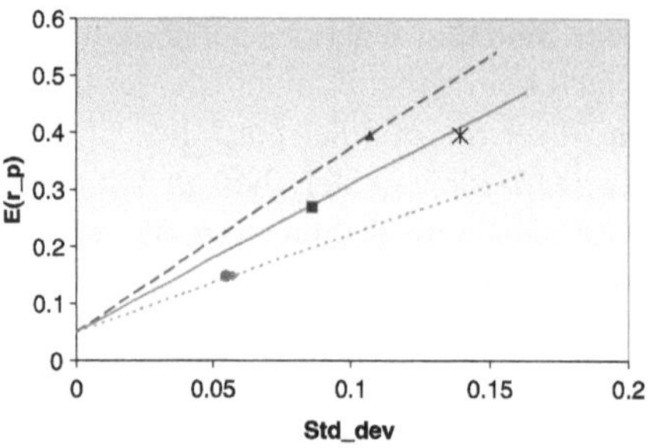

(b1) $(\theta_1, \theta_2) = (3,3)$

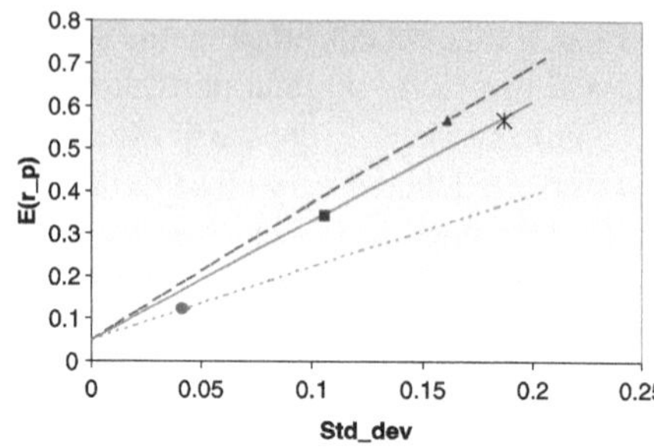

(b2) $(\theta_1, \theta_2) = (4,2)$

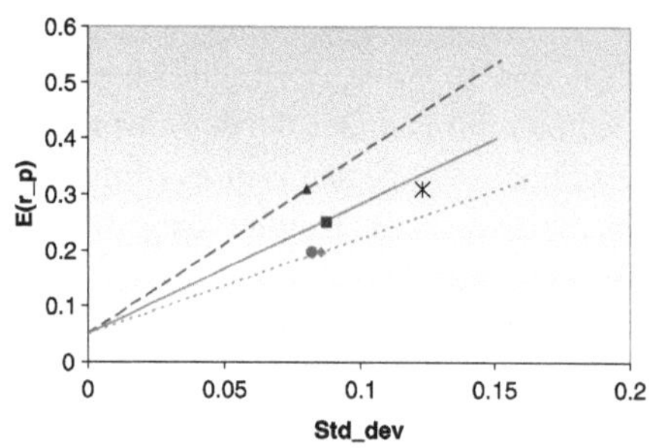

(b3) $(\theta_1, \theta_2) = (2,4)$

Fig. 2 Mean-Variance efficient frontiers, optimal portfolios and market portfolio under heterogeneous and consensus beliefs for $\mu_1 = \mu_2$ and $V_2 \leq V_1$

For convenience, we denote $V_1 \geq V_2$ if $V_1 - V_2$ is semi-positive definite. For any portfolio $\mathbf{z}$, the variance of the portfolio for investor i under his/her belief is defined by $\sigma_i^2(\mathbf{z}) = \mathbf{z}^T V_i \mathbf{z}$ for $i = 1, 2$. Therefore, $\sigma_1^2(\mathbf{z}) \geq \sigma_2^2(\mathbf{z})$ for any portfolio $\mathbf{z}$ if and only if $V_1 \geq V_2$. Consequently, we say investor 1 is less confident (or more doubtful) than investor 2.

Different from the previous case, quasi-one fund theorem holds less so when investors have different confidence levels, since the subjectively optimal portfolios are noticeably below the consensus frontier, especially for investor 1 who is the less confident investor in this case. These features are illustrated in Fig. 2 for three combinations of the risk aversion coefficients. This suggests that difference in confidence levels causes investors to choose a mixture of risky assets that is significantly different from the market portfolio of risky assets. Thus difference in confidence levels can have a larger impact on the MV efficiency of optimal portfolios than the heterogeneity in expected returns. The consensus frontier is located in between the individual frontiers and the market portfolio is located in the middle of the optimal portfolios of the two investors. If we interpret the covariance matrix as a measure of confidence, since $\mu_1 = \mu_2 = \mu_a$, one can see from Fig. 2 that market aggregation improves (worsens) the MV efficiency of the optimal portfolio for the less (more) confident investor, comparing to the case under his/her subjective belief.

Overall, we see that heterogeneity in variances and covariances has a significant impact on the consensus frontier and the MV efficiency of the optimal portfolios, while the ARAs determine the positions of individuals' optimal portfolios under both their own beliefs and the consensus belief.

3.3 The Joint Impact of Heterogeneous Expected Returns and Variances/Covariances

We now combine Examples 3.1 and 3.2 together and examine the joint impact of the heterogeneity in the expected returns and the covariance matrices. Consider the following case: investor 2 is optimistic but less confident in the sense that $\mu_2 > \mu_1$ and $V_2 > V_1$, Fig. 3 illustrates the situation for three combinations of $(\theta_1, \theta_2) = (3, 3)$, (4, 2) and (2, 4). Apart from those features observed in the previous two cases, the combined heterogeneity in both expected returns and variances/covariances have more significant impact on the portfolio frontiers in the sense that the individual frontiers are much more apart comparing to the previous two cases. In market equilibrium, both investors' MV efficiency worsens. However, when investor 1 is more risk tolerant, his optimal portfolio is very close to the consensus frontier, indicating that his/her portfolio choice of risky assets almost coincides with the market portfolio. He and Shi (2009) also investigate the case where one investor is optimistic and confident, they show that this investor will dominate the market in the sense that his/her optimal portfolio will be much closer to the consensus frontier.

Overall, one can see that when multiple sources of heterogeneity are considered, the effect on the market equilibrium is complex. For example, an investor's belief can be very different from the consensus belief, however, in some cases, he/she makes portfolio choice of risky assets that is very similar to the market portfolio, hence his/her subjectively optimal portfolio locates very close to the consensus frontier.

3.4 Miller's Hypothesis

According to Miller (1977), assets with higher dispersion in beliefs have higher market price and lower expected returns comparing to otherwise similar stocks. The justification of this hypothesis is that negative opinions are not fully reflected in the

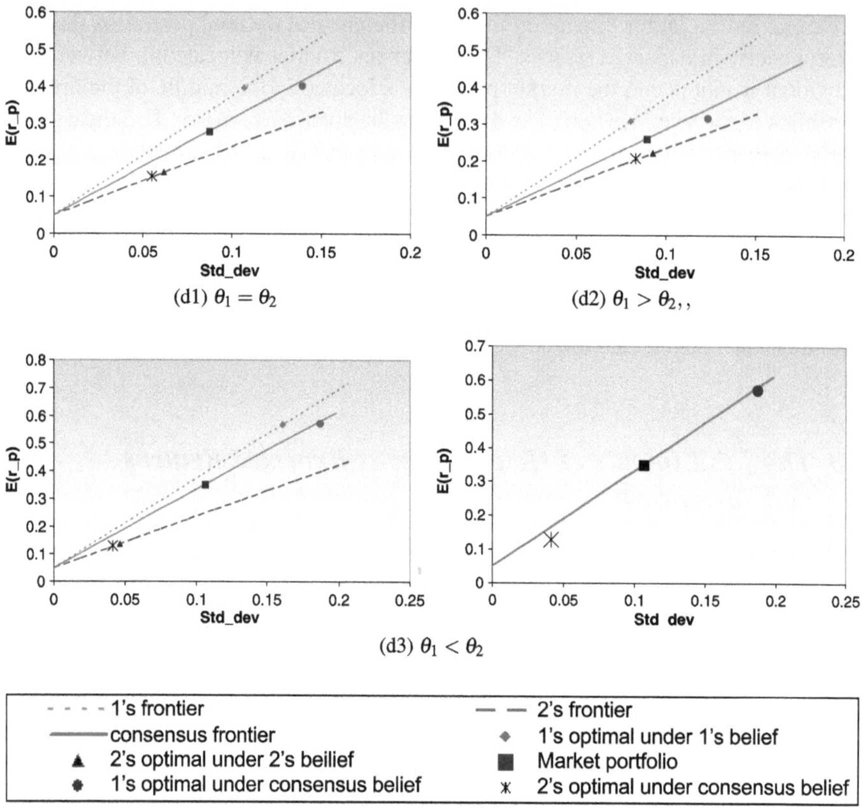

Fig. 3 Mean-Variance efficient frontiers, optimal portfolios and market portfolio under heterogeneous and consensus beliefs for $\mu_1 < \mu_2$, $V_1 < V_2$

asset price because of short sell constraints. For a case of two investors, by considering a *mean preserving spread* in the beliefs of the expected payoff, He and Shi (2009) show that Miller's hypothesis holds if the more optimistic investor (investor whose belief in the expected future payoff is higher) is also less risk averse compared to the pessimistic investor. With the average belief in expected payoffs unchanged, the investor who is optimistic and less risk averse dominates the market, consequently, consensus belief of the expected payoff is higher, leading to a higher equilibrium price and lower expected future return. The analysis provides a convincing framework in supporting Miller's hypothesis.

We show in the following that Miller's hypothesis does not hold when the heterogeneous beliefs are formed in terms of future asset returns, even if more optimistic investor is also less risk-averse. We consider an example analogous to Example 3.4 in He and Shi (2009).

Example 3.3 Assume two investors form their beliefs in terms of asset returns, $\mathscr{B}_i := \mathscr{B}(V_i, E_i(\tilde{\mathbf{r}})), i = 1, 2)$. For $\varepsilon > 0$, consider two assets j and k with $E_2(\tilde{r}_j) < E_1(\tilde{r}_j)$, and $E_1(\tilde{r}_k) = E_1(\tilde{r}_j) + \varepsilon$ and $E_2(\tilde{r}_k) = E_2(\tilde{r}_j) - \varepsilon$. This implies that the dispersion of the belief of the expected return is greater for asset k than for asset j. Let $V_1 = V_2 = V_o$, then

$$E_a(\tilde{r}_j) = \frac{\tau_1}{\tau_a} E_1(\tilde{r}_j) + \frac{\tau_2}{\tau_a} E_2(\tilde{r}_j), \qquad E_a(\tilde{r}_k) = \frac{\tau_1}{\tau_a}(E_1(\tilde{r}_j) + \varepsilon) + \frac{\tau_1}{\tau_a}(E_2(\tilde{r}_j) - \varepsilon).$$

Hence

$$E_a(\tilde{r}_j) - E_a(\tilde{r}_k) = \frac{\varepsilon}{\theta_1^{-1} + \theta_2^{-1}}(\theta_2^{-1} - \theta_1^{-1}) \tag{5}$$

showing that $E_a(\tilde{r}_j) < E_a(\tilde{r}_k)$ if and only if $\theta_1 < \theta_2$. Therefore, divergence of opinion actually increases the expected return of asset k compared to an otherwise similar stock when the more optimistic investor 1 is also less risk averse. With everything else equal, $E_a(\tilde{r}_j) < E_a(\tilde{r}_k)$ also implies a higher equilibrium price for asset k.

Example 3.3 illustrates that Miller's hypothesis is conditional on the formation of the heterogeneous beliefs. The intuition is that market tends to reflect the opinions of the less risk averse investors who are active in the market. Therefore, if the less risk averse investors are also relatively more optimistic about the expected future asset returns, then the consensus belief of expected returns will also be higher.

Based on the above discussions, we can summarize the impact of the heterogeneity on the market as follows. If we treat investors with different beliefs as fund managers, our analysis illustrates that, when the market consists of these investors, their subjectively optimal portfolios are often not MV efficient when the market is in equilibrium, unless their beliefs coincide with the consensus belief. This implies that it is difficult for managed funds to out-perform the market systematically, as observed in markets (see Sharpe 2007). In some cases, their optimal portfolios can be very close to the consensus frontier, leading to the quasi-one fund theorem which is a very interesting feature. On the one hand, the market is determined endogenously by all the market investors with heterogeneous beliefs. It is the bounded rationality and heterogeneity of the investors that makes the investors hardly achieve the same performance as the market (measured by the MV efficiency), reflecting the market dysfunctionality. On the other hand, in aggregation, the market always performs better than individuals and, in some situations, individuals are able to perform almost as good as the market, characterized by the quasi-one fund theorem. Also different aspects of heterogeneity affect the market differently and divergence of opinion may not necessarily lead to higher equilibrium price and lower expected return.

4 A Statistic Analysis on the Diversified Beliefs

In the previous section, investors' beliefs are given deterministically. However, when there is uncertainty associated with agents' beliefs, characterization of the heterogeneous beliefs is a difficult issue, leading to the *wilderness of heterogeneity*. To overcome this problem, we introduce a mean-preserved spread distribution in beliefs, motivated by Brock et al. (2005) and Diks and van der Weide (2005).

By conducting a statistical analysis based on Monte Carlo simulations, this section examines the impact of the mean-preserved spread distribution in beliefs on the market through the statistics of return distributions, the beta coefficients, and two performance measures, Sharpe and Treynor ratios under the consensus belief. The Sharpe (Treynor) ratio is defined as the marginal rate of substitution between excess portfolio return and its standard deviation (beta), i.e. for any portfolio p, its Sharpe Ratio equals the value of $E_a(\tilde{r}_p - r_f)/\sigma_a(\tilde{r}_p)$ and its Treynor ratio equals the value of $E_a(\tilde{r}_p - r_f)/\beta_p$. Since the CAPM relation is valid under the consensus belief, Treynor ratio for any portfolio p is equal to the excess market return, i.e. $E_a(\tilde{r}_p - r_f)/\beta_p = E_a(\tilde{r}_m - r_f)$.

In particular, we examine the impact of the diversity in beliefs on the performance of the market portfolio and the optimal portfolios of investors. We assume that there are two investors, one risk-free asset and three risky assets in the market. For the benchmark case, let $\theta_1 = \theta_2 = \theta_o = 3$, the expected return μ_o and the return covariance matrix V_o are as defined in Example 3.1.

4.1 Diversified Beliefs in the Expected Asset Returns

We first examine the impact of the diversified beliefs about the expected asset returns. Assume the two investors are homogeneous in their characteristics except for their beliefs in the expected returns, $\tilde{\mu}_i = \mu_o + \tilde{\delta}_i$, where $\tilde{\delta}_i = (\delta_{i1}, \delta_{i2}, \delta_{i3})^T$ with $\tilde{\delta}_{i,j} \overset{\text{iid}}{\sim} \sigma_{\delta_i}\mathcal{N}(0, 1)$ for $i = 1, 2$, $j = 1, 2, 3$. Hence investor i is more confident about his/her belief of the expected asset returns if σ_{δ_i} is smaller. The diversity in beliefs among the two investors are measured by $(\sigma_{\delta_1}, \sigma_{\delta_2})$. We consider the following combinations of $(\sigma_{\delta_1}, \sigma_{\delta_2}) = (1\%, 1\%), (1\%, 2\%), (1\%, 3\%), (0, 2\%)$ and $(0, 3\%)$ to conduct two types of comparison. The first type corresponds to the combinations of $(\sigma_{\delta_1}, \sigma_{\delta_2}) = (1\%, 1\%), (1\%, 2\%)$ and $(1\%, 3\%)$ to examine the impact of the diversity as σ_{δ_2} increases. The second type examines the impact of diversity in $(\sigma_{\delta_1}, \sigma_{\delta_2})$ in which the average of σ_{δ_1} and σ_{δ_2} is unchanged but the spreads among them increase, as in between $(1\%, 1\%)$ and $(0, 2\%)$, and between $(1\%, 2\%)$ and $(0, 3\%)$. For each given $(\sigma_{\delta_1}, \sigma_{\delta_2})$, we run 10,000 simulations to obtain the summary statistics for both returns and beta coefficients. The results, together with detailed discussions, can be found in He and Shi (2008). Based on the summary statistics, we observe a very interesting phenomena that both the average Sharpe and Treyor ratios increase systematically for the market portfolio M as the diversity between σ_{δ_1} and σ_{δ_2} increases and also the market portfolio M has the highest average Sharpe ratio. This phenomena is clearly illustrated in Fig. 4(a1) and (a2) (left panel). In fact, it follows from Proposition 2.1 that the Treynor ratios are the same for given $(\sigma_{\delta_1}, \sigma_{\delta_2})$ across all the assets and portfolios. However, the average Treynor ratio increases when the dispersion in $(\sigma_{\delta_1}, \sigma_{\delta_2})$ increases. This suggests that, in terms of average Sharpe and Treyor ratios, the market benefits from the diversity in the heterogeneous beliefs and higher dispersion in beliefs increases both the average Sharpe and Treyor ratios of the market portfolio. We also observe that

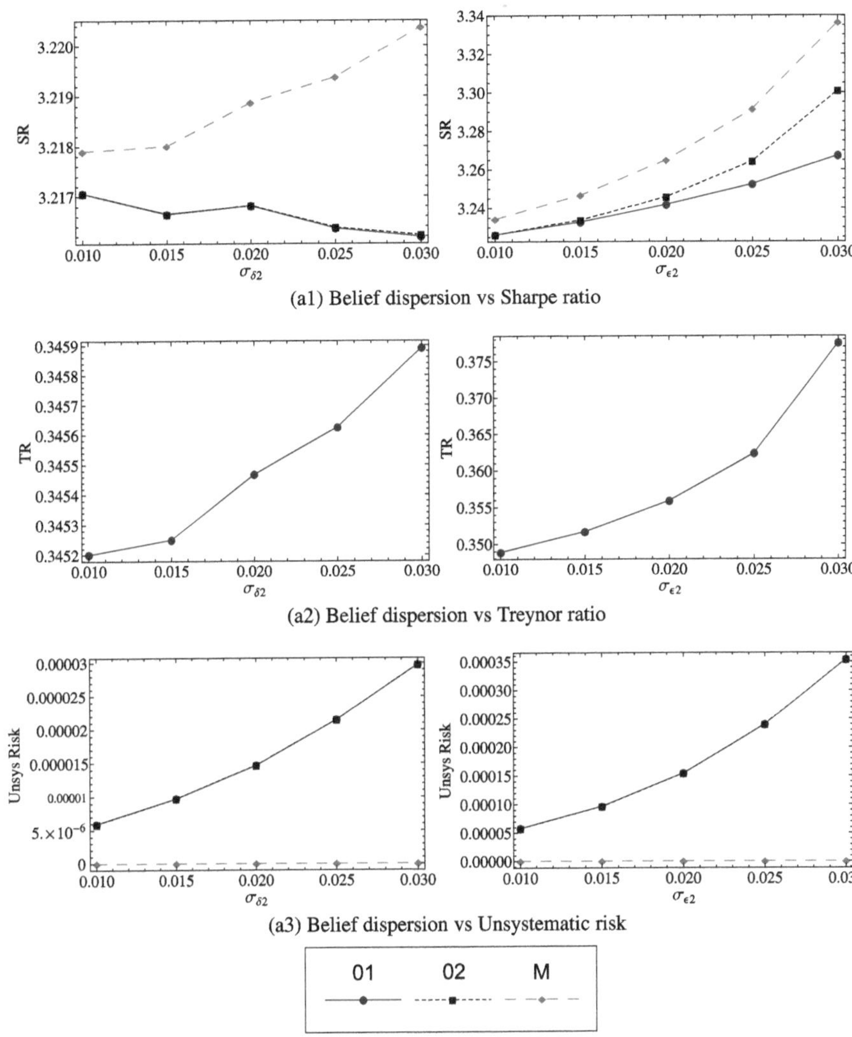

Fig. 4 Effect of belief dispersion on the average Sharpe, Treynor ratios and unsystematic risk when (i) investor 1 has a constant dispersion in expected returns ($\sigma_{\delta_1} = 1\%$) and investor 2's dispersion $\sigma_{\delta_2} \in [1\%, 3\%]$ (*left panel*), (ii) investor 1 has a constant dispersion in variance of asset returns ($\sigma_{\varepsilon_1} = 1\%$) and investor 2's dispersion $\sigma_{\varepsilon_2} \in [1\%, 3\%]$ (*right panel*)

the Sharpe ratios of the optimal portfolios of the two investors are very close to that of the market portfolio. In regards to the beta coefficients, first two risky assets have betas less than 1 while the third risky asset has beta coefficient larger than 1. The mean values for the beta coefficients of all three assets and portfolios decrease systematically as the dispersion of beliefs increases, leading to a lower systematic risk. On the other hand, Fig. 4(a3) (left panel) clearly indicates that there is an insignificant increase in the unsystematic risks of the optimal portfolios as the dispersion in beliefs increases, while the unsystematic risk of the market portfolio is always zero. This result illustrates that the quasi-one fund theorem holds statistically.

We now provide an explanation for the above results. Since the expected return is the only source of heterogeneity, the covariance between asset return and the aggregate market return under the consensus belief is given by $V_o \mathbf{w}_m = \frac{1}{\theta_o W_{m0}} \frac{1}{2} \sum_i^2 E_i(\tilde{\mathbf{r}} - r_f \mathbf{1})$, see Chiarella et al. (2009b). On average both investors' beliefs of the expected returns equal to $E_o(\tilde{\mathbf{r}})$. Thus, regardless of the dispersion in the beliefs, the average of the covariances between assets and the aggregate market is given by $V_o \mathbf{w}_m = \frac{1}{\theta_o W_{m0}} E_o(\tilde{\mathbf{r}} - r_f \mathbf{1})$. On the other hand, the market variance under the consensus belief $\sigma_{a,m}^2 = \mathbf{w}_m^T V_o \mathbf{w}_m$ is a quadratic function of $E_i(\tilde{r}_j - r_f)$ which is the risk premium of asset j perceived by investor i. Consequently, we expect $\sigma_{a,m}^2$ to increase as the uncertainty in the belief of expected asset returns increases, leading to higher average Sharpe and Treynor ratios for the market portfolio according to (3), illustrated in Fig. 4(a1) and (a2) (left panel), respectively. This explains the under-performance of investors' optimal portfolios comparing to the market portfolio. Also, illustrated by Fig. 4(a3) (left panel), the systematic risk of the risky assets and portfolios decrease while the unsystematic risks of the optimal portfolios increase, though insignificantly. The economic intuition is that, comparing to the benchmark case, there is a greater risk associated with the future return of the market when there is large dispersion in investors' beliefs, therefore a higher risk premium is required as a compensation. The diversity in the expected asset returns provides a potential explanation to the *Risk Premium Puzzle* since we have demonstrated that a higher dispersion of beliefs can lead to a higher market risk premium.

4.2 Diversified Belief in Variances/Covariances of Asset Returns

We now assume that the investors are homogeneous except in their beliefs of covariance matrices of asset returns. Let $\theta_1 = \theta_2 = \theta_o = 3$ and $\mu_1 = \mu_2 = \mu_o$. Assume the beliefs of the correlation structure of the asset returns are also homogeneous, however the beliefs of the volatilities of asset returns are independently normally distributed. More precisely, let $V_o = D_o C D_o$ and $\tilde{V}_i = \tilde{D}_i C \tilde{D}_i$, where $D_o = \text{diag}(\sigma_{o1}, \sigma_{o2}, \sigma_{o3})$, C is the correlation matrix, $\tilde{D}_i = D_o + \varepsilon_i \mathbf{I}$, and $\varepsilon_i \overset{\text{iid}}{\sim} \mathcal{N}(0, \sigma_{\varepsilon_i}^2)$. That is the volatility of asset j's return under investor i's belief follows the distribution $\tilde{\sigma}_{ij} \sim \mathcal{N}(\sigma_{oj}, \sigma_{\varepsilon_i}^2)$, which is independent for each investor i. A summary on the resulting statistics from Monte Carlo simulations and related discussions can be found in He and Shi (2008). Different from the previous case for the dispersion of beliefs in expected asset returns, both the average Sharpe and Treynor ratios increase systematically for all assets and portfolios, not only the market portfolio, when the dispersion of beliefs in asset volatilities increases. This is clearly illustrated by Fig. 4(a1) (right panel) and (a2) (right panel). Similar to the previous case, the unsystematic risks of the optimal portfolios increase, but not significantly, as the dispersion of beliefs in variances of asset returns increases, demonstrated by Fig. 4(a3) (right panel).

We now provide some justifications to the above observations. Since $\theta_i = \theta_o$ and $E_i(\tilde{\mathbf{r}}) = E_o(\tilde{\mathbf{r}})$ for $i = 1, 2$, the covariance between assets' return and the aggregate market return under the consensus belief is given by

$$V_a \mathbf{w}_m = \frac{E_o(\tilde{\mathbf{r}} - r_f \mathbf{1})}{\theta_o W_{m0}/I}, \tag{6}$$

which is actually a constant. On the other hand, the variance of the market portfolio is given by

$$\mathbf{w}_m^T V_a \mathbf{w}_m = \frac{1}{(\theta_o W_{m0}/I)^2} E_o(\tilde{\mathbf{r}} - r_f \mathbf{1})^T \left(\frac{1}{2} \sum_i^2 V_i^{-1} \right) E_o(\tilde{\mathbf{r}} - r_f \mathbf{1})$$

with $V_i = D_i\ C_o\ D_i = (D_o + \varepsilon_i \mathbf{I}) C_o (D_o + \varepsilon_i \mathbf{I})$. Obviously, increasing dispersion in beliefs implies that there are more chances for the beliefs in asset volatility being very close to zero, which will lead to an increase in the market variance, thus a dramatic increase in Treynor ratio, see Fig. 4(a2) (right panel). Essentially, the covariance between asset returns and the market returns under the consensus belief is a constant, while the variance of the market portfolio increases when the dispersion increases, leading to higher market risk premium and higher average Sharpe and Treynor ratios. The increase in the risk premia as the dispersion of beliefs increases is clearly higher than the previous case, hence the market requires a higher compensation in terms of expected returns for uncertainty given that variances/covariances are believed to be more predictable than expected returns.

4.3 Diversified Risk Aversions

In the homogeneous case when $V_i = V_o$ and $\mu_i = \mu_o$ for all i, it is clear from Proposition 2.1 that any changes in the ARA coefficients will not affect the consensus belief $\mathscr{B}_a$ and the standard CAPM holds. However, this is no longer the case when either the beliefs in the expected returns or variance/covariance of returns are heterogeneous. To understand the joint impact of the heterogeneities on the market, we consider heterogeneous ARA coefficients in three cases: (i) $\mu_1 \neq \mu_2$, $V_o = V_1 = V_2$; (ii) $\mu_o = \mu_1 = \mu_2$, $V_1 \neq V_2$; and (iii) $\mu_1 \neq \mu_2$, $V_1 \neq V_2$. A summary on the resulting statistics from Monte Carlo simulations and related discussions can be found in He and Shi (2008). In all three cases, we find that the dispersion in ARA coefficients affect the skewness and kurtosis for the expected returns of the optimal portfolios in different ways, but the average Treynor ratios, rather than the average Sharpe ratios, increase systematically as the dispersions of the beliefs in ARA coefficients increase. This is probably due to the fact that higher dispersion in risk aversion reduces the aggregate market risk aversion, which in turn offsets the increase in the market volatility.

Based on the above analysis, we obtain the following overall features on the impact of the diversified beliefs. (i) Measured by the average Sharpe and Treynor ratios, dispersion of beliefs improves the performance of the market portfolio, leading to higher market risk premium for bearing the diversity in investors' beliefs. The "cost" of uncertainty on beliefs in the variances/covariances of asset return is higher than that in expected returns. (ii) Diversified risk aversion does not have any impact on the market when beliefs are homogeneous. However, when combined with diversified beliefs in the expected returns and variances, it can improve the average Treynor ratio when dispersions increase. In addition, the resulting statistics from Monte Carlo simulations in He and Shi (2008) (not reported here) also show that the diversified beliefs have greater impact on the distribution of the expected returns for the optimal portfolios than for the individual risky assets. In addition, market aggregation of heterogeneous beliefs can lead to non-normal return distributions for the market portfolio as well as the individual optimal portfolios.

5 Conclusion

Within the framework of Chiarella et al. (2009b) on MV analysis, this paper examines the impact of the heterogeneity and bounded rationality on the market equilibrium and MV efficiency of the optimal portfolios. The heterogeneity is characterized by the heterogeneous beliefs about the returns of the risky assets, while the bounded rationality corresponds to the MV optimization of investors based on their beliefs. Through numerical examples and statistical analysis based on Monte Carlo simulations, we examine the MV efficiency of the optimal portfolios of investors and diversification effect of the heterogeneous beliefs. We provide some evidence on the mean variance inefficiency of the optimal portfolios of the heterogeneous investors. However, the optimal portfolios of investors can be very close to the consensus frontier in some cases. This implies that, in some situations, investors' selections of the optimal portfolio under their subjective beliefs can be almost perfectly rational under the market aggregation. This may help us to understand the empirical finding that the managed funds tend to under-perform the market portfolio on average, though some managed funds can perform as close as the market. In general, the consensus frontier is located in between the investors' frontiers under their subjective beliefs, while different aspect of heterogeneity plays different roles. The heterogeneity in the covariance matrices plays the most important role in determining the relative positions of the individual frontiers and the consensus frontier, while the heterogeneity in expected returns plays the second important role, which is controlling how far apart are the individual frontiers from the consensus frontier. The risk aversion coefficients determine the relative positions of the individual optimal portfolios to the market portfolio. Most interestingly, we found that an increase in the dispersion of beliefs in the expected returns and/or variances can improve the performance of the market portfolio measured by the average Sharpe and Treynor ratios, leading to higher market risk premium. This indicates a diversification effect of the diversified beliefs. In He and Shi (2008), a similar analysis is also conducted when the heterogeneous beliefs are formed in the asset payoffs and we found that both setups share many similar features, though the diversification effect is more significant for the return setup.

It would be interesting to extend the analysis of this paper to an intertemporal model by following the HAMs literature to incorporate expectations feedback mechanism into the beliefs. By allowing investors to switch among different expectations based on certain performance measure, it is not clear how the MV efficiency of the optimal portfolios is improved or whether the diversification effect of the heterogeneous beliefs still holds. We leave those tasks for future research.

Acknowledgements We thank the editors, Herbert Dawid and Willi Semmler, two anonymous referees, the seminar participants at Peking University and the National Chengchi University, and participants at the Inaugural conference on Investment Strategies and Financial Market Dysfunctionality (Sydney, December 2007) and the 14th International Conference on Computing in Economics and Finance (Paris, June 2008) for helpful comments. Financial support from the Australian Research Council (ARC) under Discovery Grant (DP0773776) and Paul Woolley Centre for Capital Market Dysfunctionality at the University of Technology, Sydney are gratefully acknowledged.

References

Abel, A. (2002). An exploration of the effects of pessimism and doubt on asset returns. *Journal of Economic Dynamics and Control*, *26*, 1075–1092.

Alfarano, S., Lux, T., & Wagner, F. (2005). Estimation of agent-based models: the case of an asymmetric herding model. *Computational Economics*, *26*, 19–49.

Ang, A., Hodrick, R., Xing, Y., & Zhang, X. (2006). The cross-section of volatility and expected returns. *Journal of Finance*, *61*(1), 259–299.

Bart, J., & Masse, I. (1981). Divergence of opinion and risk. *Journal of Financial and Quantitative Analysis*, *16*, 23–34.

Böhm, V., & Chiarella, C. (2005). Mean variance preferences, expectations formation, and the dynamics of random asset prices. *Mathematical Finance*, *15*, 61–97.

Böhm, V., & Wenzelburger, J. (2005). On the performance of efficient portfolios. *Journal of Economic Dynamics and Control*, *29*, 721–740.

Brock, H., & Hommes, C. (1997). A rational route to randomness. *Econometrica*, *65*, 1059–1095.

Brock, H., & Hommes, C. (1998). Heterogeneous beliefs and routes to chaos in a simple asset pricing model. *Journal of Economic Dynamics and Control*, *22*, 1235–1274.

Brock, W., Hommes, C., & Wagener, F. (2005). Evolutionary dynamics in financial markets with many trader types. *Journal of Mathematical Economics*, *41*, 7–42.

Chiarella, C., & He, X. (2002). Heterogeneous beliefs, risk and learning in a simple asset pricing model. *Computational Economics*, *19*, 95–132.

Chiarella, C., & He, X. (2003). Heterogeneous beliefs, risk and learning in a simple asset pricing model with a market maker. *Macroeconomic Dynamics*, *7*, 503–536.

Chiarella, C., Dieci, R., & Gardini, L. (2002). Speculative behaviour and complex asset price dynamics. *Journal of Economic Behavior and Organization*, *49*, 173–197.

Chiarella, C., Dieci, R., & Gardini, L. (2005). The dynamic interaction of speculation and diversification. *Applied Mathematical Finance*, *12*(1), 17–52.

Chiarella, C., Dieci, R., & He, X. (2006a). *Aggregation of heterogeneous beliefs and asset pricing theory: a mean-variance analysis* (Technical Report 186). Quantitative Finance Research Center, University of Technology, Sydney.

Chiarella, C., He, X., & Hommes, C. (2006b). A dynamic analysis of moving average rules. *Journal of Economic Dynamics and Control*, *30*, 1729–1753.

Chiarella, C., Dieci, R., & He, X. (2007). Heterogeneous expectations and speculative behaviour in a dynamic multi-asset framework. *Journal of Economic Behavior and Organization, 62*, 402–427.

Chiarella, C., Dieci, R., & He, X. (2009a). Heterogeneity, market mechanisms and asset price dynamics. In T. Hens & K. R. Schenk-Hoppe (Eds.), *Handbook of financial markets: dynamics and evolution* (pp. 277–344). Amsterdam: Elsevier.

Chiarella, C., Dieci, R., & He, X. (2009b). A framework for CAPM with heterogeneous beliefs. In G. I. Bischi, C. Chiarella, & L. Gardini (Eds.), *Nonlinear dynamics in economics, finance and social sciences: essays in honour of John Barkley Rosser Jr.* (pp. 353–369). Berlin: Springer.

Detemple, J., & Murthy, S. (1994). Intertemporal asset pricing with heterogeneous beliefs. *Journal of Economic Theory, 62*, 294–320.

Diether, K., Malloy, C., & Scherbina, A. (2002). Differences of opinion and cross section of stock returns. *Journal of Finance, 57*, 2113–2141.

Diks, C., & van der Weide, R. (2005). Herding, a-synchronous updating and heterogeneity in memory in a CBS. *Journal of Economic Dynamics and Control, 29*, 741–763.

Gaunersdorfer, A. (2000). Endogenous fluctuations in a simple asset pricing model with heterogeneous agents. *Journal of Economic Dynamics and Control, 24*, 799–831.

Gaunersdorfer, A., & Hommes, C. (2007). A nonlinear structural model for volatility clustering. In G. Teyssiere & A. Kirman (Eds.), *Long memory in economics* (pp. 265–288). Berlin: Springer.

He, X., & Li, Y. (2007). Power-law behaviour, heterogeneity, and trend chasing. *Journal of Economic Dynamics and Control, 31*, 3396–3426.

He, X., & Shi, L. (2008). *Heterogeneity, bounded rationality, and market dysfunctionality* (Technical Report 233). Quantitative Finance Research Center, University of Technology, Sydney.

He, X., & Shi, L. (2009). *Portfolio analysis and zero-beta CAPM with heterogeneous beliefs* (Technical Report 244). Quantitative Finance Research Center, University of Technology, Sydney.

Hommes, C. (2001). Financial markets as nonlinear adaptive evolutionary systems. *Quantitative Finance, 1*, 149–167.

Hommes, C. (2006). Heterogeneous agent models in economics and finance. In L. Tesfatsion & K. L. Judd (Eds.), *Handbook of computational economics: Vol. 2. Agent-based computational economics* (pp. 1109–1186). Amsterdam: North-Holland.

Horst, U., & Wenzelburger, J. (2008). On no-ergodic asset prices. *Economic Theory, 34*(2), 207–234.

Huang, C.-F., & Litzenberger, R. (1988). *Foundations for financial economics*. Amsterdam: Elsevier/North-Holland.

Johnson, T. (2004). Forecast dispersion and the cross section of expected returns. *Journal of Finance, 59*, 1957–1978.

LeBaron, B. (2006). Agent-based computational finance. In L. Tesfatsion & K. L. Judd (Eds.), *Handbook of computational economics: Vol. 2. Agent-based computational economics* (pp. 1187–1233). Amsterdam: North-Holland.

Lintner, J. (1965). The valuation of risk assets and the selection of risky investments in stock portfolios and capital budgets. *Review of Economic Studies, 47*, 13–37.

Lintner, J. (1969). The aggregation of investor's diverse judgements and preferences in purely competitive security markets. *Journal of Financial and Quantitative Analysis, 4*, 347–400.

Miller, E. (1977). Risk, uncertainty, and divergence of opinion. *Journal of Finance, 32*, 1151–1168.

Mossin, J. (1966). Equilibrium in a capital asset market. *Econometrica, 35*, 768–783.

Pagan, A. (1996). The econometrics of financial markets. *Journal of Empirical Finance, 3*, 15–102.

Rubinstein, M. (1974). An aggregation theorem for securities markets. *Journal of Financial Economics, 1*, 225–244.

Rubinstein, M. (1975). Security market efficiency in an Arrow-Debreu economy. *American Economic Review, 65*, 812–824.

Rubinstein, M. (1976). The strong case for the generalized logarithmic utility model as the premier model of financial markets. *Journal of Finance, 31*, 551–571.

Sharpe, W. (1964). Capital asset prices: a theory of market equilibrium under conditions of risk. *Journal of Finance*, *19*, 425–442.
Sharpe, W. (2007). *Investors and markets, portfolio choice, asset prices, and investment advice*. Princeton: Princeton Univ. Press.
Wenzelburger, J. (2004). Learning to predict rationally when beliefs are Heterogeneous. *Journal of Economic Dynamics and Control*, *28*, 2075–2104.
Wenzelburger, J. (2009). Perfect forecasting, behavioral heterogeneity, and asset prices. In T. Hens & K. R. Schenk-Hoppe (Eds.), *Handbook of financial markets: dynamics and evolution* (pp. 345–401). Amsterdam: Elsevier.
Westerhoff, F. (2004). Multiasset market dynamics. *Macroeconomic Dynamics*, *8*, 591–616.
Westerhoff, F., & Dieci, R. (2006). The effectiveness of Keynes-Tobin transaction taxes when Heterogeneous agents can trade in different markets: a behavioral finance approach. *Journal of Economic Dynamics and Control*, *30*, 293–322.
Williams, J. (1977). Capital asset prices with Heterogeneous beliefs. *Journal of Financial Economics*, *5*, 219–239.
Zapatero, F. (1998). Effects of financial innovations on market volatility when beliefs are Heterogeneous. *Journal of Economic Dynamics and Control*, *22*, 597–626.

Can Investors Benefit from Using Trading Rules Evolved by Genetic Programming? A Test of the Adaptive Efficiency of U.S. Stock Markets with Margin Trading Allowed

Stan Miles and Barry Smith

Abstract This paper employs genetic programming to develop trading rules, then uses these rules to test the efficient markets hypothesis. Unlike most similar research, the study both incorporates margin trading and returns trading rules that are more than simple buy-sell signals. Consistent with the standard portfolio model, a trading rule is defined here as the proportion of an investor's total wealth that is held in the form of stocks; because margin trading is allowed, the proportion can be greater than 1. The results show that the 24 individual stock markets studied were adaptively efficient between 1985 and 2005.

1 Introduction

A number of studies (e.g., Allen and Karjalainen 1999; Gençay 1998, 1999; and Sullivan et al. 1999, 2001, 2003) have tested the efficient market hypothesis (EMH) by examining the out-of-sample performance of technical trading rules. High risk-adjusted out-of-sample performance of these rules is interpreted as evidence against EMH, because if EMH is true, investors cannot benefit from using publicly available in-sample information to derive profitable trading rules out-of-sample. Adaptive efficiency, a weaker version of EMH, was developed by Daniel and Titman (1999). A market is said to be adaptively efficient if profit opportunities disappear soon after they become apparent.

In this study, we test the adaptive efficiency of U.S. stock markets by examining the out-of-sample returns of technical trading rules constructed by genetic programming (GP). Many of the previous studies that tested EMH were limited to trading rules that returned simple buy-sell signals; such rules switch between investing all wealth in a single risky asset and investing all wealth in a single riskless asset. In contrast, the rules in our study are defined as setting the proportion of wealth to be held in the form of stocks; any wealth not held in the form of stocks is invested in a riskless asset. If adhering to a trading rule requires that stock holdings exceed wealth, the trader takes out a margin loan.

S. Miles (✉)
Department of Economics, School of Business and Economics, Thompson Rivers University, 900 McGill Road, P.O. Box 3010, Kamloops, BC, Canada V2C 5N3
e-mail: stanmiles@tru.ca

H. Dawid, W. Semmler (eds.), *Computational Methods in Economic Dynamics*, Dynamic Modeling and Econometrics in Economics and Finance 13,
DOI 10.1007/978-3-642-16943-4_5,

Past studies that tested EMH usually adjusted the out-of-sample trading rule returns for risk, in a variety of manners. We adopt a fitness criterion that is based on the investor's expected utility and incorporates risk aversion; hence, our adjustment of the out-of-sample trading rule returns is consistent with the standard portfolio model. In summary, our model fits within the existing literature but is more realistic than most previous models because it allows for margin trading, and it is a stricter test of adaptive efficiency because it allows for trading rules that are more complex than the simple buy-sell signals generated by the rules in most previous research.

1.1 Background

Koza (1992) introduced GP as a modification of genetic algorithms. GP employs a computerized version of the working of principles of natural selection to search for candidate solutions to problems, in a nonlinear fashion. The methodology is designed for particular problems: the set of possible solutions consists of computer programs or analytical expressions that can be expressed as decision trees. GP uses tree-like structures that are hierarchical compositions of functions to represent solution candidates. GP does not specify a priori the structure of the solution candidates. The process, which is described in detail in Sect. 3.1, operates to "evolve" decision trees that become increasingly more adept at solving the problem of interest.

Compared to the classic optimization methods, evolutionary algorithms (of which GP is a subset) offer several advantages. Gauss–Newton and other gradient-type methods cannot be applied to problems with a discontinuous objective function, but GP can handle such problems. Whereas gradient-like methods encounter difficulties on problems with objective functions that have multiple local optima, because they converge to local maxima, GP can be applied successfully. GP and other evolutionary algorithms also are said to often be successful in cases when other optimization methods fail due to the large size of the search space.

Some qualifications concerning use of GP and other evolutionary algorithms are as follows: GP is not guaranteed to find the global maximum. Special-purpose algorithms in well-understood domains usually have better performance than GP and other evolutionary algorithms that encapsulate little problem-specific knowledge. Because GP requires constantly populating a pool of solution candidates, the objective function must be evaluated multiple times; as a result, the required computation time can be large.

Researchers have applied GP to diverse problems in econometrics, economics, and finance, as well as to numerous problems in other fields that are beyond the scope of this paper. Chen and Yeh (2002) applied GP to evolve populations of traders who learn over time as a means of demonstrating how emergent properties can be shown in an agent-based artificial stock market. Chen and Yeh (1997) also formalized the notion of unpredictability in the efficient market hypothesis through use of GP. Álvarez-Díaz and Álvarez (2005) combined forecasts generated by GP and neural networks to forecast exchange rates. Lensberg (1999) investigated the usefulness of GP for solving highly irregular optimization problems and for generating hypotheses about rational behavior in situations where explicit maximization is not well defined. Lensberg et al. (2006) and McKee and Lensberg (2002) used GP to construct an effective bankruptcy prediction model.

One interesting application of GP is in the area of financial asset trading strategies. These strategies can be used to test weak-form financial market efficiency. GP has been applied widely in related applications in the S&P 500 market, including studies by Allen and Karjalainen (1999); Fyfe et al. (2005); Neely (2003); Ready (2002); and Wang (2000). One of the first studies of the out-of-sample returns of ex ante optimal trading rules evolved by GP is by Allen and Karjalainen. They concluded that, after figuring in transaction costs associated with the trading suggested by their rules, the rules generated in their study did not outperform the simple buy-and-hold strategy. Fyfe et al. (2005) and Neely (2003) extended the experiments presented by Allen and Karjalainen by using a more complex fitness criterion, one that adjusts trading rule returns for risk, so as to evolve ex ante optimal trading rules. Both studies found that when the out-of-sample returns of trading rules are adjusted for risk, the rules cannot beat the buy-and-hold strategy. Allen and Karjalainen's study was further extended by Ready, who tested the performance of GP rules under conditions of higher transaction costs and potential price slippage between the time when the trading signals are generated and the time when the corresponding trades can be completed. Once again, trading rules could not outperform the buy-and-hold strategy. Wang used GP to generate trading and hedging rules in S&P 500 spot and futures markets. This study found the S&P 500 spot market to be efficient, as most GP rules that evolved simply duplicated the buy-and-hold strategy.

Researchers also have employed GP to study the properties of prices in individual stock markets. Kaboudan (2000) used GP to produce one-day-ahead stock price forecasts for six individual stocks, then evaluated trading strategies based on these forecasts; these strategies yielded higher returns than that of the buy-and-hold strategy. Fyfe et al. (1999) employed GP to evolve trading rules for one UK stock and found that risk-adjusted returns are inferior to that of the buy-and-hold rule. Potvin et al. (2004) applied GP to evolve trading strategies for stocks in 14 Canadian companies. Rules evolved by GP were found to outperform the buy-and-hold strategy when the market was falling or when it was stable, but these rules were dominated by the buy-and-hold approach during times when the market was rising. Though the out-of-sample returns were positive for 9 out of 14 stocks, the average out-of-sample return for the 14 stocks in this study, applying the GP rules, was -3.59%.

One category of trading rules is "bang-bang" strategies, simplistic rules according to which investors switch back and forth between investing all of their wealth in a risky asset and investing it all in the riskless asset. Academics and practitioners who have studied technical trading rules have defined their rules as bang-bang strategies so often that Skouras (2001) defined technical analysis as a bang-bang strategy. Samuelson (1997) proved that the expected utility of the investor who employs a constant diversification trading rule is necessarily higher than the expected utility of the investor who uses a bang-bang strategy. Gollier (1997) proved that the bang-bang strategy consisting of investing in one asset in the first period and in another asset in the second period is second-order stochastically dominated by the strategy of splitting one's wealth evenly between the two assets during the two periods. These two results illustrate that bang-bang strategies are dominated by strategies that are allowed to diversify between the risky and the riskless assets at every point in time. Studies that test EMH by evaluating the performance of bang-bang trading rules therefore are biased toward accepting EMH. A proper test of EMH would involve examining the performance of technical trading rules that have proved to be more efficient than the simplest bang-bang strategies, which allow no diversification at a given point in time.

Unlike studies that use GP to find trading rules for stock indices and individual stocks as a means of studying the performance of GP rules themselves, Allen and Karjalainen (1999) arrived at their conclusions regarding market efficiency by examining both the performance of single GP rules themselves and the performance of portfolios of GP trading rules. For the latter, Allen and Karjalainen used GP to evolve and save 100 rules for the S&P 500 index, using daily data. They then examined the out-of-sample returns of a portfolio that assigned an equal weight in the portfolio to each rule that had satisfied the selection criteria used in the study. The portfolio thus invested in the risky asset a proportion of funds set by the proportion of rules that returned a signal to invest all of the funds in the risky asset. In this two-step approach, the ability of GP to find good portfolio rules could be diminished because the objective (high out-of-sample returns from a portfolio of trading rules) is different from the actual fitness function that GP uses as it evolves individual bang-bang rules.

Most studies that tested EMH by evaluating the returns generated by technical analysis rules employed simple rules that returned 0–1 signals, or bang-bang strategies. Studies such as those by Fyfe et al. (2005) and Potvin et al. (2004) used GP to search within the space of such trading rules. Samuelson's (1997) results indicate that the out-of-sample performance of the rules could be improved by relaxing the bang-bang restriction to allow rules that return a proportion of wealth (not restricted to 0% or 100%) to be invested into the risky asset, and we employ that in our experiments. Our experiments add realism to the trading simulations of those studies by allowing margin trading such that the investor can set the proportion of wealth allocated to the risky asset to be any number between 0% and 200% (under the assumption of a maximum loan of 50% of a portfolio's value; in other words, an investor can use 100% of wealth as collateral for a margin loan of the same amount).

This article is organized as follows: Section 2 presents background information on the environment in which stock trading takes place, and Sect. 3 describes the methodology employed. The empirical results and their implications for market efficiency of 24 U.S. stock markets are detailed in Sect. 4. Finally, some concluding remarks are presented in Sect. 5.

2 The Trading Environment

The opportunities to trade on margin are subject to regulatory oversight. In the United States, the margin requirement for stocks is set by the Federal Reserve

Board (FRB) under Regulation T. In general, an initial margin requirement is that collateral must be deposited on the day the stock transaction is opened, and a maintenance margin requirement must be maintained every day thereafter. The maintenance margin is a fraction of the initial margin. Because the stock margin requirements are set with respect to the "loan value" of the position, the initial margin requirement for stocks is expressed in terms of a percentage of the current stock price.

Since 1974, the Board of Governors of the Federal Reserve System has set the initial margin requirement for stocks at 50%. This means that investors must have equity in their accounts equal to or greater than 50% of the value of securities held. At the New York Stock Exchange (NYSE), the broker-dealers at member firms are obligated to insist that their customers have a maintenance margin equal to at least 25% (30%) for long (short) stock positions. Broker-dealers may set house margin requirements for selected volatile stocks and for concentrated accounts (nondiversified portfolios containing a small number of stocks) above the mandatory exchange margins.

Security price declines set off maintenance margin calls. An investor who receives a margin call must either (a) deposit new collateral in the form of cash or another security with enough margin value or (b) close part of his or her open stock positions. Investors who fail to meet a margin call on time may have their stock holdings liquidated at the market price. When traders choose to meet the margin call by selling part of their securities, they must sell at least the number of stock shares that would bring the ratio of investor equity to the value of the stock position back to the maintenance margin amount.

3 Methodology

Our methodology will generate trading rules for margin trading for each of 24 stocks and then study the out-of-sample performance of these rules. We use GP to evolve the trading rules, which determine the proportion of wealth to be allocated for investment in a risky asset (i.e., one of the 24 stocks in this study), with the remaining wealth in the "portfolio" for each individual stock being invested into a riskless asset (or, in the case of a margin loan, borrowed). This is in contrast to simple binary bang-bang rules evolved in earlier studies (e.g., Dempster and Jones 2001; Fyfe et al. 2005; and Potvin et al. 2004).

Within the literature, the approach most similar to our evolution of the proportion of wealth to be allocated to a risky asset, with the possibility of using wealth as margin collateral, is Wang's (2000) use of GP to generate trading and hedging rules in the S&P 500 spot and futures markets. Wang limited GP futures trading rules to five trading signals (similar to our proportions of wealth to be held in the risky asset, but limited to only a few discrete choices): two contracts held long, one contract held long, no position, one contract held short, and two contracts held short.

Bessembinder and Chan (1998) studied markets using a narrower range of alternatives, examining the returns of a "double-or-out" strategy. For this strategy, a trader holds the Dow Jones portfolio when the technical trading rule does not return a trading signal, switches to holding T-bills when the rule returns a sell signal, and borrows (at the T-bill rate) to double the equity position when the rule returns a buy signal. Bessembinder and Chan examined the out-of-sample performance of known technical analysis rules. In this study the "break-even" trading costs computed (which would exactly cancel out increases in portfolio returns from using technical rules) are lower than the estimates of actual trading costs, which implies that the study confirmed EMH. In the present paper, rather than studying known rules, we study the out-of-sample performance of the technical rules evolved by GP.

3.1 Genetic Programming Setup

The GP method begins by generating a population of random candidate solutions to the given problem, referred to as the initial generation. The only requirements for candidate solutions is that they be well defined and produce output appropriate to the problem of interest. Most of these random solutions will be quite poor at solving the problem; some obviously will be better than the rest, and some, purely by chance, will be moderately good or even quite good. From that initial population, the next generation of solution candidates is created, in a process described below. The set of solutions is then allowed to "evolve," using crossover and mutation operators, with the "fittest" members of each generation being assigned higher levels of probability of "mating" to create members of the subsequent generation from their component parts and from random elements.

The crossover operator uses two parent solution candidates to build offspring solution candidates in the next generation by replacing a randomly selected subtree in one of the parent solution candidates with a subtree from another parent solution candidate. The mutation operator is used in addition to the crossover operator to create offspring solution candidates. The mutation operator (employed with a small probability) ensures that genetic diversity is not reduced, by inserting a randomly generated subtree into the offspring.

Through this process of using relatively more "fit" candidate solutions to produce each successive generation of candidate solutions, the decision trees in each successive generation tend to become more adept at solving the problem. GP continues to produce populations this way until a termination criterion is satisfied.

In our experiments, GP constructs trading rules by assembling Boolean, probability, and real-valued functions as the building blocks in a tree structure. Each function takes its inputs from the functions below it in the tree. The building blocks used in all of the experiments consist of numerical constants, arithmetic and logical operators, and simple functions of past price data. Table 1 lists these building blocks and other particulars of the experiments we conducted. To guarantee that a trading rule is well defined, the root node (the "top of the tree") of each GP decision tree must be constrained to be a function that has an output of the probability type; that is, it returns a number (a proportion) between 0 and 1, inclusive, at the beginning of every trading day. To this end, all root nodes are constrained to be one of the functions in the set {And, AND, GT, If–Then, If–Then–Else, IF–THEN, IF–THEN–ELSE, Not, NOT, LT, Or, OR, SRatio, pconstant}. (See Table 1 for details of the workings of the functions that constitute the function set.)

Our experiments take the probability returned by each GP solution candidate decision tree and convert it to a rule stating the fraction of wealth that the investor will allocate to be held as shares of stock. If this number is 1, for example, it indicates that the investor should hold as many shares of stock as possible. If the initial margin is constrained to be 50% of the value of shares of stock in the investor's portfolio, the investor would buy shares of stock valued at 200% of his or her wealth, using all wealth as collateral and borrowing an equal amount from his or her stock broker as a margin loan.

At the bottom of the tree are functions from the terminal set (functions requiring no inputs). Their output type, like that of all functions below the top of the tree, matches the input type of the function above. The terminal set consists of numerical constants and of variables in the set {stock price, stock return, Days-remaining}. The function set contains real-valued functions, Boolean functions, and probability functions that are constrained to return a number between 0 and 1. It is important to realize that not all logical functions return a Boolean output. Functions in the set {and, or, not, if–then, if–then–else} have Boolean inputs and outputs. Functions in the set {And, Or, Not, If–Then, If–Then–Else} convert Boolean arguments into a probability output of 1 or 0. Functions in the set {AND, OR, NOT, IF–THEN, IF–THEN–ELSE} take probability inputs and compute probability outputs. Lastly, functions in the set {>, <} convert real numbers into Boolean values, and functions in the set {GT, LT} convert real numbers into probabilities.

The real-valued functions in the function set include arithmetic and mathematical operators in the set {+, −, /, ∗, absolute value, ln, Power}. Also included are functions for maximum and minimum, a lag function that returns the value of the variable argument as it was n days ago (n is the second, integer-valued, argument), and a function that returns a moving average of the variable argument (Moving_Av) in a window defined by the second, integer-valued, argument.

The function and terminal sets identified in Table 1 enable GP to search for trading strategies in the space of complex and nonlinear decision trees. This setup allows GP to potentially identify factors that are important for successful trading strategies, as well as to put these factors together in ways that form decision rules that correspond to profitable trading strategies.

3.2 Data

In our experiments, we employ GP using the most recent 5 years of data to evolve trading rules, which are then applied in the following year. We divide the data into subperiods of 1 year each and sub-subperiods of 3 months each, the assumed length of the investor's trading horizon. Throughout the experiments, these data

Table 1 Genetic programming building blocks

Building block	Input data type	Input	Output data type	Output
+	Real	a, b	Real	$a + b$
−	Real	a, b	Real	$a - b$
*	Real	a, b	Real	$a \times b$
/	Real	a, b	Real	If $\|b\| > 0$, output a/b; else, output 1
Absolute value	Real	a	Real	$\|a\|$
Lag	Variable (a), Integer (n)	a, n	Real	Value of the variable a, n days ago
ln	Real	a	Real	If $a > 0$, output $\ln(a)$; else, output 0
Maximum	Real	a, b	Real	$\text{Max}(a, b)$
Minimum	Real	a, b	Real	$\text{Min}(a, b)$
Moving_Av	Variable (a), Integer (n)	a, n	Real	Average of the last n observations of the variable a
Power	Real	a, b	Real	a^b
Return	Variable	a	Real	$\ln(a_t/a_{t-1})$
>	Real	a, b	Boolean	If $a > b$, output true; else, output false
<	Real	a, b	Boolean	If $a < b$, output true; else, output false
And	Boolean	a, b	Boolean	If a is true and b is true, output true; else, output false
If–then	Boolean	a, b	Boolean	If a is true, output b; else, output false
If–then–else	Boolean	a, b, c	Boolean	If a is true, output b; else, output c
Not	Boolean	a	Boolean	If a is true, output false; else, output true
Or	Boolean	a, b	Boolean	If a is true or b is true, output true; else, output false
And	Boolean	a, b	Probability	If a is true and b is true, output 1; else, output 0
AND	Probability	a, b	Probability	$a \times b$
GT	Real	a, b	Probability	If $a > b$, output 1; else, output 0
If–Then	Boolean (a), Probability (b)	a, b	Probability	If a is true, output b; else, output 0

Table 1 (Continued)

Building block	Input data type	Input	Output data type	Output
IF–THEN	Probability	a, b	Probability	If $a = 1$, output b; else, output 0
If–Then–Else	Boolean (a), Probability (b, c)	a, b, c	Probability	If a is true, output b; else, output c
Not	Boolean	a	Probability	If a is true, output 1; else, output 0
IF–THEN–ELSE	Probability	a, b, c	Probability	If $a = 1$, output b; else, output c
LT	Real	a, b	Probability	If $a < b$, output 1; else, output 0
NOT	Probability	a	Probability	$1 - a$
Or	Boolean	a, b	Probability	If a is true or b is true, output 1; else, output 0
OR	Probability	a, b	Probability	$(a + b) - (a \times b)$
SRatio	Real	a, b	Probability	If $b = 0$, or if a and b are of opposite sign, output 0. Otherwise, output 1 if $\|a\| \geq \|b\|$; else, output a/b
Pconstant		None	Probability	Real number between -1 and 1
Days-remaining		None	Variable	Number of days remaining until end of sub-subperiod
P_t		None	Variable	Current value of asset price
R		None	Variable	Current value of riskless rate
W_t		None	Variable	Current value of investor's wealth

sub-subperiods are used to train the GP methodology (training periods), select the fittest candidate to be applied out-of-sample (selection periods), and evaluate the fitness of the GP rules using out-of-sample data (from a testing period). To evaluate the "fitness" of candidate solutions in a given time period, we use a criterion that involves averaging utilities of the wealth accumulated, through use of the trading rules generated by GP, at the ends of sub-subperiods that constitute the appropriate time period. The trading horizon of 3 months was chosen arbitrarily. The choice of a longer trading horizon (i.e., longer sub-subperiods) would result in fewer terms being averaged, so that each term would carry more weight. On the positive side, each term would carry more information because it includes more trading days; on the negative side, an "outlier" term could more seriously bias the results. Currently we are conducting research to examine the sensitivity of results to changes in the trading horizon and to changes in the number of training and selection subperiods.

For each of the 24 stocks used in this study, the data set spans the years 1980–2005. Thus, allowing for training and selection periods during which trading rules are evolved, we have 21 testing subperiods and 84 testing sub-subperiods (as there are 4 sub-subperiods of 3 months each per subperiod of 1 year) with which to work. The training and selection periods each consist of 2.5 subperiods, and each testing period is composed of 1 subperiod. The selection period follows the training period, and the testing period follows the selection period.

As a specific example, an investor at the beginning of 1985 has access to 5 years of historical data (1980–1984). The investor assigns the first half of this data set to the training period and the remainder to the selection period. Ten GP trials (to be discussed in Sect. 3.3) are run on this subset of the data, using the periods specified this way. If threshold criteria, defined in Sect. 3.6, are satisfied for any of the rules generated in these 10 trials, one rule (which best meets the fitness criterion, as discussed in Sect. 3.4) is selected to be applied out-of-sample. The investor then uses this rule to trade in 1985, the testing period. That completes one round of rule evolution and testing. At the beginning of 1986, all periods are reassigned by being rolled forward one year: The testing period is now 1986, and the years 1981–1985 are now referred to as training and selection periods. Once again, 10 GP trials are run, in the manner described above, and one rule is selected to be applied out-of-sample (again, if threshold criteria are satisfied for any of the rules generated in these 10 trials); that rule is applied to trades in the testing period, which is now 1986. We continue rolling our window forward in this manner until we use the last year in our data set, 2005, as the testing period. In summary, we use 5 years of data to evolve a trading rule to be applied 1 year ahead, doing this 21 times for every stock (the data set contains 26 years, 1980–2005 inclusive; the first testing period is 1985, and the last is 2005, for a total of 21 testing periods).

During each experiment, each sub-subperiod is split evenly into an observation phase and a trading phase (operationally defined below). The observation phase ends when the trading phase begins. On the first day of the trading phase, the GP algorithm has access to all of the stock prices during the observation phase that has just ended. From then on, every day GP can use all of that stock price information, as well as all stock price information from the current trading phase, up to and including data from the previous day, to make its recommendation for wealth allocation. Each observation phase and each trading phase is 60 trading days (approximately 3 calendar months) in length; therefore, each sub-subperiod (consisting of an observation phase followed by a trading phase) is approximately 6 calendar months long.

For these experiments, we chose 24 companies traded on the NYSE. We chose well-known companies operating in a variety of industries. To ensure that the companies came from a variety of industries, we picked two stocks each from the 12 industries in Fama and French's industry classification scheme.[1] Specifically, two companies were selected from each of the following industries: Consumer Durables, Consumer Non-Durables, Manufacturing, Energy, Chemicals, Business Equipment, Telephone and Television, Utilities, Shops, Healthcare, Finance, and

[1]Refer to http://mba.tuck.dartmouth.edu/pages/faculty/ken.french/Data_Library/det_12_ind_port.html.

Table 2 Individual stocks used for the GP experiments

Industry	Company	Symbol
Consumer non-durables	Altria group	MO
Consumer non-durables	Pepsico	PEP
Consumer durables	General motors	GM
Consumer durables	Whirlpool	WHR
Manufacturing	Eastman kodak	EK
Manufacturing	Goodyear tire & rubber	GT
Energy	Exxon mobil	XOM
Energy	Halliburton	HAL
Chemicals	Dow chemical	DOW
Chemicals	DuPont	DD
Business equipment	IBM	IBM
Business equipment	Xerox	XRX
Telephone and television	AT&T Inc.	T
Telephone and television	Sprint	S
Utilities	American electric	AEP
Utilities	Duke energy	DUK
Shops	Target	TGT
Shops	Wal-mart stores	WMT
Healthcare	Johnson and Johnson	JNJ
Healthcare	Pfizer	PFE
Finance	Bank of America	BAC
Finance	Merrill Lynch	MER
Other	Disney	DIS
Other	Hilton hotels	HLN

Other. We chose from among the companies that were active in the market for the entire period between the start of 1980 and the end of 2005. For each stock, our data set comprises daily prices for the time period 1980–2005. Table 2 lists the companies used in this study, along with their corresponding industries. These data, along with 3-month T-bill rates, were taken from Datastream.

The stock prices in these data sets are not adjusted for dividends. Bessembinder and Chan (1998) estimated the dividend yield to be 0.016% per day for the Dow Jones Industrial Average (DJIA). When the trading rules evolved by GP result in not being fully invested in the stock, the decision not to include the dividends in the data set has the effect of underestimating returns to a greater extent for the buy-and-hold trading rule than for the rules evolved by GP. Conversely, when the GP rules call for obtaining a margin loan, not including the dividends in the data set has the opposite effect: Returns are underestimated to a greater extent for the GP rules than for the buy-and-hold rule. Because both of these scenarios can occur, it is difficult to determine the overall influence of exclusion of dividends from the data set on the results of our study in regard to the GP rules versus the buy-and-hold rule. The effect is ambiguous even for a given rule, which might return a signal less than 0.5 (in which case the investor's portfolio is not fully invested in the stock) on one trading day and a signal greater than 0.5 (in which case the investor obtains a margin loan to buy stocks) on a different day. Not including dividends in the data set always has the effect of underestimating returns for the buy-on-margin-and-hold rule (defined in Sect. 3.4) to a greater extent than for the GP rules.

3.3 Operationalization of Genetic Programming Method

Every GP experiment conducted as part of this study involves 10 trials, and each trial consists of 50 generations. Every generation uses a population size of 50,000 trading rules. The tree depth of the solution candidate decision trees was limited to 25 levels. To create rules for each generation, we use the crossover operator and the mutation operator.

A set of 10 GP trials comprises the following steps:

Step 1 Generate 50,000 random rules, evaluate their fitness in the training and selection periods, and identify and save all of the rules that satisfy the first six threshold criteria (described in Sect. 3.6 and in Table 3). If more than 50 rules satisfy the criteria, save only the 50 rules that have the highest fitness in the selection period.

Step 2 Attach to each rule a probability of being chosen to be used to create "offspring" rules in the next generation, with the probability correlating with the rule's fitness during training and selection periods. Choose rules from the current generation randomly, using the attached probabilities, and apply to these rules either the crossover operator (with probability 95%) or the mutation operator (with probability 5%), so as to generate 50,000 rules for the next generation. As above, evaluate the fitness of the rules in this population in the training and selection periods, then save all of the rules that satisfy the first six threshold criteria (up to a maximum of 50).

Step 3 If this is not Generation 50, go back to Step 2 to create the population of trading rules in the next generation. If this is Generation 50, begin the next trial by going back to Step 1, unless this is Trial 10.

Step 4 If this is Generation 50 of Trial 10, take the rules that were saved during the 10 trials and discard all of the rules that do not satisfy the last two threshold criteria. If any rules remain, select the rule that achieves the highest fitness in the selection period. Study the performance of this rule in the testing period.

Use of "data mining" techniques such as the ones we employ raises potential difficulties, in that the rules chosen may work very well for the data on which they were developed and would be expected to provide high rates of return on that data set. That is, the data might not be representative, and the solutions found may apply well only to those nonrepresentative data. Studies by Neely et al. (1997) and Neely and Weller (1999, 2003) used one training, one selection, and one testing period. Because these studies used limited data sets, they are subject to the criticisms associated with data mining. We adopt an approach similar to that of Allen and Karjalainen (1999) to address these potential difficulties in the choice of time periods. They used 10 sets of successive training, selection, and testing periods. We examine multiple training, selection, and testing periods for each market studied, and we conduct experiments for multiple stock markets.

3.4 Criterion of Fitness

We assume that the investor's preferences are characterized by the logarithmic utility of terminal wealth (W_T) on the day that trading ends. We assume a simple utility function given by

$$U(W_T) = \ln(W_T). \tag{1}$$

The goal of our experiments is to investigate whether we can find a way for investors to increase their utility over the span of their trading horizon by switching from trading in accordance with simple buy-and-hold rules to trading in accordance with a rule evolved by GP. In these experiments, GP provides trading signals to rebalance the trading portfolio between the risky stock asset and the riskless 3-month T-bill asset at the end of every trading day, throughout the investment horizon. Our investment model examines traders whose preferences are characterized by (1) and whose trading horizon is 3 months. We evaluate a rule's fitness in a certain training (or selection or testing) period by averaging the utilities of terminal wealth attained at the ends of sub-subperiods of 3 months that make up that training (or selection or testing) period. This type of fitness criterion takes risk into account by making an adjustment to the raw returns corresponding to the trading rules.

We use two simple buy-and-hold rules as benchmarks in this study: a buy-and-hold rule by which the investor holds all of his or her wealth in the stock, without taking out a margin loan, and a buy-on-margin-and-hold rule by which the investor uses all of his or her wealth as margin collateral, and as a result obtains maximum leverage allowed by the margin regulations.

In studies that evaluate the out-of-sample performance of trading rules evolved by GP as a means to test EMH, various criteria for trading rule performance have been used. We present several of these performance criteria, from some representative studies, to provide a sense of the types of criteria that have been used in previous studies. Allen and Karjalainen (1999) and Potvin et al. (2004) used as a fitness criterion the excess return of trading by the rule versus trading using the buy-and-hold strategy. The measure of performance that adjusted trading returns for risk employed by Fyfe et al. (2005) was the Sharpe ratio (Sharpe 1966), and the measure employed by Dempster and Jones (2001) was a modified Stirling ratio, which is a function of the ratio of return to maximum drawdown. Relevant to this discussion, Neely (2003) used GP to generate three sets of rules that maximize three corresponding fitness criteria that adjust for risk: the Sharpe ratio, the X^* statistic (Sweeney and Lee 1990), and the X_{eff} criterion (Dacorogna et al. 2001).

The risk-adjustment criterion introduced by Dacorogna et al. (2001), the X_{eff} criterion, is related to the criterion of fitness employed in our study. The X_{eff} criterion measures the utility derived from a trading strategy by an investor (whose preferences are characterized by constant absolute risk aversion) over a weighted average of return horizons. Criterion X_{eff} originates from utility theory, except for its reliance on a weighting function that assigns relevant importance to different return horizons. This weighting function is chosen somewhat arbitrarily, may be arbitrarily changed for trading models with different trading frequencies, and does not originate in the standard portfolio model. In the present study, we do not consider multiple trading horizons; hence, we choose to use a fitness criterion that is related to expected utility maximization in a more straightforward fashion.

3.5 Mechanics of the Trading Process

We simulate the trading process in our experiments in the following manner: The trading setup described is used to evaluate the fitness of one candidate trading strategy solution in one sub-subperiod, be it a training, a selection, or a testing sub-subperiod. On the first day of the trading phase, the value of the investor's cash account is set to W_0. For each of our stock experiments, W_0 is set to \$100,000. We make an important assumption that the activities of our simulated trader have negligible influence on the stock price.

We define the investor's wealth at the end of day t, W_t, as the value of the shares of stock in the portfolio at the end of day t plus the value of the cash account (the cash account is negative if the investor has outstanding margin debt). Suppose that on trading day t, the investor's wealth is W_t and the stock's price is P_t. The initial margin regulations (which require margin collateral in the investor's account to be at least 50% of the value of all shares of stock held on margin) imply that the investor can have at most $\text{int}(W_t/(0.5P_t))$ shares of stock on trading day t in his or her portfolio. (The "int" function truncates its input, to give the largest integer not exceeded by the input.)

The portfolio trading rule generated by GP determines the proportion of wealth that the investor will allocate to stock holdings. The rule output for day t is computed using information from the start of the observation phase and up to day $t-1$, inclusive of both the start and end dates. If, on day t, the rule output is α_t, the investor is guided to have N_t shares of stock in his or her portfolio; that is,

$$N_t = \text{int}((\alpha_t W_t)/(0.5P_t)). \tag{2}$$

If the current number of shares of stock in the portfolio is different from this amount, the portfolio is rebalanced accordingly, at the end of day t, at the closing price of day t.

After the investor allocates the amount $[P_t \times \text{int}((\alpha_t W_t)/(0.5P_t))]$ to buy stocks, the remainder of W_t is held in the cash account. The higher this remaining amount, the lower the probability that the investor will receive a margin call. From (2) it can be seen that as long as α_t is below 0.5, the investor's wealth, W_t, is sufficient to obviate the need for the investor to make a margin loan. If $\alpha_t < 0.5$, we assume that the investor receives daily interest payments on the amount remaining in the cash account. If $\alpha_t > 0.5$, the investor makes a margin loan, and we assume that the interest on this margin debt is deducted from the cash account every day.

For simplicity, it is assumed that traders can lend and borrow at the same interest rate, equal to the 3-month T-bill rate. We recognize that this assumption contradicts an economic model of what determines margin loan rates, presented in Fortune (2000) and described further below, as well as being contrary to Fortune's empirical data on interest rates. The simplifying assumption also contradicts empirical findings reported by Kubler and Willen (2006) and Ayres and Nalebuff (2008). All three of these studies noted that the investors with the brokerage houses in the studies faced different interest rates when lending and when borrowing funds to be used as margin to buy equity from their broker.

Kubler and Willen (2006) mention margin loan characteristics, and specifically interest rates on margin loans, at various brokerage houses. They note considerable diversity in the difference between interest rates on collateralized debt and rates on the riskless asset, both across different brokerage houses and by the size of the loan. They point out that this difference is especially significant for small investors. Ayres and Nalebuff (2008) report data that reiterate and provide support for the findings of Kubler and Willen, but they compare the rates that brokers charge on margin loans to the brokers' "call money" rates, rather than to the rate on a risk-free asset.

Fortune (2000, p. 31) points out that "The premium over the lender's cost of money, however defined, covers the broker's cost of recording, monitoring, and managing the loan, as well as a risk premium for the possibility that the customer's assets might become insufficient to repay the margin loan." The model presented in Fortune (2000) demonstrates that the act of a broker providing a margin loan can be interpreted to be equivalent to the broker giving an investor an implicit put option on the account. Under this setup, following the decrease of the value of an investor's account, the investor can allow forced sales of securities or can abandon the account. This implies that the margin loan rate should include a premium that corresponds to the credit risk corresponding to the margin debt. The author goes on to evaluate the impact of this implicit put option on the margin loan rates charged by brokerage houses. The author shows that this rate is related to the value of the put option, which in turn depends on the volatility of the return on underlying securities and on the account's leverage, which is measured by the size of the margin loan relative to the value of securities. In other words, according to this model, brokers should offer margin loans at different rates that reflect the differing volatility and leverage of individual accounts. After examining the rules at various brokerage houses, Fortune presents a "margin loan mystery": In spite of concerns that appear important in theory, brokers' primary consideration in setting margin loan rates seems to be the absolute loan size, rather than market conditions or the level of leverage in an investor's account.

Although it would be useful, and empirically more accurate, in future studies to relax this assumption of equal borrowing and lending rates, the assumption of unlimited borrowing and lending at the risk-free interest rate underlies security valuation and option pricing models, and it is established in the literature. Furthermore, we do not expect the assumption to make any significant difference in the results of the study. It should bias the results toward trading rules that involve more borrowing on margin (because there is no premium charged on borrowing money, as opposed to lending), but by and large, we believe that rules that are profitable will tend to be profitable at different but realistic assumed rates of interest.

In addition to interest rates on the risk-free asset and on margin loans, transaction costs also must be considered. When the investor buys shares of stock, both the cost of the shares and the transaction costs are subtracted from the cash account. Neely et al. (1997) have pointed out that adopting higher transaction costs in the training and selection periods would decrease the proportion of retained rules that trade heavily. Rules that trade heavily are more likely than those that trade less heavily to be overfitting the data. Following Neely, Weller, and Ditmar, we adopt unrealistically high transaction costs in the training and selection periods, as a means of avoiding retaining rules that overfit the data, then use realistic transaction costs in the testing period, so that the rules are tested in a realistic setting. For training and selection periods, we use the following (deliberately unrealistically high) transaction cost structure: a one-way transaction cost of 0.5% of the value of the transaction plus a two-way flat rate of $5 per share of stock. In the testing period, we choose to use the same transaction cost structure used by Allen and Karjalainen (1999) to simulate trading in the S&P 500 index: a one-way transaction cost of 0.25%. Allen and Karjalainen's transaction cost structure, in turn, was motivated by Sweeney (1988), who found that one-way transaction costs for institutional traders were in the range 0.1–0.2%. Allen and Karjalainen argued that a one-way transaction cost of 0.25% incorporates all costs at realistic levels, including the cost of the market impact. Wang (2000) stated that the transaction cost structure for his S&P 500 index trading simulations corresponds to a one-way transaction cost of 0.12%, and that this is a realistic assumption for institutional investors.

We assume that the following activities take place on trading day t: First, the interest payment is added into the cash account (or, in the case of a margin loan, deducted from it). This interest payment is a function of the balance in the cash account (or the total amount of the margin loan, in the latter case) on day $t-1$ and the 3-month T-bill rate. Second, the trading signal, α_t, is generated. Third, the portfolio is rebalanced at the close of day t. Fourth, the day's trading costs are deducted from the cash account, and the cash account is credited (debited) accordingly when stock is sold (bought).

On the last day of the trading phase of each sub-subperiod, the investor sells the stock in the portfolio, and we compute the terminal wealth, W_T, and the investor's utility of terminal wealth, $U(W_T) = \ln(W_T)$. To evaluate a rule's fitness in the training (selection) period, we average the utilities of terminal wealth attained at the end of sub-subperiods that make up the training (selection) period for this stock. To evaluate the out-of-sample fitness of a specific rule evolved by GP to be applied in a certain testing subperiod, we average the utilities of terminal wealth for the sub-subperiods that constitute the testing subperiod.

According to the methodology followed in these experiments, a rule's performance in the selection period sub-subperiods determines whether or not that rule gets saved to be applied out-of-sample. Section 3.6 clarifies the process by which a rule's performance in-sample is used to select the rules to be applied out-of-sample in the testing period.

3.6 Rule Selection Process and Thresholds for Saving Rules

In our experiments, we are testing whether GP can use past price data to evolve trading rules that work well out-of-sample. In accordance with Daniel and Titman's (1999) definition of adaptive efficiency, we are testing whether rules that attain high fitness in-sample continue to have high fitness out-of-sample. The studies conducted by Neely et al. (1997), Allen and Karjalainen (1999), and Neely and Weller (1999) adopted an approach of saving one rule (the one with the highest fitness in the selection period) per trial and applying it out-of-sample if it outperforms a benchmark in the selection period. The benchmark was the buy-and-hold rule in the case of the Allen and Karjalainen study, which applied GP to the S&P 500 index. In contrast, the benchmark in the studies by Neely et al. (1997) and Neely and Weller (1999) was the strategy of not trading and earning the riskless interest rate. These studies apply GP to foreign exchange markets. These authors appear to be using a simple threshold criterion for determining which rule, if any, is selected to be tested out-of-sample. Their threshold criterion, however, doesn't seem to be the most intuitive one to follow. Few risk-averse real-world investors would be willing to switch from investing in accordance with the buy-and-hold rule to investing in accordance with a rule evolved by GP that marginally outperforms the buy-and-hold rule in-sample. Consequently, in this paper we use more sophisticated threshold criteria that must be satisfied in-sample to select the rules to be applied to the out-of-sample period.

The goal is to find rules with the same performance (or better) in-sample as the performance the investor would like to see out-of-sample (that is, performance that is better than a chosen benchmark, as measured by one or more criteria). In addition to looking for the rule that produces a high (on average) utility of terminal wealth at the end of the trading horizon of 3 months, the investor might want to search for a rule that satisfies certain money management criteria (e.g., the rule is profitable a certain minimum fraction of the time; when a loss occurs, it doesn't exceed a certain maximum allowed amount; or the rule gains a certain minimum return at longer horizons). The underlying goal is assumed to be to find a trading strategy that consistently produces high returns without the risk of extreme losses. Each of the four threshold criteria above (high average utility and the three criteria related to money management) is a different way of specifying this goal.

Table 3 formally presents the set of threshold criteria, to be satisfied in-sample (four criteria each in both the training and the selection periods, for a total of eight

Table 3 Parameter settings for the thresholds[a]

Threshold	Threshold value
Minimum average utility at the end of a subperiod for training period	$11.537618 = \ln(102, 500)$
Minimum average utility at the end of a subperiod for selection period	11.537618
Minimum fraction of profitable training subperiods	90%
Minimum fraction of profitable selection subperiods	90%
Minimum wealth observed during the training period	$90,000
Minimum wealth observed during the selection period	$90,000
Minimum wealth at the end of the training period	$125,000
Minimum wealth at the end of the selection period	$125,000

[a]The thresholds in this table had to be satisfied in the training and selection periods, as indicated, while the following (deliberately unrealistically high) transaction cost structure was used: a one-way transaction cost of 0.5% of the value of the transaction plus a two-way flat rate of $5 per share of stock

criteria), that we use in the 24 experiments with individual stocks. We use these threshold criteria to home in on the rules to be tested out-of-sample. The actual threshold values were chosen arbitrarily. A sensitivity study of how the out-of-sample fitness of the rules being saved is influenced by the threshold values is beyond the scope of the present study. We select a single rule for each stock (if at least one rule meets the threshold criteria), and the rules could be different for all 24 stocks. The procedure is explained in detail in the paragraphs that follow.

As described above, for each stock, corresponding to each testing period, we conduct one GP run comprising 10 trials, with each trial consisting of 50 generations. For every generation, we evaluate the fitness of all of the rules, then discard all the rules that do not satisfy the following six threshold criteria (two sets of three each for the training and selection periods; see Table 3): (a) the average utility attained at the end of both the training and the selection sub-subperiods (each 3 months long) must have a certainty equivalent of at least 102.5% of the initial wealth, (b) 90% of training and 90% of selection sub-subperiods must be profitable, and (c) the minimum wealth observed on any day during the training and the selection periods must be greater than 90% of the initial wealth. We rank the remaining rules according to their fitness in the selection period and save the 50 rules with the highest selection period fitness. If fewer than 50 rules satisfy the threshold criteria of our study, we save all of the rules. If none of the rules that make up the population in a given generation satisfies these three criteria, we don't save any rules. Following creation of 50 generations in each of the 10 trials, we discard all the saved rules that do not satisfy the fourth threshold criterion (namely, that the rule results in terminal wealth of at least 125% of the initial wealth at the end of both the total training and selection periods). From the rules that are retained, if any, we then select, to be tested out-of-sample, the rule with the highest selection-period fitness.

Thus, we are searching for a trading strategy, α_t, to be applied out-of-sample in the testing period. This trading strategy must maximize the quantity

$$\max_{\alpha_t} \frac{\sum_{i=1}^{n} U(W_T^i(\alpha_t))}{n}, \tag{3}$$

such that the constraints listed in Table 3 are satisfied in-sample, in the training and selection periods; n is the number of selection sub-subperiods, and $U(W_T^i(\alpha_t))$ is the utility of terminal wealth (given by $\ln(W_T^i(\alpha_t))$) at the end of selection sub-subperiod i.

4 Results

The goal of this study is to investigate whether investors whose trading horizon is 3 months, and whose preferences are characterized by the logarithmic utility of terminal wealth at the end of the trading horizon, can increase their expected utility by switching from trading in accordance with the simple buy-and-hold strategy (without using margin loans for leverage) or the buy-on-margin-and-hold strategy (a strategy that uses the maximum leverage allowed by margin regulations) to trading in accordance with a rule evolved by GP. For each of the 24 stocks, Table 4 provides the average utility of terminal wealth at the end of each testing period for our GP methodology.

As can be seen from Table 4, we employed 21 testing periods, corresponding to the 21 years spanning the period 1985–2005, inclusive. The blank spaces in Table 4 indicate testing periods corresponding to training periods for which no rules satisfying the thresholds in Table 3 were evolved by GP. Use of the thresholds presented in Table 3 to determine which rules get saved resulted in GP saving rules in 231 training periods (of the possible 504, corresponding to all 24 stocks × 21 years). Table 4 presents the utility of terminal wealth averaged over four testing sub-subperiods, corresponding to the testing periods that in turn correspond to the training periods in which rules were found that satisfied the thresholds presented in Table 3.

We compared the expected utility of using the GP methodology with the expected utilities of using the buy-and-hold methodology and the buy-on-margin-and-hold methodology. For each methodology, we computed the average of 24 average out-of-sample utilities of the terminal wealth achieved by applying each of these two methodologies to each of the 24 stock markets examined as part of this study. Specifically, to compute the expected utility for the buy-and-hold and the buy-on-margin-and-hold rules, we computed the average of the utilities of terminal wealth attained at the end of sub-subperiods that made up 21 testing periods for each stock (i.e., we averaged 21 [testing periods per stock] × 1 [subperiod per testing period] × 4 [sub-subperiods per subperiod] × 24 [stocks] = 2,016 utilities of terminal wealth). We interpret these averages as the estimates of the expected utility (for an investor whose preferences are characterized by the logarithmic utility function) of using the buy-and-hold rule and the buy-on-margin-and-hold rule. It should be noted that this

Table 4 Average testing sub-subperiod utility of terminal wealth for GP rules, with $U(W_T) = \ln(W_T)$ and initial wealth = $100,000

Panel A: Consumer non-durables, consumer durables, and manufacturing

Year	Altria group (MO)	Pepsico (PEP)	General motors (GM)	Whirlpool (WHR)	Eastman kodak (EK)	Goodyear tire & rubber (GT)
1985						
1986						
1987						
1988						
1989	11.5884					
1990	11.5038	11.5358			11.5308	
1991	11.5163	11.5735				
1992	11.5963	11.5217				11.5041
1993	11.1760					
1994		11.5392				
1995	11.5259	11.4971				
1996	11.5807	11.5248				
1997	11.5247					
1998	11.4578	11.4763			11.5360	
1999	11.5937	11.5127	11.5234		11.5654	
2000	11.4230	11.6014			11.5025	
2001	11.6343	11.5251			11.5033	
2002	11.5182	11.5180	11.4414		11.3112	
2003	11.3314	11.3636	11.2022	11.5161		
2004	11.4829	11.5151		11.5151		
2005	11.5177	11.5062	11.5177			
$E(U(W_T))$	11.4982	11.5151	11.4212	11.5156	11.4915	11.5041

approach of comparing expected utilities of methodologies is completely accurate only if all three methodologies–that is, using a GP-generated rule versus applying either the buy-and-hold strategy or the buy-on-margin-and-hold strategy–were to produce a rule in each training period for every stock. (For some subperiods, no rule meets all the threshold criteria presented in Table 3; therefore, in these subperiods, no comparison can be made between the results of GP-generated rules and benchmarks.) To get around this problem and evaluate the expected utility of using GP to evolve trading rules to be used out-of-sample, we can compute the average (across 21 testing subperiods and across 24 stocks) out-of-sample utility of terminal wealth using one of the three strategies below.

Strategy 1 involves using the GP rule to trade in the out-of-sample periods corresponding to the in-sample periods for which GP is able to find a rule that satisfies the threshold criteria in Table 3, but investing in T-bills in out-of-sample periods

Table 4 (Continued)

Panel B: Energy, chemicals, and business equipment

Year	Exxon mobil (XOM)	Halliburton (HAL)	Dow chemical (DOW)	DuPont (DD)	IBM (IBM)	Xerox (XRX)
1985		11.5420			11.5137	
1986		11.4366			11.5167	
1987						
1988	11.5283	11.5999			11.5282	
1989		11.5319			11.5321	
1990						
1991						
1992	11.5108	11.5217	11.5217			11.5217
1993						
1994						
1995						
1996						
1997						
1998		11.4280				11.5032
1999	11.5234				11.5235	11.4336
2000	11.5743	11.5883			11.3732	11.2820
2001	11.6171				11.5251	
2002	11.4260	11.5596	11.5171		11.3109	11.5427
2003	11.4653	11.5233	11.5161		11.4703	11.5161
2004	11.5151			11.4636	11.5151	11.5151
2005	11.5170	11.5140	11.5177		11.5177	11.5177
$E(U(W_T))$	11.5197	11.5245	11.5182	11.4636	11.4842	11.4790

corresponding to in-sample periods for which GP does not find a satisfactory rule. Strategy 2 is similar, but it uses the buy-and-hold strategy in out-of-sample periods corresponding to in-sample periods for which GP does not find a satisfactory rule, rather than using a default of investing in T-bills. Strategy 3 is similar to Strategy 2, the difference being that the buy-on-margin-and-hold strategy is used as the default. Note that in order to ensure that path dependency is not a factor, these trading simulations assume that on the first day of the trading phase of every sub-subperiod, the value of the investor's cash account, W_0, is reset to \$100,000.

For each of the 24 stocks chosen for this study, Table 5 provides expected utilities of using Strategy 1, Strategy 2, Strategy 3, the buy-and-hold strategy, and the buy-on-margin-and-hold strategy to trade out-of-sample. The 24 expected utilities corresponding to each stock and to each methodology can be averaged to obtain the expected utility of using a particular methodology to trade out-of-sample, for a port-

Table 4 (Continued)

Panel C: telephone and television, utilities, and shops

Year	AT&T Inc. (T)	Sprint (S)	American electric (AEP)	Duke energy (DUK)	Target (TGT)	Wal-mart stores (WMT)
1985	11.5304				11.5304	11.5736
1986	11.5270				11.5043	11.5463
1987					11.5265	11.4068
1988					11.5283	11.5282
1989					11.5640	11.5932
1990					11.4920	
1991					11.5418	11.7275
1992					11.5217	11.5461
1993					11.5199	11.5644
1994	11.5216				11.5425	11.4662
1995					11.5262	11.5139
1996						11.5249
1997					11.7266	11.5804
1998	11.5248				11.6072	11.4655
1999					11.6177	11.5451
2000	11.4771				11.4349	11.5577
2001	11.4708				11.4688	11.4886
2002	11.5182	11.5182			11.6651	11.5505
2003	11.4540				11.5646	11.5284
2004	11.4414			11.4636	11.5151	11.4968
2005	11.5177	11.5177			11.5177	11.5191
$E(U(W_T))$	11.4983	11.5180		11.4636	11.5458	11.5362

folio consisting of 24 trading funds, each one devoted to a single stock. These average utilities are presented in Table 6. The average utility corresponding to the riskless strategy of holding T-bills in every testing subperiod is invariant across stocks; it is reported in Table 6 for comparison purposes.

The results presented in Tables 5 and 6 show that the markets for the 24 stocks in our study were characterized by adaptive efficiency between 1985 and 2005. According to our trading simulations, stock investors could not benefit from identifying trading strategies (based on past prices) that worked in-sample, and then investing according to these strategies out-of-sample. According to Table 6, the buy-and-hold strategy achieves the highest expected utility (11.5306, certainty equivalent \$101,783.17) of all six strategies presented. The riskless strategy of investing all of one's wealth in T-bills (expected utility 11.5247, certainty equivalent \$101,184.41) proved to be superior to Strategy 1 (expected utility 11.5209, certainty equivalent

Table 4 (Continued)

Panel D: Healthcare, finance, and other

Year	Johnson and Johnson (JNJ)	Pfizer (PFE)	Bank of America (BAC)	Merrill Lynch (MER)	Disney (DIS)	Hilton hotels (HLN)
1985	11.5304	11.5304		11.5304		11.5302
1986	11.5269	11.5251		11.5592	11.6479	
1987	11.5265				11.5265	
1988	11.4860	11.6180		11.5283	11.5283	
1989	11.5426	11.5136			11.5319	
1990	11.5306				11.5459	11.5045
1991	11.5479	11.5344			11.5746	
1992	11.5126	11.4991		11.5217	11.5768	11.5217
1993	11.5316	11.5165			11.5005	11.5199
1994	11.5216	11.5581	11.5216	11.3610	11.5216	
1995	11.5629				11.6196	11.5259
1996	11.6881			11.5012	11.5248	
1997	11.5537	11.5680	11.5255	11.5247	11.5068	11.5247
1998	11.6263	11.7972	11.5248	11.6064	11.5250	11.5248
1999	11.5703	11.4378	11.2897	11.1600	11.4884	
2000	11.4598	11.5951	11.5254	11.4920	11.4527	
2001	11.5500	11.5250	11.6201	11.3597	11.3306	
2002	11.5163	11.5182	11.4680	11.3390	11.5182	11.5182
2003		11.4391	11.5161	11.5721	11.6244	
2004	11.5151	11.5587	11.5151	11.5001	11.5151	11.5151
2005	11.5177	11.4704	11.5245	11.5177	11.5177	11.5177
$E(U(W_T))$	11.5408	11.5415	11.5031	11.4716	11.5289	11.5203

$100,800.64). Continuing the pairwise comparison of matching strategies, the expected utility of Strategy 2 (11.5246, certainty equivalent $101,174.29) is lower than the expected utility of the buy-and-hold strategy (11.5306, certainty equivalent $101,783.17), whereas the expected utility of Strategy 3 (11.5145, certainty equivalent $100,157.58) is higher than the expected utility of the buy-on-margin-and-hold strategy, but lower than the expected utility of the riskless strategy.

According to Table 5, using GP to identify trading rules to be used to trade out-of-sample and then using either Strategy 1, Strategy 2, or Strategy 3 does not generally outperform the simple benchmark strategies for the majority of the 24 individual stocks. The following are the exceptions: For the stock with the ticker symbol TGT, employing Strategy 1 achieves a higher expected utility than investing all of one's wealth into T-bills, trading in accordance with the buy-and-hold strategy, or trading in accordance with the buy-on-margin-and-hold rule. Using Strategy 2 while trad-

Table 5 Average sub-subperiod utility of terminal wealth using gp strategies and simple trading rules, with $U(W_T) = \ln(W_T)$, initial wealth = \$100,000, and utility of the riskless strategy[a] = 11.5247[b]

Panel A: Consumer non-durables, consumer durables, and manufacturing

Company	Buy-and-hold strategy (no leverage)[c]	Buy-on-margin-and-hold strategy (maximum leverage)[d]	Strategy 1[e]	Strategy 2[f]	Strategy 3[g]
Altria group (MO)	11.5457	11.5414	11.5050	11.5141	11.5180
Pepsico (PEP)	11.5500	11.5536	11.5190	11.5354	11.5439
General motors (GM)	11.5085	11.4633	11.5055	11.5022	11.4793
Whirlpool (WHR)	11.5187	11.4849	11.5241	11.5202	11.4909
Eastman kodak (EK)	11.5063	11.4614	11.5146	11.5119	11.4921
Goodyear tire & rubber (GT)	11.5120	11.4607	11.5232	11.5083	11.4555

[a]Investing the entire wealth into T-bills

[b]The utility from always investing in T-bills, averaged across all subperiods

[c]Investing the entire wealth into the given stock, then holding these shares until the end of the trading horizon (with no margin trading)

[d]Buying as many shares of the corresponding stock as the margin regulations allow (which, by definition, involves margin trading)

[e]Investing one's initial wealth, during the testing period, in accordance with a GP rule when a GP rule is found during the training period, and investing one's initial wealth into T-bills otherwise

[f]Investing one's initial wealth, during the testing period, in accordance with a GP rule when a GP rule is found during the training period, and investing one's initial wealth in accordance with a simple buy-and-hold rule (with no margin trading) otherwise

[g]Investing one's initial wealth, during the testing period, in accordance with a GP rule when a GP rule is found during the training period, and investing one's initial wealth in accordance with a buy-on-margin-and-hold rule (that involves margin trading, and buying as many shares of the stock as the margin regulations allow) otherwise

ing the stocks with the ticker symbols DD, S, HAL, HLN and TGT leads to higher expected utility than using the three benchmark strategies. For the stocks with the ticker symbols DD, TGT and XOM, employing Strategy 3 achieves a higher expected utility than do the three benchmark strategies. The stock with the ticker symbol TGT appears in all three lists presented in this paragraph. For this stock, using Strategy 3 led to the highest expected utility. It should be noted that the buy-on-margin-and-hold rule had the lowest expected utility for most stocks, followed by Strategy 3.

Table 5 (Continued)

Panel B: Energy, chemicals, and business equipment

Company	Buy-and-hold strategy (no leverage)	Buy-on-margin-and-hold strategy (maximum leverage)	Strategy 1	Strategy 2	Strategy 3
Exxon mobil (XOM)	11.5370	11.5333	11.5234	11.5352	11.5382
Halliburton (HAL)	11.5203	11.4628	11.5243	11.5306	11.5160
Dow chemical (DOW)	11.5340	11.5202	11.5240	11.5335	11.5248
DuPont (DD)	11.5318	11.5178	11.5300	11.5412	11.5403
IBM (IBM)	11.5188	11.4878	11.5035	11.5079	11.5005
Xerox (XRX)	11.5178	11.4632	11.5084	11.5041	11.4743

Panel C: Telephone and television, utilities, and shops

Company	Buy-and-hold strategy (no leverage)	Buy-on-margin-and-hold strategy (maximum leverage)	Strategy 1	Strategy 2	Strategy 3
AT&T Inc. (T)	11.5288	11.5126	11.5127	11.5212	11.5212
Sprint (S)	11.5274	11.4962	11.5241	11.5328	11.5115
American electric (AEP)	11.5176	11.4961	11.5241	11.5176	11.4961
Duke energy (DUK)	11.5279	11.5158	11.5216	11.5251	11.5134
Target (TGT)	11.5445	11.5315	11.5448	11.5483	11.5508
Wal-Mart stores (WMT)	11.5526	11.5533	11.5359	11.5379	11.5385

Panel D: Healthcare, finance, and other

Company	Buy-and-hold strategy (no leverage)	Buy-on-margin-and-hold strategy (maximum leverage)	Strategy 1	Strategy 2	Strategy 3
Johnson and Johnson (JNJ)	11.5505	11.5576	11.5397	11.5385	11.5355
Pfizer (PFE)	11.5416	11.5340	11.5387	11.5413	11.5391
Bank of America (BAC)	11.5355	11.5206	11.5155	11.5237	11.5193
Merrill Lynch (MER)	11.5407	11.5177	11.4874	11.4968	11.4952
Disney (DIS)	11.5535	11.5364	11.5289	11.5338	11.5381
Hilton hotels (HLN)	11.5230	11.4859	11.5228	11.5297	11.5155

Table 6 Overall average[a] sub-subperiod utility of terminal wealth, certainty equivalent wealth, and annualized rate of return for GP strategies and simple trading rules, with $U(W_T) = \ln(W_T)$ and initial wealth = \$100,000

Strategy	Overall average sub-subperiod utility of terminal wealth	Certainty equivalent wealth	Annualized rate of return (%)
Riskless[b]	11.5247	101,184.41	4.82
Buy-and-hold, no leverage[c]	11.5306	101,783.17	7.33
Buy-and-hold, maximum leverage[c]	11.5087	99,578.34	−1.68
Strategy 1[c]	11.5209	100,800.64	3.24
Strategy 2[c]	11.5246	101,174.29	4.78
Strategy 3[c]	11.5145	100,157.58	0.63

[a]Averaged over 24 stocks

[b]Averaged over 21 sub-subperiods

[c]Averaged over $21 \times 24 = 504$ sub-subperiods

4.1 Examination of Results in Bull Versus Bear Markets

It is also of interest to study the behavior of the evolved trading rules conditional on the market state (i.e., bull or bear) in training, selection, and testing periods. We examine the signals returned by the rules in each set of subperiods for which rules were found. We studied the distribution of the signals, splitting the signal into six possible ranges: $\alpha = 0$, $0 < \alpha \leq 0.25$, $0.25 < \alpha \leq 0.50$, $0.50 < \alpha \leq 0.75$, $0.75 < \alpha < 1$, and $\alpha = 1$.

Recall that because margin trading is allowed, the signal $\alpha = 1$ is interpreted as using 100% leverage—buying as many shares of the stock on margin as possible. This is achieved by borrowing an amount equal to one's wealth, and then using one's wealth as well as the loan to buy shares of the stock. When the rule returns a signal of $\alpha = 0.50$, it means that the simulated trader buys as many shares of stock as possible with his or her wealth, without buying any shares on margin. The signal of $\alpha = 0$ is interpreted as staying away from the stock and investing all wealth in the riskless asset.

For each saved rule, for each stock, for each day in the training, selection, and testing periods, we generate the data regarding the GP signal for the day, the rebalancing of the portfolio that was done in response to that signal, the value of the portfolio, the amount of the margin loan, and the interest earned or paid. To study the distribution of rule signals conditional on market state, we use the procedure introduced by Lunde and Timmermann (2004) to partition the price data for the 24 stocks included in the present study into mutually exclusive and exhaustive subsets of "bull" and "bear" market states.

Every day is assigned to either the bull or bear market state. Every day, the price is compared to the latest local maximum price ($P^{\max}$) [if the state is "bull"] or to the latest local minimum price ($P^{\min}$) [if the state is "bear"]. The simulations assume that the market starts in a bull state. For a positive constant λ, the "bull" state is switched to "bear" if the price falls below the level $(1-\lambda)P^{\max}$, and this "bear" state is retroactively applied to all days following the day when the price was at a local maximum. Conversely, the "bear" state is switched to "bull" if the price rises above the level $(1+\lambda)P^{\min}$, and this "bull" state is retroactively applied to all days following the day on which the price was at a local minimum.

Lunde and Timmermann (2004) experiment with λ levels of 0.10, 0.15, and 0.20. Their paper looked at much longer trading horizons than the 3 months used in our paper. Thus, we set $\lambda = 0.10$ here. (Investigation showed that using $\lambda = 0.05$ achieved similar results.) This definition of bull and bear states partitions the data on stock prices into mutually exclusive and exhaustive bull and bear market subsets based on sequences of first passage time.

Each value in the bull market portion of Table 7 is obtained by dividing the number of days when the rules in a certain period (training, selection, or testing) [of all subperiods for which a rule had been saved, for all 24 stocks] return a signal in a given range of α, on days when the market was classified to be in the "bull" state, by the total number of days that are classified to be in the "bull" state in this period. That value [(number of days in a given range of α)/(total number of "bull"

Table 7 Distribution of rule signals conditional on market state[a]

	Alpha range	Training	Selection	Testing
Bull market	$\alpha = 0$	66.77	60.96	66.87
	$0 < \alpha \leq 0.25$	5.29	4.28	4.37
	$0.25 < \alpha \leq 0.50$	0.47	0.51	0.59
	$0.50 < \alpha \leq 0.75$	1.75	1.69	1.81
	$0.75 < \alpha < 1$	5.31	7.30	6.32
	$\alpha = 1$	20.41	25.26	20.04
Bear market	$\alpha = 0$	86.20	83.03	67.10
	$0 < \alpha \leq 0.25$	4.45	5.41	3.89
	$0.25 < \alpha \leq 0.50$	0.29	0.40	0.49
	$0.50 < \alpha \leq 0.75$	0.74	0.64	2.06
	$0.75 < \alpha < 1$	1.26	2.18	5.66
	$\alpha = 1$	7.06	8.34	20.80

[a]For each of the six alpha ranges, this table displays the percentage of the days (in training, selection, and testing subperiods for which rules were saved) on which the trading rules constructed by GP returned a signal in that range. Alpha is defined as follows: The extreme value of 1 corresponds to full leverage (using one's entire wealth to buy the stock and borrowing an amount equal to wealth to buy an identical amount of the stock); a value of 0.5 corresponds to investing one's entire wealth in the stock while not buying any shares of the stock on margin; and the extreme value of 0 implies that the simulated trader is not trading the stock, and instead is investing in the riskless asset. "Bull" and "bear" market states refer to evaluations of the market state using criteria adapted from Lunde and Timmermann (2004)

days)] is multiplied by 100 to get a percentage, as shown in Table 7. The values in the bear market portion of Table 7 are obtained in a similar manner.

One striking finding of this analysis is the proportion of trading days for which the generated rules returned signals at the extreme values of the possible range, that is, 0% and 100%. In this study, we set out to generate rules that returned signals in the intermediate range rather than the two extreme values. In both "bull" and "bear" market states, however, the signal returned by the rules was at one of the extreme values more than 80% of the time. We did not determine the reason for this unexpected behavior of the simulations. An avenue for future research is improving our methodology to ensure that the setup is not biased to generate extreme rules of 0% or 100%.

An implication is that in all periods (training, selection, and testing), the rules are unlikely to return a signal of 50%. Thus the rules' behavior is very different from that of the buy-and-hold strategy with no leverage.

As expected, in the in-sample periods (training and selection), the rules are more likely to recommend maximum leverage on days when the market is classified to be in the "bull" state. For the training period, during the "bull" state 20.41% of the rule signals indicated use of maximum leverage, and during the "bear" state only 7.06% of the rule signals indicated use of maximum leverage. The corresponding values for the selection period were 25.26% for the "bull" state and 8.34% for the "bear" state. For these in-sample periods, the rules were also more likely to recommend staying out of the market during the "bear" market state than during the "bull" market state. For the training (selection) period, the rules signaled not investing in the stock on 86.20% (83.03%) of days classified to be part of the "bear" market state, compared to 66.77% (60.96%) of days classified to be part of the "bull" state of the market.

Table 7 also reveals that GP rules had trouble distinguishing between the "bull" market state and the "bear" market state in the out-of-sample (testing) period. During the "bull" ("bear") state of the market, the rules recommended staying out of the market during 66.87% (66.10%) of the testing period trading days, and to employ maximum leverage during 20.04% (20.80%) of the testing period trading days. These findings also imply that GP rules behaved like the buy-on-margin-and-hold strategy using maximum leverage on approximately 20% of the out-of-sample trading days, independently of the state of the market.

The scope of our stock study was broad, as we looked at 504 in-sample periods (24 stocks × 21 in-sample periods per stock). Our comprehensive study leads us to the conclusion that the 24 stock markets examined were adaptively efficient between 1985 and 2005.

5 Conclusion

In this paper, we used GP to study adaptive efficiency of stock markets. To this end, we applied GP to the trading of 24 stocks and examined whether the algorithm can discover trading strategies with good out-of-sample performance. Our GP search was thorough: We examined the algorithm's performance in a total of 504 testing periods for 24 stocks, using a population size of 50,000 trading rules in each generation, substantially larger than the 500 or fewer trading rules employed in most earlier studies.

In the trading simulations we presented, a trading strategy is assumed to be the proportion of wealth allocated to a risky asset (a single stock). One of the contributions of the present study is that it allows GP to trade stocks in a model with realistic margin regulations, a feature not included in any of the studies examined in the literature review. None of the literature reviewed mentioned studies that had included this feature, so we are relatively certain that it has not been incorporated in any major published research. As mentioned earlier, the most recent research shows that trading strategies that diversify between the risky and the riskless assets at every point in time are superior to bang-bang strategies. For this reason, our definition of a trading strategy allowed us to test adaptive efficiency of the stock markets that we examined in this study without the testing being subject to the biases encountered by other studies (e.g., those of Dempster and Jones 2001; Fyfe et al. 2005; and Potvin et al. 2004), which limited their GP strategies to simple buy-sell signals).

Our study complements the research done by Allen and Karjalainen (1999); Neely et al. (1997); Neely and Weller (1999, 2003); and Neely (2003). Those studies saved a number of buy-sell rules, evolved using GP, and then considered returns earned by portfolio rules formed using the signals derived from the saved rules, or the in-sample return characteristics of those saved rules.

Recent studies (e.g., Fyfe et al. 2005 and Neely 2003) have used GP to evolve trading rules using a number of fitness criteria that adjusted trading rule returns for risk. In this study, we used GP to find trading rules using a new fitness criterion that differently adjusted trading rule returns for risk: We maximized the average utility of terminal wealth. This criterion is closest to, but distinct from, one of the risk adjustment measures used by Neely, namely, the X_{eff} measure.

Another contribution of the present paper is that, in our experiments, we extended the simple threshold criterion of earlier studies (e.g., save a rule only if it outperforms the buy-and-hold rule in the selection period) to more complex threshold criteria. Our study looked for opportunities to trade profitably in an out-of-sample period, based on using trading rules with an unusually high return for a given level of risk in an in-sample period. The current study extends past research because we went beyond simply saving rules that outperform the buy-and-hold rule (as done in earlier studies such as those of Allen and Karjalainen 1999; Fyfe et al. 2005; Neely and Weller 1999; Neely et al. 1997; and Ready 2002). We saved rules that satisfy various money management criteria, in addition to choosing rules with the highest expected utility.

According to our results, the stock markets studied can, in general, be characterized by adaptive efficiency. An investor who buys and holds stocks usually achieves a higher expected utility than an investor who uses a rule saved by a GP algorithm in accordance with our methodology. This result is not unexpected: Fyfe et al. (2005) and Neely (2003) found that when the trading rule returns of the rules generated by GP are adjusted for risk, the results are consistent with market efficiency. It is important to note, however, the possibility that the results might change with changes in GP parameters (e.g., number of generations, population size, the values of the threshold criteria) or GP settings (e.g., the number of building blocks GP is allowed to use to create trading rules).

One of the more interesting extensions of this research would use a variety of other relevant time series as building blocks when applying GP to evolve trading strategies for individual stocks. For example, it seems possible that the price of gold may be an important factor determining investment in the stock of a gold mining company. Applying GP methodology to other financial markets (e.g., option markets or stock markets in developing countries that previous research has demonstrated to be less efficient than U.S. stock markets) also seems to offer potential for useful research.

To eliminate the possibility that we would obtain results that are simply artifacts of the periods chosen, we adopted a "sliding window" approach that allowed us to run our GP experiments for many combinations of training, selection, and testing periods for a given data set. In the research presented here, we used 5 years as training and selection periods and 1 year as a testing period. We looked only at trading horizons of 3 months. Extensions of the current study, some of which are being conducted by the authors, could examine how the results change when the trading horizon is changed or when lengths of the various (training, selection, and testing) periods are changed.

Acknowledgements We gratefully acknowledge financial support from the Canadian Social Sciences and Humanities Research Council. We thank Ian Davis for assistance with the computer coding. We thank, for their comments, seminar participants in the 14th International Conference on Computing in Economics and Finance, the Canadian Economics Association 2008 Annual Meeting, and the Fifth World Congress of the Bachelier Finance Society.

References

Allen, F., & Karjalainen, R. (1999). Using genetic algorithms to find technical trading rules. *Journal of Financial Economics*, *51*, 245–271.

Álvarez-Díaz, M., & Álvarez, A. (2005). Genetic multi-model composite forecast for non-linear prediction of exchange rates. *Empirical Economics*, *30*, 643–663.

Ayres, I., & Nalebuff, B. (2008). *Buying stock on margin can reduce retirement risk*. Working paper.

Bessembinder, H., & Chan, K. (1998). Market efficiency and the returns to technical analysis. *Financial Management*, *27*, 5–17.

Chen, S. H., & Yeh, C. H. (1997). Toward a computable approach to the efficient market hypothesis: an application of genetic programming. *Journal of Economic Dynamics and Control*, *21*, 1043–1063.

Chen, S. H., & Yeh, C. H. (2002). On the emergent properties of artificial stock markets: the efficient market hypothesis and the rational expectations hypothesis. *Journal of Economic Behavior and Organization*, *49*, 217–239.

Dacorogna, M. M., Gençay, R., Müller, U. A., & Pictet, O. V. (2001). Effective return, risk aversion and drawdowns. *Physica A*, *289*, 229–248.

Daniel, K., & Titman, S. (1999). Market efficiency in an irrational world. *Financial Analysts Journal*, *55*, 28–40.
Dempster, M. A. H., & Jones, C. (2001). A real-time adaptive trading system using genetic programming. *Quantitative Finance*, *1*, 397–413.
Fortune, P. (2000). Margin requirements, margin loans, and margin rates: practice and principles. *New England Economic Review*, 19–44.
Fyfe, C., Marney, J. P., & Tarbert, H. F. E. (1999). Technical analysis versus market efficiency: a genetic programming approach. *Applied Financial Economics*, *9*, 183–191.
Fyfe, C., Marney, J. P., & Tarbert, H. F. E. (2005). Risk adjusted returns from technical trading: a genetic programming approach. *Applied Financial Economics*, *15*, 1073–1077.
Gençay, R. (1998). The predictability of security returns with simple technical trading rules. *Applied Financial Economics*, *5*, 347–359.
Gençay, R. (1999). Linear, non-linear and essential foreign exchange rate prediction with simple technical trading rules. *Journal of Empirical Finance*, *47*, 91–107.
Gollier, C. (1997). On the inefficiency of bang–bang and stop-loss portfolio strategies. *Journal of Risk and Uncertainty*, *14*, 143–154.
Kaboudan, M. A. (2000). Genetic programming prediction of stock market prices. *Computational Economics*, *16*, 207–236.
Koza, J. R. (1992). *Genetic programming: on the programming of computers by means of natural selection*. Cambridge: MIT Press.
Kubler, F., & Willen, P. (2006). *Collateralized borrowing and life-cycle portfolio choice*. NBER working paper.
Lensberg, T. (1999). Investment behavior under Knightian uncertainty: an evolutionary approach. *Journal of Economic Dynamics and Control*, *23*, 1587–1604.
Lensberg, T., Eilifsen, A., & McKee, T. E. (2006). Bankruptcy theory development and classification via genetic programming. *European Journal of Operational Research*, *169*, 677–697.
Lunde, A., & Timmermann, A. (2004). Duration dependence in stock prices: an analysis of bull and bear markets. *Journal of Business and Economic Statistics*, *22*, 253–273.
McKee, T. E., & Lensberg, T. (2002). Genetic programming and rough sets: a hybrid approach to bankruptcy classification. *European Journal of Operational Research*, *138*, 436–451.
Neely, C. J. (2003). Risk-adjusted, ex ante, optimal technical trading rules in equity markets. *International Review of Economics and Finance*, *12*, 69–87.
Neely, C. J., & Weller, P. A. (1999). Technical trading rules in the European monetary system. *International Review of Economics and Finance*, *18*, 429–458.
Neely, C. J., & Weller, P. A. (2003). Intraday technical trading in the foreign exchange market. *Journal of International Money and Finance*, *22*, 223–237.
Neely, C. J., Weller, P., & Ditmar, R. (1997). Is technical analysis in the foreign exchange market profitable? A genetic programming approach. *Journal of Financial and Quantitative Analysis*, *32*, 405–426.
Potvin, J. Y., Soriano, P., & Vallee, M. (2004). Generating trading rules on the stock markets with genetic programming. *Computers and Operations Research*, *31*, 1033–1047.
Ready, M. J. (2002). Profits from technical trading rules. *Financial Management*, *31*, 43–62.
Samuelson, P. A. (1997). Proof by certainty equivalents that diversification-across-time does worse risk corrected, than diversification-throughout-time. *Journal of Risk and Uncertainty*, *14*, 129–142.
Sharpe, W. F. (1966). Mutual fund performance. *Journal of Business*, *39*, 119–138.
Skouras, S. (2001). Financial returns and efficiency as seen by an artificial technical analyst. *Journal of Economic Dynamics and Control*, *25*, 213–244.
Sullivan, R., Timmermann, A., & White, H. (1999). Data snooping, technical trading rule performance, and the bootstrap. *The Journal of Finance*, *54*, 1647–1691.
Sullivan, R., Timmermann, A., & White, H. (2001). Dangers of data-mining: the case of calendar effects in stock returns. *The Journal of Finance*, *105*, 249–286.
Sullivan, R., Timmermann, A., & White, H. (2003). Forecast evaluation with shared data sets. *International Journal of Forecasting*, *19*, 217–227.

Sweeney, R. J. (1988). Some new filter rule tests: methods and results. *Journal of Financial and Quantitative Analysis*, *23*, 285–300.

Sweeney, R. J., & Lee, E. J. Q. (1990). International dimensions of securities and currency markets. In R. Aggarwal & C. F. Lee (Eds.), *Advances in financial planning and forecasting series* (Vol. 4, pp. 55–79). Greenwich: JAI Press.

Wang, J. (2000). Trading and hedging in S&P 500 spot and futures markets using genetic programming. *The Journal of Futures Markets*, *20*, 911–942.

Bankruptcy Prediction: A Comparison of Some Statistical and Machine Learning Techniques

Tonatiuh Peña, Serafín Martínez, and Bolanle Abudu

Abstract We are interested in forecasting bankruptcies in a probabilistic way. Specifically, we compare the classification performance of several statistical and machine-learning techniques, namely discriminant analysis (Altman's Z-score), logistic regression, least-squares support vector machines and different instances of Gaussian processes (GP's)—that is GP classifiers, Bayesian Fisher discriminant and Warped GPs. Our contribution to the field of computational finance is to introduce GPs as a competitive probabilistic framework for bankruptcy prediction. Data from the repository of information of the US Federal Deposit Insurance Corporation is used to test the predictions.

1 Introduction

Corporate bankruptcy is an active area of financial research because an event of this nature will always provoke adverse effects on the economy and pose a credibility challenge to financial authorities. In fact, the forecast of bankruptcies is a subject of paramount importance for different types of governmental and commercial organisations because a failed corporation can cause contagious failures to the rest of the financial system and thus lead to a systemic crisis. Such importance has been further increased by regulations such as the Basel capital accord (or Basel II) of 1994, which suggests financial institutions to build their credit portfolios based on the default assessment of their clients. As a consequence, the development of analytical tools to determine which financial information is more relevant to predict financial distress has gained popularity along with the design of early warning systems that predict bankruptcy.

Along the years two main methodologies have been developed to assist in the process of estimating financial distress (i.e. predicting bankruptcies): the first one uses accounting information while the second one, market information. Among the former, financial ratio analysis is a technique that studies relations of the type X/Y

T. Peña (✉)
Dirección General de Investigación Económica, Banco de México, Mexico City, Mexico
e-mail: tpena@banxico.org.mx

H. Dawid, W. Semmler (eds.), *Computational Methods in Economic Dynamics*, Dynamic Modeling and Econometrics in Economics and Finance 13,
DOI 10.1007/978-3-642-16943-4_6,

where $X, Y \in \mathbb{R}$ are variables selected from an enterprise's financial statement. Although there is no consensus for defining or calculating financial ratios we can still divide them into four categories: efficiency, profitability, short term and long term solvency ratios. The seminal work on prediction of corporate failure through financial ratio analysis was proposed by Beaver (1966) and it can be thought of as a univariate classification technique to estimate the probability of failure. Subsequently Altman (1968) worked on a generalisation through the estimation of a multivariate statistic known as Z-score.

While these two methods have proved useful for the last forty years, the advent of new regulations such as Basel II justifies the use of more sophisticated techniques to predict financial distress. Among such novel methodologies a group with an important computational component has been recently developed. For example the problems of asset valuation, portfolio allocation and bankruptcy prediction have been approached from different perspectives, like genetic algorithms (GA's), artificial neural networks (ANN's), decision trees, among others. We will use the term *computational finance* (Tsang and Martinez-Jaramillo 2004; Chen 2002) to refer to the development and application of these type of techniques to solve financial problems and some literature on the topic can be found at (Serrano-Cinca et al. 1993; Back et al. 1996; Joos et al. 1998; Varetto 1998; Atiya 2001; Shin and Lee 2002; Park and Han 2002; Yip 2003; Quintana et al. 2007).

Up to our knowledge, this is the first work to apply the Gaussian process formalism for data inference to estimate bankruptcy probabilities. From a Bayesian perspective, GP's provide a natural way for learning a regression or classification function in terms of functional priors and some very good monographies on the topic have been written in recent years with (Rasmussen and Williams 2006) as an example. Our work makes a contribution to the field of computational finance by presenting a comparison of classical statistical techniques for classification against some recently developed machine learning algorithms. More specifically, we introduce GP's as a powerful and competitive probabilistic framework for bankruptcy prediction. As an added bonus of working within the realm of GP's, we come up with a feature that allows to determine the relevance of the different financial ratios in an automatic way, something known as automatic relevance determination (ARD) in the neural networks literature.

Although the methods herein presented are applicable to any type of company that handles financial ratios, data availability made us focus on the banking sector.[1] Analysing bankruptcies in the banking sector implies taking into account that this type of institutions must satisfy very specific legal and accounting requirements imposed to them by financial authorities, central banks, supervisory institutions, etc.; so it is adequate to take them as a special case within the universe of corporate bankruptcy. In fact generalising this task to the banking sector of different countries is made even more difficult when we consider that some of their own regulations do not contemplate the existence of bankruptcies.

[1] The work by Estrella et al. (2000) has a similar scope to ours.

The rest of the paper is organised as follows: Sect. 2 introduces bankrupcty prediction as a statistical classification problem. Sections 3 and 4 are devoted to the description of some well-known statistical techniques used for bankruptcy prediction, namely discriminant analysis and logistic regression. Section 5 describes the technical details of how a family of stochastic processes, i.e. Gaussian ones, might be used to classify data and therefore applied to our problem domain. Section 6 describes experiments carried out on a set of data from the Federal Deposit Insurance Corporation in order to assess how Gaussian processes fare with respect to the other type of classifiers. Section 7 is a discussion about how GP's could be integrated into commercially available credit risk models. Finally, Sect. 8 draws some conclusions about the proposed methods.

2 Bankruptcy Prediction as a Classification Problem

We are interested in forecasting the failure of banks and also on assigning a probability value to quantify our degree of belief that this event will happen. In order to do so, we approach the bankruptcy prediction problem as a binary classification one, whereby each instance of a set of observed data belongs to a group of predefined classes (bankrupt or non-bankrupt) and the objective is to separate one class from the other with the minimum amount of error. Thus we aim to have a system that predicts whether an institution will go bankrupt or not according to some type of financial information, for example through the institution's financial ratios. This type of task is known as supervised learning within the machine learning community. In the following sections we review some of the most widespread methods to classify data, Fisher's discriminant analysis along with logistic regression. In the subsequent, we will assume the following: (i) a classification task whereby a new observation $O^\star$ needs to be allocated to one of k available classes—that are known a priori; (ii) that such classes are mutually exclusive; (iii) that for some reason the allocation procedure depends on the application of an indirect method. By *indirect* we mean that a vector of features $\mathbf{x}^\star$ is used instead of $O^\star$. We will assume the availability of correctly labelled training data and consequently that an exact way to classify the observations exists, but that for some reason is not feasible to apply. Indeed, medical diagnosis[2] and prognosis[3] are typical examples where direct classification is not feasible, as mentioned by MacLachlan (1991). Another suitable case for indirect classification is the determination of the level of financial stress of a corporation because a straightforward assessment is almost impossible to produce. Instead it is more suitable to resort to some indirect means, like the corporation's financial ratios to determine whether the corporation will go bankrupt or not.

[2]Identifying a disease.

[3]Estimating the prospect of recovery.

3 Fisher's Discriminant Analysis

Discriminant analysis is a classification technique originally devised by Fisher (1936) with the aim of solving a bone classification problem that he was requested to address.[4] This technique is concerned with the relationship between a set of data and their corresponding label values (MacLachlan 1991) and its goal is to specify such relationship in terms of a function that ideally separates each instance of the training data according to their label. In the remainder of the paper we will refer to discriminant analysis as FDA. In this section we briefly review FDA for the specific case of binary classification and in such a way that lays the ground for the introduction of logistic regression and Gaussian processes for classification. We concentrate on discriminant analysis because it forms the basis of Altman's Z-score, which is one of the best well-known techniques to assess financial distress.

3.1 Problem Setup

Consider a set of training data $\mathcal{D} = (\mathbf{X}, \mathbf{y}) = \{(\mathbf{x}^{(n)}, y^{(n)})\}_{n=1}^{N}$ and denote by $\mathbf{x}^{(n)} \in \mathcal{X}$ a single observation in a d-dimensional space and by $y^{(n)} \in \{1, 0\}$, the categorical variable or label assigned to the observation. An observation $\mathbf{x}^{(n)}$ consists of the set of financial ratios recorded at a fixed point in time for a given bank n, which was at that time either bankrupt or not, i.e. $y^{(n)}$. Mathematically, discriminant analysis aims to assign a new observation $O^{\star}$ into one of the $k = 2$ available classes and the discriminant will do so by finding a vector of parameters $\mathbf{w}$ that will be optimal in some sense. In fact, the space $\mathbb{R}^d$ will be divided into $k-1$ regions by hyperplanes in $\mathbb{R}^{d-1}$ to do the separation.

The process is best explained in a pictorial way. Figure 1 shows a dataset composed of two classes being separated by a discriminant function $D(\mathbf{w})$ perpendicular to $\mathbf{w}$. Each data point $\mathbf{x}^{(n)}$ is projected over $\mathbf{w}$, such that the distance between the projected means $d = (\mu_0 - \mu_1)$ is as wide as possible while the scatter around the projections $(\sigma_0^2 + \sigma_1^2)$ is as small as possible as well. The projection is achieved by taking the dot product $f^{(n)} = \mathbf{w}^T\mathbf{x}^{(n)}$ $(\forall n)$, thus the quality of the solution depends on the tilt of the vector $\mathbf{w}$. Observe that a classifier might be obtained by verifying the sign of the projected points with respect to $D(\mathbf{w})$, i.e. assign every instance on $D(\mathbf{w}) \geq 0$ to class 1 and to class 0 otherwise. Posterior class probabilities $p(\mathcal{C}_1|\mathbf{x})$ and $p(\mathcal{C}_0|\mathbf{x}) = 1 - p(\mathcal{C}_1|\mathbf{x})$, may also be derived by assuming the projections come from Gaussian densities.

Under this setting, Fisher (1936) was the first to conclude that the vector $\mathbf{w}$ is given by maximising the ratio of between to within-class variances,

$$J = \frac{(\mu_1 - \mu_0)^2}{\sigma_1^2 + \sigma_0^2}. \qquad (1)$$

[4] Some human remains discovered in a burial site in Egypt were required to be sexed, i.e. determined whether they belonged to female or male specimens (Fisher 1936).

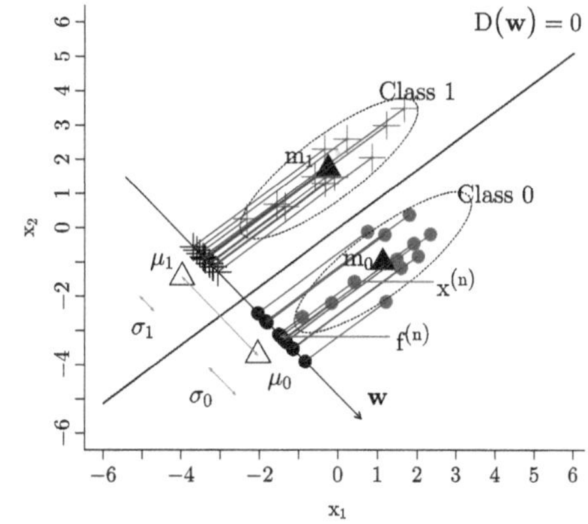

Fig. 1 Fisher discriminant analysis example. Two clusters of data being projected onto the direction of discrimination $\mathbf{w}$. Members of each class are represented as '*pluses*' or '*dots*'. The quality of the discriminant depends on the separation between the projected class means μ_0 and μ_1 and the scatter of the projected classes σ_0^2 and σ_1^2. In the plot, the projection of $\mathbf{x}^{(n)}$ over $\mathbf{w}$ is referred as $f^{(n)}$

Given that $\mu_q = \sum_{n\in q} \frac{1}{N_q}\mathbf{w}^T\mathbf{x}_q^{(n)}$ and $\sigma_q^2 = \sum_{n\in q} \frac{1}{N_q}(\mathbf{w}^T\mathbf{x}_q^{(n)} - \mu_q)^2$, for $q = \{1, 0\}$, coefficient J can be expressed in terms of $\mathbf{w}$ and with some straightforward manipulation we arrive to

$$J(\mathbf{w}) = \frac{\mathbf{w}^T\mathbf{\Sigma}_B\mathbf{w}}{\mathbf{w}^T\mathbf{\Sigma}_w\mathbf{w}}, \tag{2}$$

where the matrices $\mathbf{\Sigma}_B = (\mathbf{m}_1 - \mathbf{m}_0)(\mathbf{m}_1 - \mathbf{m}_0)^T$ and $\mathbf{\Sigma}_w = \sum_{q\in\{0,1\}} \sum_{n=1}^{N_q} (\mathbf{x}_q^{(n)} - \mathbf{m}_q)(\mathbf{x}_q^{(n)} - \mathbf{m}_q)^T$ are known as between and within-class covariance matrices, respectively. A solution to the discriminant problem consists of taking the derivative of (2) w.r.t. $\mathbf{w}$ and solving. Zeroing the gradient and through some rearrangement we get

$$\hat{\mathbf{w}} \propto \mathbf{\Sigma}_w^{-1}(\mathbf{m}_0 - \mathbf{m}_1), \tag{3}$$

which is the expression we are looking for.

Therefore class predictions for new observations $\mathbf{x}^\star$ are readily available by projecting the data point over the estimated direction of discrimination $\hat{\mathbf{w}}$ and verifying the sign of the projection, i.e. $f^\star = \hat{\mathbf{w}}^T\mathbf{x}^\star \geq D(\hat{\mathbf{w}})$. Note that FDA does not yield a direct estimate of class probabilities and in this sense it is a non-probabilistic method.

4 Discriminative Models for Classification

We now focus our attention on probabilistic methods for classification. That is, we want predictons on data to take directly the form of class probabilities and not of values that need a post processing stage to be interpreted as such, as it happens with FDA. We first observe that classification problems might be addressed in similar terms to those of standard regression, that is by explicitly specifying a likelihood function (or cost function) that models the data generation process of the observations one can proceed with parameter estimation through the application of techniques such as maximum likelihood. In this section we introduce logistic regression, which is probably one of the most popular probabilistic methods for classification.

4.1 Logistic Regression

Going back to the allocation problem of Sect. 2, we still want to make a class assignment for observation O and the most natural approach is to consider $\mathbf{x}$ and y as random variables and work with the joint density $p(\mathbf{x}, y)$ that arises from them.[5] Applying the rules of probability, the joint can be factorised as $p(\mathbf{x}|y)p(y)$ or as $p(y|\mathbf{x})p(\mathbf{x})$ and from these representations stem the two different approaches for probabilistic data classification. The first approach is usually referred to as *generative* because it models the data generating process in terms of the class conditional density $p(\mathbf{x}|y)$, which combined with the class prior $p(y)$ allows to obtain the posterior

$$p(y|\mathbf{x}) = \frac{p(\mathbf{x}|y)p(y)}{p(\mathbf{x}|y=1)p(y=1) + p(\mathbf{x}|y=0)p(y=0)}.$$

The second approach is called *discriminative* because it focuses on modelling $p(y|\mathbf{x})$ directly and will be the one we will concentrate on in this paper. Nevertheless it is worth noting that in both the generative and discriminative approaches it is necessary to make modelling assumptions, for example deciding what type of density to use for representing $p(\mathbf{x}|y)$ or $p(y|\mathbf{x})$.

A straightforward way to obtain a discriminative classifier is to convert the output of a regression function into the class probability being sought, for example by applying a response function.[6] That is consider a regression function $f(\cdot)$ whose domain is $(-\infty, \infty)$ then by 'squashing' it into the range $[0, 1]$ we will have obtained the desired classifier. An example is the logistic regression model

$$p(y=1|\mathbf{x}) = g(\mathbf{w}^T\phi(\mathbf{x})), \tag{4}$$

whose response function is

$$g(z) = \frac{1}{1+\exp(-z)}. \tag{5}$$

Note that (4) is a combination of a linear model, parameterised by $\mathbf{w}$, a basis function $\phi(\cdot)$ and the logistic response function g. An alternative function is the cumulative Gaussian $\Phi(z) = \int_{-\infty}^{\infty} \mathcal{N}(x|0, 1)dx$ which produces what is known as a probit model.

---

[5]We recall that $\mathbf{x}$ is a vector of observed features obtained through indirect means whereas y is a canonical variable representing the class.

[6]The response function is the inverse of the *link* function used in statistics.

Given a training set $\mathcal{D} = (\mathbf{X}, \mathbf{y})$, with $y^{(n)} \in \{1, 0\}$, we can use the problem setup of Sect. 3 to interpret how logistic regression works. We can think back again that the goal is to find a vector of weights, such that projections of data over it will be separated maximally according to a specified criterion. However, the criterion will not be Rayleigh's quotient (1) anymore but rather the maximum likelihood function and therefore a new optimisation problem will arise,

$$\begin{aligned}\hat{\mathbf{w}} &= -\arg\min_{\mathbf{w}} \ln p(\mathbf{y}|\mathbf{X}, \mathbf{w}) \\ &= -\arg\min_{\mathbf{w}} \sum_{n=1}^{N} \left\{ y^n \ln \sigma(a_n) + (1 - y^n) \ln(1 - \sigma(a_n)) \right\}, \end{aligned} \tag{6}$$

where $a_n = \mathbf{w}^T \mathbf{x}^{(n)}$.

Notice there is no closed-form solution for problem (6) but nevertheless an estimate $\hat{\mathbf{w}}$ may be obtained through numeric methods (Bishop 2006). In contrast with FDA, predictions are available by feeding the estimate $\hat{\mathbf{w}}$ and the test point $\mathbf{x}^\star$ into the logistic function (5) and this time a probability of class-membership will be automatically produced. Supposing the basis $\phi(\cdot)$ is the identity, the probability becomes $p(y^\star = 1|\mathbf{x}^\star) = g(\hat{\mathbf{w}}^T \mathbf{x}^\star)$.

5 Gaussian Processes for Regression and Classification

Gaussian processes are a generalisation of multivariate Gaussian densities to infinite continuous function sets (Rasmussen 2004) and have been used for data inference tasks for at least one hundred years; for example Thiele (1931) was one of the earliest proponents. However modern applications of GP's began with the work of mining engineer Krige (1996) and later with that of Kimeldorf and Wahba (1970), O'Hagan (1978) and Wahba (1990). The term *process* is used to refer to a collection of indexed random variables $[f^{(1)}, \ldots, f^{(N)}]$ that (i) can be defined through a common probability density—in this case a Gaussian—and (ii) that satisfy some consistency and permutation properties (Grimmett and Stirzaker 2004).

Gaussian processes keep close connections with ANN's whenever the two of them are treated from a Bayesian viewpoint (Neal 1996). However, in contrast with ANN's, Gaussian processes offer the advantage of flexible modelling without the overhead of having to adapt a large number of parameters, something that has commonly hindered the application of ANN's in many problem domains. Some work of computational finance that specifically addresses bankruptcy prediction is Atiya (2001).

In this section we discuss linear regression and its complementary approach, GP regression, both from a Bayesian perspective. In fact, it can be shown that both approaches are equivalent but that under certain circumstances it is more convenient to apply one over the other. The ensuing discussion will enable the introduction of some different guises of GP's for data classification: Gaussian process classifiers, least-squares support vector machines, among others. The Bayesian approach to linear regression is discussed in texts like (Box and Tiao 1973) for example, whereas GP regression in more modern ones like (Mackay 2003; Rasmussen and Williams 2006).

5.1 Bayesian Linear Regression: The Parameter Space Approach

Let us consider what may be called generalised linear regression because we will be using a fixed set of basis functions $\{\phi_i(\mathbf{x})\}_{i=1}^{m}$ (Williams 1999). Suppose then a set of training data $\mathcal{D} = \{(\mathbf{x}^{(n)}, t^{(n)})\}_{n=1}^{N}$, an underlying function f, which we are interested to infer and that inputs and targets are related in a linear way through $t^{(n)} = f^{(n)} + \epsilon$; with $f^{(n)} = \mathbf{w}^T\phi(\mathbf{x}^{(n)})$ and $\epsilon \sim \mathcal{N}(0, \sigma_v^2)$. Then an embodiment of the information extracted from the data will be given by the posterior distribution over the parameters $\mathbf{w}$, which is expressed in terms of Bayes' rule as

$$p(\mathbf{w}|\mathcal{D}) = \frac{p(\mathcal{D}|\mathbf{w})p(\mathbf{w})}{p(\mathcal{D})}; \tag{7}$$

where $p(\mathcal{D}|\mathbf{w})$ is known as the likelihood function and $p(\mathbf{w})$ as the prior. If observations are i.i.d. the likelihood may very well be represented by $t^{(n)} \sim \mathcal{N}(\mathbf{w}^T\phi(\mathbf{x}^{(n)}), \sigma_v^2)$, whereas the prior as $\mathbf{w} \sim \mathcal{N}(\mathbf{0}, \mathbf{\Sigma}_{wt})$. Under such assumptions it is very easy to show that the posterior will take the form

$$p(\mathbf{w}|\mathcal{D}) = \mathcal{N}(\mathbf{w}_{\text{MAP}}, \mathbf{A}_r),$$

where mean the vector

$$\mathbf{w}_{\text{MAP}} = \beta \mathbf{A}_r^{-1}\mathbf{\Phi}^T\mathbf{t}, \tag{8}$$

and the covariance matrix $\mathbf{A}_r = \mathbf{\Sigma}_{wt}^{-1} + \beta\mathbf{\Phi}^T\mathbf{\Phi}$. The matrix $\mathbf{\Phi} \in \mathbb{R}^{N\times d}$ is usually termed the *design matrix* while $\beta = 1/\sigma_v^2$, as the *precision*.

From a data modelling perspective, the ultimate purpose is not to derive the posterior distribution but rather make predictions $f^\star$ for unobserved data $\mathbf{x}^\star$, which in the present case is done by evaluating

$$\begin{aligned} p(f^\star|\mathcal{D}) &= \int p(f^\star|\mathcal{D}, \mathbf{w})p(\mathbf{w}|\mathcal{D})\partial\mathbf{w} \\ &= \mathcal{N}(\bar{f}^\star, (\sigma^\star)^2). \end{aligned} \tag{9}$$

Note the above integral is a weighted average of conditional expectations over the posterior.[7] Expressions for the mean and variance are given by

$$\bar{f}^\star = \mathbf{w}_{\text{MAP}}^T\phi(\mathbf{x}^\star), \tag{10}$$

[7]We have omitted dependencies on $\mathbf{x}^\star$ to keep the notation uncluttered.

and

$$\sigma_f^2(\mathbf{x}^\star) = \phi(\mathbf{x}^\star)^T \mathbf{A}_r^{-1} \phi(\mathbf{x}^\star), \tag{11}$$

respectively. Regarding the mean result, if we consider a classification setting, it is straightforward to show $\mathbf{w}_{\mathrm{MAP}}$ (8) is equivalent to $\hat{\mathbf{w}}_{\mathrm{FDA}}$ (3) by simply clamping the targets to the label values (Bishop 1995). It should be noted that in order to obtain the predictive variance $\operatorname{var} t(\mathbf{x}^\star)$ it is necessary to add σ_v^2 to $\sigma_f^2(\mathbf{x}^\star)$ to account for the additional variance due to the noise, since the two sources of variation are uncorrelated (Williams 1999).

5.2 Gaussian Processes for Regression: The Function Space Approach

In the previous section we saw how the uncertainty in a typical regression problem was described in terms of a probability distribution over the parameters $\mathbf{w}$. It is also possible to deal directly with uncertainty with respect to the function values at the points we are interested in and this is the function-space (or GP) view of the problem, as stated by Williams (1999). The key point for departing from the parameter-based approach for data modelling is to realise the projections $f^{(n)}$ can also be treated as random variables. Specifically, by assuming a finite instantiation $\mathbf{f} = [f^{(1)}, \ldots, f^{(N)}]^T$ defined in a consistent way we will have a random process, which will be a GP, if $\mathbf{f}$ is described by a multivariate Gaussian density (Mackay 1998).

In particular, we will assume that every $f^{(n)}$ depends of an input $\mathbf{x}^{(n)}$ with index n, such that $f^{(n)} = f(\mathbf{x}^{(n)})$. Note this definition implies that parameterising the function values with $\mathbf{w}$ is irrelevant for the modelling process. Nevertheless, the justification of the GP assumption might be supported by the fact that placing a Gaussian prior over the parameters $\mathbf{w}$ induces a Gaussian prior distribution over the set of instantiations $\mathbf{f}$, provided that $\mathbf{f}$ is a linear function of $\mathbf{w}$.

Thus assuming training data $\mathcal{D}$ has been observed, a posterior distribution will need to be inferred in similar tenets to those of Sect. 5.1. Regarding the specification of a prior of the GP type, it will be defined by a mean function $m(\mathbf{x})$ and a covariance function $k(\mathbf{x}, \mathbf{x}')$. In other words $p(\mathbf{f}) = \mathcal{N}(\mathbf{0}, \mathbf{K})$ with matrix $\mathbf{K} \in \mathbb{R}^{N \times N}$ populated with entries of the form $k(\mathbf{x}^i, \mathbf{x}^j) \forall i, j$. If the likelihood $p(\mathcal{D}|\mathbf{f})$ is Gaussian, that is if $\mathcal{D}$ is composed of a set of noisy observations $t^{(n)} = f^{(n)} + \epsilon$, with $\epsilon \sim \mathcal{N}(0, \sigma_v^2)$, it can be demonstrated that application of Bayes' rule will lead to

$$\begin{aligned} p(\mathbf{f}|\mathcal{D}) &\propto p(\mathcal{D}|\mathbf{f}) p(\mathbf{f}) \\ &= \mathcal{N}(\mathbf{K}(\sigma_v^2 \mathbf{I} + \mathbf{K})^{-1} \mathbf{t}, \sigma_v^2 (\sigma_v^2 \mathbf{I} + \mathbf{K})^{-1} \mathbf{K}), \end{aligned} \tag{12}$$

where we have used vectors $\mathbf{f} = [f(\mathbf{x}^{(1)}), \ldots, f(\mathbf{x}^{(N)})]^T$ and $\mathbf{t} = [t^{(1)}, \ldots, t^{(N)}]^T$, (Seeger 2004). The posterior distribution is thus influenced by the prior and this is ascertained in (12) by observing that posterior mean and covariance depend on the matrix $\mathbf{K}$, which is the prior covariance.

So far, the posterior over the training data $p(\mathbf{f}|\mathcal{D})$ has been inferred but the most important task is to predict test points. This only requires that once we observe $\mathcal{D}$ we determine the posterior predictive distribution for a point $f^\star = f(\mathbf{x}^\star)$, that is outside the training set. This is readily done by applying

$$p(f^\star|\mathcal{D}) = \int p(f^\star|\mathbf{f})p(\mathbf{f}|\mathcal{D})\partial\mathbf{f},$$

$$= \mathcal{N}\big(\mathbf{k}(\mathbf{x}^\star)^T(\mathbf{K}+\sigma_v^2\mathbf{I})^{-1}\mathbf{t}, k(\mathbf{x}^\star,\mathbf{x}^\star)+\mathbf{k}(\mathbf{x}^\star)^T(\mathbf{K}+\sigma_v^2\mathbf{I})^{-1}\mathbf{k}(\mathbf{x}^\star)\big), \quad (13)$$

where the vector $\mathbf{k}(\mathbf{x}^\star) \in \mathbb{R}^{N\times 1}$ is filled with scalars of the form $\{k(\mathbf{x}^{(n)},\mathbf{x}^\star)\}_{n=1}^{N}$. We remit the avid reader to Williams (1999) for the demonstration of the equivalence of results (9) and (13).

Given that the weight and function space view are equivalent, it is worth asking which one is more convenient to apply. From a computational perspective, both approaches rely on a matrix inversion, which in the weight-space approach is that of $\mathbf{\Sigma}_{wt}$, an $m \times m$ matrix; whereas in the function space it is that of $\boldsymbol{K}$, an $N \times N$ matrix. In general, for many types of regression, $m \ll N$ and the weight space approach will be preferred. However for certain types of linear prediction, m will be infinite and the only possible approach will be the function-space view. Further insights into the convenience of the function space approach to regression is contained in Mackay (1998).

5.2.1 The Covariance Function

Most applications of GP's assume the mean function $m(\mathbf{x})$ to be centred around $\mathbf{0}$, so the core of the formalism lies on the type of covariance function being used. Therefore it is worth analysing some of their features. For example in this work we only use *isotropic* functions of the form $k(\mathbf{x},\mathbf{x}') = k(r)$, with $r = \|\mathbf{x}-\mathbf{x}'\|$. In isotropic covariances, the correlation between observations is independent of their absolute position; only their difference measured in terms of a norm counts. For example, by taking an Euclidean norm we ensure that points $\mathbf{x}$ and $\mathbf{x}'$ lying close to each other will give rise to high correlation, therefore making $f(\mathbf{x})$ and $f(\mathbf{x}')$ close to each other as well. An example of an isotropic covariance we use is

$$k(f(\mathbf{x}^i), f(\mathbf{x}^j)) = k(\mathbf{x}^i,\mathbf{x}^j) = \theta_1 \exp\left(-\frac{\theta_2}{2}\|\mathbf{x}^i-\mathbf{x}^j\|^2\right), \quad (14)$$

also known as RBF or radial basis function covariance. The parameters $\mathbf{\Theta}_k = \{\theta_1,\theta_2\}$ adjust the scale and the width of the radial function, which in this case is a Gaussian. The inverse of θ_2 is also known as the bandwidth parameter σ.

In order to compare how prior and posterior GP's are affected by the choice of covariance function, Fig. 2 shows samples from both of them; the former defined

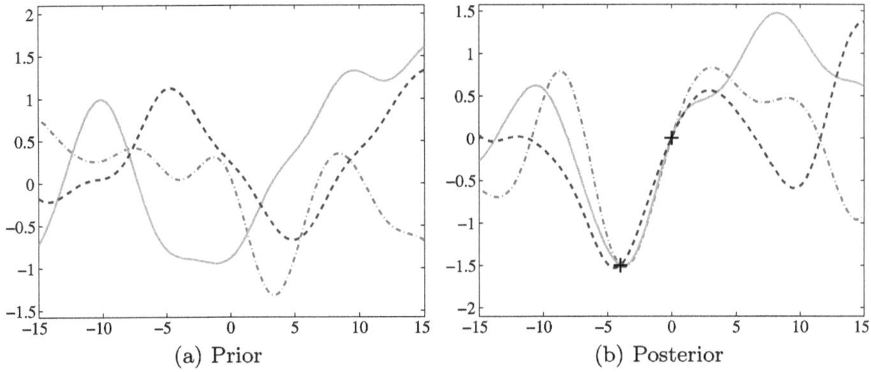

Fig. 2 The plot shows 3 samples taken from prior and posterior GP's. (**a**) Samples from a prior $p(\mathbf{f}) = \mathcal{N}(\mathbf{0}, \mathbf{K})$. (**b**) Given some training data $\mathcal{D}$, the plot shows samples taken from the posterior $p(f^\star|\mathcal{D})$, (13). In *both plots* an RBF covariance (14) was used to compute matrix $\mathbf{K}$. Note that in (**b**) the functions continue to be smooth, but this time are pinned down by the observed points

as $p(\mathbf{f}) = \mathcal{N}(\mathbf{0}, \mathbf{K})$ and the latter as $p(f^\star|\mathcal{D})$, specified in (13). An RBF covariance (14) was used to take the samples. In plot (a) the functions can take up any shape, provided they are smooth, whereas in plot (b) the functions must also be smooth but pinned down by the observed points. In both cases, the bandwidth of the RBF was adjusted to $\log \sigma^{-1} = -2.3026$.

5.3 Gaussian Processes for Classification

We can think of GP regression as a generalisation of the more well-known Bayesian linear one and in similar terms, GP classification can be thought of as a generalisation of logistic regression. Recall that in Sect. 4 the activation of the logistic function was given by $a = \mathbf{w}^T \phi(\mathbf{x})$; thus following a similar rationale to that of the previous section, a Gaussian process may allow to non-linearise a by working directly over the space of functions. Thus by considering a collection of latent variables a_n for $n \in [1, N]$, we can replace the linear models $\mathbf{w}^T \phi(\mathbf{x}^{(n)})$ by a Gaussian process $\mathbf{f}$. Furthermore, given a new observation $\mathbf{x}^\star$ we are interested in determining its probability of class membership $\pi(\mathbf{x}^\star) = p(y = 1|\mathbf{x}^\star) = \sigma(f(\mathbf{x}^\star))$. The inference process is performed in an analogue way to the one previously described, thus the distribution over $f^\star$ is computed as

$$p(f^\star|\mathcal{D}) = \int p(f^\star|\mathcal{D}, \mathbf{f}) p(\mathbf{f}|\mathcal{D}) \partial\mathbf{f}, \qquad (15)$$

where $p(\mathbf{f}|\mathcal{D}) \propto p(\mathcal{D}|\mathbf{f}) p(\mathbf{f})$ is the posterior obtained through the application of Bayes' rule. However, in contrast to the regression case of Sect. 5.2, the noise model that needs to be specified is that for classification, i.e. a Bernoulli distribution of the form

$$p(\mathcal{D}|\mathbf{f}) = \prod_{n=1}^{N} \sigma(f^n)^{y^n}\left[1 - \sigma(f^n)^{(1-y^n)}\right]. \tag{16}$$

This density is equivalent to that presented as argument in the optimisation problem of (6), but with parameterisations of the form $\mathbf{w}^T\phi(\mathbf{x})$ replaced by f's.

The posterior (15) is used subsequently to estimate a probabilistic prediction of the class label, that is

$$\pi^\star = p(y^\star = 1|\mathcal{D}, \mathbf{x}^\star) = \int p(y^\star|f^\star)p(f^\star|\mathcal{D})\partial f^\star. \tag{17}$$

Both integrals (15) and (17) are not analytically tractable and thus have to be computed in an approximate way. However, whereas (15) is usually computed through stochastic methods, such as Markov Chain Monte Carlo or deterministic approaches like Laplace approximation; (17) being one dimensional can be evaluated through standard numeric techniques like quadrature. More references on GP classification can be found at Williams and Barber (1998).

5.4 Some Other Types of GP's

Perhaps the simplest approach to have an approximation of the non-tractable integrals just mentioned consists of making a quadratic expansion around the mode of the posterior $p(\mathbf{f}|\mathcal{D})$, and this is commonly referred as Laplace approximation. However, it has been proved by several authors (e.g. Minka 2001) that such types of approximation many times fail to capture the true nature of the distribution, thus producing bad predictive results. Several alternative methods exist in the literature, with one of them approximating the Bernoulli likelihood $p(\mathcal{D}|\mathbf{f})$ with Gaussian densities. This method yields a classifier with comparable properties to those of FDA and can produce competitive results in some problem domains, as shown by Peña Centeno and Lawrence (2006). In the subsequent we will refer to this method as Bayesian Fisher discriminant (BFD).

Another type of GP technique is the so-called least squares support vector machine of Suykens and Vandewalle (1999), which is formulated as an optimisation problem with equality constraints. The motivation the so-called LS-SVM is to find a faster and simpler way to solve the QP-problem that involves solving standard support vector machines (Cortes and Vapnik 1995). The simplification consists of replacing the inequality constraints of a standard support vector machine with equality ones. In this way the LS-SVM is less computationally intensive to solve, at the expense of losing sparseness.

Finally, one of the main drawbacks of applying GP regression stems from the fact that they assume Gaussian noise and unfortunately most problem domains do not show this characteristic. Snelson et al. (2003) generalised the GP framework for regression by learning a non-linear transformation of the outputs, so that non-Gaussian noise could still be modelled with a GP. The generalisation, as Snelson states, consists of learning a *GP regressor in latent space and simultaneously a transformation or warping space for the outputs*; in this way other types of noise are accounted for. This strategy will be termed warped Gaussian processes or WGP's.

These three methods are just a set of algorithmic tools that have been developed by the machine learning community to solve regression and classification problems. In Sect. 6 we will go back to them and test their effectiveness on the problem of classifying a real dataset.

5.5 Adaptation of Hyperparameters

In all the GP-based methods presented, it is only after a solution for the posterior predictive distribution $p(f^{\star}|\mathcal{D})$ has been obtained that the issue of setting the hyperparameters $\mathbf{\Theta}_k$ of the covariance function is addressed. Bayesian methodology dictates these parameters should be set in a hierarchical way, however the conditional parameter distributions arising from a covariance of the type in (14) are not amenable to Gibbs sampling. Thus practitioners have looked for more straightforward methods for parameter estimation, for example Williams (1999) recommends the use maximum likelihood or generalised cross-validation. More details about maximum likelihood estimation are given in this section, while the application of generalised cross-validation is described in Rasmussen and Williams (2006). In this work, we selected hyperparameters for all the GP algorithms through maximum likelihood.

In the simplest example of all, the regression case, given some training data $\mathcal{D} = (\mathbf{X}, \mathbf{t})$, a noise model of the form $p(\mathcal{D}|\mathbf{f}) = \mathcal{N}(\mathbf{f}, \sigma_v^2\mathbf{I})$ and a prior $p(\mathbf{f}) = \mathcal{N}(\mathbf{0}, \mathbf{K})$, it can be proved that the marginal likelihood is

$$p(\mathcal{D}|\mathbf{\Theta}_k) = \int p(\mathcal{D}|\mathbf{f})p(\mathbf{f}|\mathbf{\Theta}_k)\mathbf{f}$$
$$= \frac{1}{(2\pi)^{N/2}|\mathbf{K}+\sigma_v^2\mathbf{I}|^{1/2}} \exp\left\{-\frac{1}{2}\mathbf{t}^T(\mathbf{K}+\sigma_v^2\mathbf{I})\mathbf{t}\right\}.$$

Therefore, the log of $p(\mathcal{D}|\mathbf{\Theta}_k)$ that will be subject to optimisation may be computed analytically

$$l = \log p(\mathcal{D}|\mathbf{\Theta}_k) = -\frac{1}{2}\log|\mathbf{K}+\sigma_v^2\mathbf{I}| - \frac{1}{2}\mathbf{t}^T(\mathbf{K}+\sigma_v^2\mathbf{I})^{-1}\mathbf{t} - \frac{N}{2}\log 2\pi. \quad (18)$$

As there is no closed form solution for the maximisation of l w.r.t. $\mathbf{\Theta}_k$, one needs to rely on numeric methods such as conjugate gradients to find a local maximum. Indeed the gradient of (18) will be used and is written explicitly as

$$\frac{\partial l}{\partial \theta_i} = -\frac{1}{2}\mathbf{t}^T(\mathbf{K}+\sigma_v^2\mathbf{I})^{-1}\mathbf{t} + \mathbf{t}(\mathbf{K}+\sigma_v^2\mathbf{I})^{-1}\frac{\partial \mathbf{K}}{\partial \theta_i}(\mathbf{K}+\sigma_v^2\mathbf{I})^{-1}\mathbf{t}.$$

The strategy for parameter specification in the case of Gaussian process classifiers and variants (i.e. WGP, BFD) follows the same lines as that of regression. In other words, the idea is to maximise the marginal likelihood of the data, but now with the specific noise model defined by each method. For example in the case of GPC's it will be (16).

5.6 Automatic Relevance Determination

Adapting the values of the hyperparameters is important if one wants to have good generalisation results and a better understanding of the data. Indeed for some families of covariance functions there is a hyperparameter associated with each input dimension, such that each one represents the characteristic length scale of the data[8], thus by applying a parameter adaptation method like maximum likelihood the relative importance of the inputs will be inferred. For instance

$$k\left(\mathbf{x}^i,\mathbf{x}^j\right)=\theta_1\exp\left(-\frac{\theta_2}{2}\left(\mathbf{x}^i-\mathbf{x}^j\right)^T\mathbf{\Theta}_{ard}\left(\mathbf{x}^i-\mathbf{x}^j\right)\right)+\theta_3\delta_{ij}, \tag{19}$$

is a function that weighs each component of $\mathbf{\Theta}_{ard}=\text{diag}(\theta_4,\ldots,\theta_{4+d-1})$—with d being the dimension of $\mathcal{X}$—when the training is done. The parameter δ_{ij} is the Kronecker delta, which for a large enough value θ_3 ensures that $\mathbf{K}$ is positive definite and therefore invertible at all times.

This type of feature was proposed first in the context of neural networks by Mackay (1995) and Neal (1996) and is usually referred to as *automatic relevance determination* or ARD. If the selection of prior covariance is adequate, then ARD may be a very useful method for ranking and selecting features as it effectively orders inputs according to their importance and eliminates those that are deemed not. Indeed this feature might be very useful in the bankruptcy prediction problem because it can be used to rank the financial ratios in order of importance, as is done later on.

In order to understand better ARD, Fig. 3 shows samples from a covariance of the form (19) with two dimensional inputs. Panel (a) shows a sample whereby both inputs x_1 and x_2 have the same associated weights, θ_4 and θ_5; thus in average the ensemble of samples will have a roughly equal degree of variation along the axes x_1 and x_2. Panel (b) shows a sample where the value $\theta_4>\theta_5$, producing an output that varies more on the direction x_1 than on x_2. Therefore, in both cases, by observing some data $\mathcal{D}$, the fitted posterior will have weights θ_4 and θ_5 that reflect their 'real' importance to the regression.

[8]As expressed by Rasmussen and Williams (2006), the characteristic length scales can be loosely interpreted as the distance required to move along each axes in order to have uncorrelated inputs.

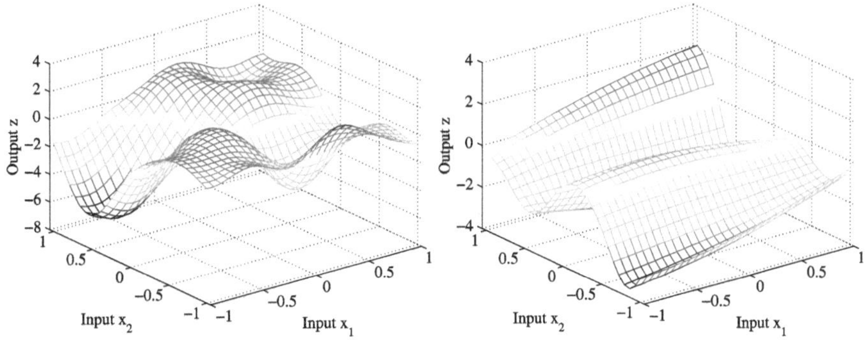

(a) $\theta_4 = 1.0$ and $\theta_5 = 1.0$ (b) $\theta_4 = 1.0$ and $\theta_5 = 0.01$

Fig. 3 Sample functions taken from a two dimensional GP prior with ARD covariance function of the form (19). Panel (**a**) shows a function with two equally important inputs x_1 and x_2 while in (**b**), input x_1 varies faster than x_2. ARD may help to determine the relevance of a feature (e.g. financial ratio) in a classification task

6 Data and Experiments

This section describes the experiments that were carried out to compare the predictive performance of the proposed algorithmic approaches with respect to discriminant analysis and logistic regression. As previously mentioned, we used data from the Federal Deposit Insurance Corporation (FDIC) and a brief analysis of the results follows.

6.1 FDIC Data

The University of Essex (UK) kindly provided[9] a data set with 243 multivariate observations. Each observation comprises a vector of dimension 11 (the number of financial ratios) and as a whole, the data was composed of roughly balanced classes (bankrupt and not). The financial ratios are described in Table 1 below. The data set was split into two parts, one for training (145 obs.) and one for testing (89 obs.). Due to the limited amount of observations we had to rely on random splits of training and test data in order to average our results and reduce as much as possible any variance effects that may have affected our results. We created 100 different pairs of training and testing sets out of the 243 observations available, keeping the same proportion of training to testing data as the original data set. Using random splitting of the data to reduce the variance of the estimates is not uncommon and is justified by the work of Efron (1979) and Stone (1974) on boot-strapping and cross-validation, respectively; (Rätsch et al. 1998) used a similar approach to ours.

[9]We thank the Centre for Computational Finance and Economic Agents (CCFEA).

Table 1 Financial ratios used in the classification experiments. Data comes from the Federal Deposit Insurance Corporation (FDIC) and was kindly provided by the Centre for Computational Finance and Economic Agents (CCFEA), University of Essex. Each ratio is described in the Appendix

Financial ratios	
1. Net interest margin	7. Efficiency ratio
2. Non-interest income to earning assets	8. Non-current assets plus other real estate owned to assets
3. Non-interest expense to earning assets	9. Cash plus US treasury and government obligations to total assets
4. Net operating income to assets	10. Equity capital to assets
5. Return on assets	11. Core capital leverage ratio
6. Return on equity	

6.2 Experimental Setup

We tested five different algorithms on the referred data: Fisher discriminant analysis (FDA), least-squares support vector machines (LS-SVM), GP's for classification (GPC), Warped GP's (WGP) and Bayesian Fisher discriminant (BFD). Every set was normalised to have zero mean and unit standard deviation. The algorithms were thus trained 100 times and tested 100 more and because of this, we considered most convenient to report the average classification performance over the 100 splits in terms of the areas under the ROC curves (AUC's). In fact AUC's are highly convenient to measure the performance of a classifier because they condense in a single figure both false positives and negatives.

6.3 Implementation and Results

The FDA, logit and probit classifiers were implemented with the Matlab function `classify` (Statistics toolbox, version 5.0.1). Whereas for LS-SVM, we used the LSSVMlab toolbox of Suykens et al. (2002). The default 10-fold cross-validation parameters were used for the training. BFD was implemented with the toolbox of Peña Centeno and Lawrence (2006). Meanwhile, the WGP implementation was that of Snelson et al. (2003), with the parameter I set to 5 function components. As WGP's are designed for regression but not classification, we clamped the targets to the label values. Finally, for GPC's we used the code of Rasmussen and Williams (2006). For all these methods, we generated ROC curves with the output values they produced, i.e. in most cases posterior class probabilities, except for FDA and WGP's.

In Table 2 we report the averages of the AUC's over the 100 testing instances of the splitted FDIC data. In this comparison, LSSVM, GPC and BFD were trained with a covariance function of the form (14). Note that in the table FDA outperforms

Table 2 Average classification results on the Federal Insurance Deposit Corporation data. We report mean, median, maximum, minimum and standard deviation of the percentage area under the ROC curve (AUC) over all testing instances of the data. The compared algorithms are: Fisher's discriminant analysis (FDA), Logistic and Probit regressions, Least-squares support vector machines (LS-SVM) and two instances of Gaussian processes (GP's): Bayesian Fisher's discriminant (BFD) and GP classifiers (GPC's). It can be observed that FDA outperforms the rest of the algorithms

	FDA	Logistic	Probit	LSSVM (rbf)	BFD (rbf)	GPC (rbf)
Mean	0.866	0.839	0.825	0.823	0.817	0.815
Median	0.877	0.841	0.838	0.818	0.816	0.815
Max	0.962	0.949	0.940	0.956	0.950	0.949
Min	0.672	0.679	0.678	0.687	0.681	0.676
STD	0.051	0.056	0.055	0.055	0.051	0.050

Table 3 Average classification results on the Federal Insurance Deposit Corporation data, with algorithms that have ARD priors (Sect. 5.6). We report mean, median, maximum, minimum and standard deviation of the percentage AUC over all testing instances. The compared methods are: Bayesian least-squared support vector machine (LS-SVM), Bayesian Fisher's discriminant (BFD) and Warped Gaussian processes (WGP's). Compare these results with those of Table 2

	BayLSSM	BFD (linard)	GPC (linard)
Mean	0.839	0.832	0.869
Median	0.853	0.831	0.873
Max	0.952	0.964	0.982
Min	0.627	0.720	0.578
STD	0.061	0.048	0.051

all the other methods. A statistical F test carried out over all the reported parameters indicated FDA to have significantly better results than the rest of methods.

From these results, we had the 'hint' the FDIC dataset could be better separated by a linear trend rather than by a non-linear one, thus instead decided to use a linear covariance of the form $k(\mathbf{x}, \mathbf{x}') = \mathbf{x}^T \boldsymbol{\Theta}_{ard} \mathbf{x}'$, with $\boldsymbol{\Theta}_{ard} = \{\theta_1, \ldots, \theta_d\}$ for the reported experiments of Table 3. This type of covariance is known as ARD (Sect. 5.6) because it assigns a hyperparameter θ_i to each dimension i of $\boldsymbol{\mathcal{X}}$.

In the second experiment (Table 3) we observe much better results for GPC and a moderate improvement for LSSVM (Bayesian) and BFD (linard), if compared with the figures of Table 2. In this case GPC performs slightly better than FDA. The figures corresponding to GPC's are statistically better at the 1% level of significance than the results reported for the methods of Tables 2 and 3; except FDA.

As a final experiment we decided to prove the WGP algorithm of Snelson et al. (2003), because in some domains it may have more expressive power than the other methods. Results of AUC's are shown in Table 4 below. It can be seen that WGP has a better predictive performance than the rest of the compared models, including FDA and GPC (Tables 2 and 3) and an F test of significance showed this was the case.

Table 4 Average classification results on the FDIC data with the warped Gaussian process algorithm (WGP) of Snelson et al. (2003). The figures reported are mean, median, maximum, minimum and standard deviation of the percentage area under the ROC curve (AUC) over all testing instances of the data. Results for this classifier are significantly better than those for the rest of methods (Tables 2 and 3)

	WGP
Mean	0.914
Median	0.978
Max	1.000
Min	0.541
STD	0.114

6.4 Analysis of Features

This section briefly describes the findings of applying ARD priors to the FDIC dataset. The study was performed on GPC's, LS-SVM's, BFD and WGP's, from the results of the experiments reported in Tables 3 and 4. However only WGP's are reported because it was the method that yielded the best classification results. Due to the random splitting of the data, a set with a hundred rankings were obtained (each member of the set being the ordering of the 11 financial ratios). Therefore it was considered most appropriate to summarise the number of times a feature was alloted to a particular rank through histograms. Figure 4 shows the histograms produced from training the WGP, with the Appendix describing each of the financial ratios of the data. It is important to consider that ARD measures the degree of variation of a feature and ranks it accordingly; it also assumes independence among features. However this does not necessarily means a low ranked feature will necessarily be irrelevant for the classification.

Figure 4 shows some regularity on the first four positions as well as on the last three. Among the first group, features six, five, seven and four, corresponding to return on equity (ROE), return on assets (ROA), efficiency ratio (ER) and net operating income (NOI), are the most frequently ranked. ROE is a relevant financial ratio because it measures the efficiency of a company to generate profits from every dollar of net assets. ROA is also a plausible feature because it measures the industry and capital requirements of insurance and banking companies and consequently, might be used to make comparisons among different type of companies. As mentioned in the Appendix, there is no consensus on how to compute the ER, however a larger value of this parameter is usually taken as a sign of corporate distress and this characteristic makes it a good candidate to predict bankrupcty. Lastly, the NOI is generally perceived as a reliable measure of a company's performance and therefore another reasonable selection.

On the opposite extreme, the group of not-so relevant features is given by the net interest margin (NIM), the non-interest income (NII) and the capital ratio (CR), corresponding to features number one, two and eleven. The low ranking of the NIM seems counterintuitive because it somehow measures the financial soundness of an

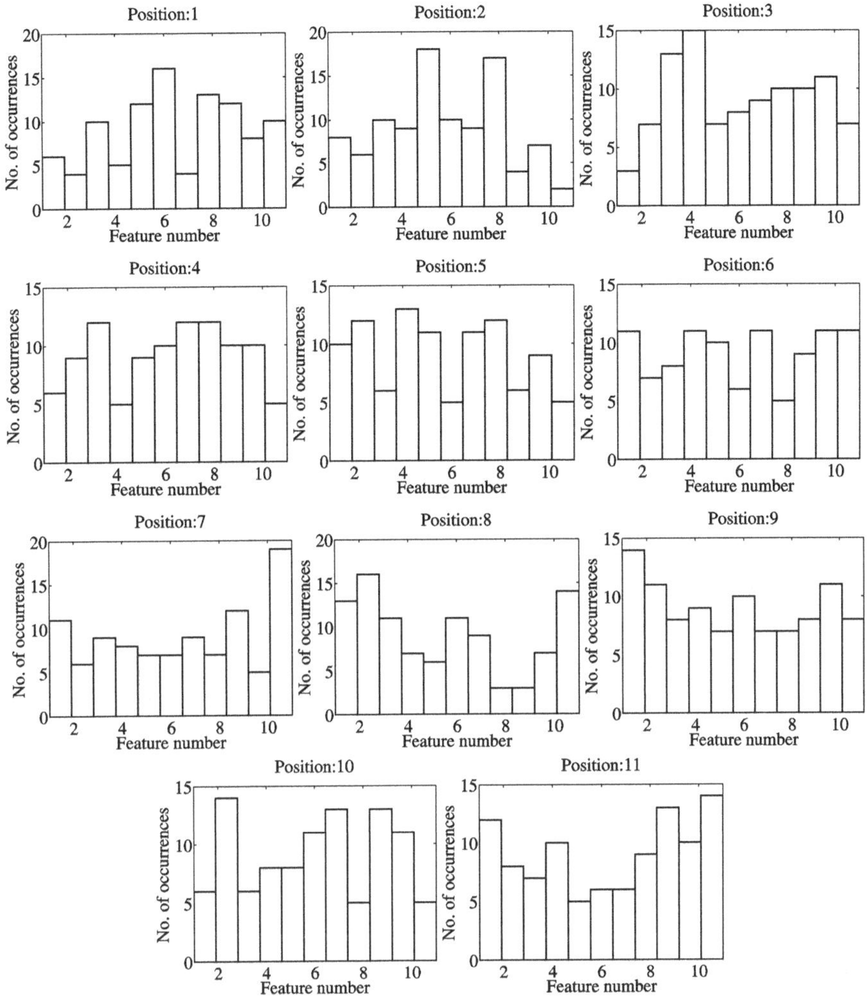

Fig. 4 Histograms of rankings (positions) produced by warped Gaussian processes (WGP) over the FDIC dataset. The way to read the results is the following: e.g. the top-left histogram shows the first ranked feature is number 6, return on equity (ROE), with 16 occurrences, while the top-middle histogram shows features 5, return on assets (ROA) and 8, non current assets (NCA) almost equally as important in the second position with 18 and 17 occurrences respectively. These results tell features six, five, seven and four are important to the classifier. Feature definitions are included in the Appendix

institution. Nevertheless, it is generally thought that modern banks should rely less on this parameter due to the competitive gains achieved by the financial sector during the last decade. Regarding NII, this ratio does not seem to have a direct relationship with the typical symptoms of financial distress a bank may have; therefore further analysis is due. Finally, although CR is probably one of the most important ratios to asses financial health, it was the one that occupied the lowest rankings.

Nevertheless, this observation might be misleading if one considers that CR is also a candidate to occupy the sixth rank and more importantly, on the fact that the feature independence assumption previously mentioned might not necessarily hold on the dataset.

7 Credit Risk in Portfolios

We have presented a new family of algorithmic techniques unknown to the computational economics community, that of Gaussian processes interpreted as a prior distribution over functional space and how they can be applied to do bankruptcy prediction in terms of a classification task. Some commercial products such as CreditMetrics^{TM} are used to quantify full credit risk, i.e. give an estimate of the losses of a portfolio through the application of a suite of different techniques; including FDA. Indeed, the CreditMetrics framework (1997) makes us realise that GP's are perfectly suitable for integration in the form of a binary classification module. Something similar would happen with other types of products such as Moody's KMV^{TM}.

8 Conclusions

This work has presented a comprehensive review of statistical methods for classification and their application to the bankruptcy prediction problem. A comparison with newly developed tools, such as various guises of Gaussian processes for classification has also been included. Justification for trying new techniques lies on the fact that standard models for estimating a classifier are based on parametric approaches. However, it was demonstrated that by taking a parametric approach a richer and more flexible class of models was being neglected, that of the non-parametric models to whom Gaussian processes belong.

GP's are a generalisation of the Gaussian density to infinite dimensional function spaces and lend themselves naturally to Bayesian inference tasks because of their simple analytic properties and ease of use. However, these characteristics do not preclude them of being applied on a set of complex problem domains, like for example separating data between classes. In this work we used data from the Federal Deposit Insurance Corporation to show how different instances of GP's yielded competitive, if not better, classification results with respect to well established techniques like the Z-score of Altman (i.e. discriminant analysis) and logistic regression.

An interesting by-product of the Bayesian formalism is that certain priors lead to the ranking and effective pruning of features when inference is done, and GP's are no exception. This by-product is known as automatic relevance determination and is enabled whenever a prior parameter is assigned to each of the dimensions of the data (in our case the dimensions were given by each of the financial ratios of the analysed data). With the aim of understanding better which financial ratios were more important to the classification, some ARD covariance functions were tried and the results showed the return on equity (ROE), return on assets (ROA), equity ratio (ER) and net operating income (NOI) as the highest ranked. The capital ratio (CR) a widely viewed relevant ratio for financial health assessment, was ranked in low positions.

We plan to expand the present work in a three-fold way: first, by assessing the financial health of Mexican banking institutions with some of these GP tools, as automated bankruptcy prediction is in its early stages in this country. Second, by expanding our datasets to include more financial ratios, in order to increase our understanding of the bankrupcty prediction task. Finally, by introducing a time-dependency component, so that this type of methods become useful for early-warning.

Appendix

A brief description of the financial ratios that compose the FDIC data follows.

Ratio 1. Net interest margin (NIM) is the difference between the proceeds from borrowers and the interest payed to their lenders.

Ratio 2. Non-interest income (NII) is the sum of the following types of income: fee-based, trading, that coming from fiduciary activities and other non-interest associated one.

Ratio 3. Non-interest expense (NIX) comprises basically three types of expenses: personnel expense, occupancy and other operating expenses.

Ratio 4. Net operating income (NOI) is related to the company's gross income associated with its properties less the operating expenses.

Ratio 5. Return on assets (ROA) is an indicator of how profitable a company is relative to its total assets. ROA is calculated as the ratio between the company's total earnings over the year and the company's total assets.

Ratio 6. Return on equity (ROE) is a measure of the rate of return on the shareholders' equity of the common stock owners. ROE is estimated as the year's net income (after preferred stock dividends but before common stock dividends) divided by total equity (excluding preferred shares).

Ratio 7. Efficiency ratio (ER) is a ratio used to measure the efficiency of a company, although not every one of them calculates it in the same way.

Ratio 8. Non current assets (NCA) are those that cannot be easily converted into cash, e.g. real estate, machinery, long-term investments or patents.

Ratio 9. It is the ratio of cash plus US treasury and government obligations to total assets.

Ratio 10. Equity capital (EC) is the capital raised from owners.

Ratio 11. The capital ratio (CR) also known as the leverage ratio is calculated as the Tier 1 capital divided by the average of the total consolidated assets.

References

Altman, E. I. (1968). Financial ratios, discriminant analysis and the prediction of corporate bankruptcy. *Journal of Finance*, *23*(4), 589–609.

Atiya, A. F. (2001). Bankruptcy prediction for credit risk using neural networks: a survey and new results. *IEEE Transactions on Neural Networks*, *12*, 929–935.

Back, B., Laitinen, T., Sere, K., & van Wezel, M. (1996). *Choosing bankruptcy predictors using discriminant analysis, logit analysis, and genetic algorithms* (Technical Report 40). Turku Centre for Computer Science, September 1996.

Beaver, W. H. (1966). Financial ratios as predictors of failures. *Journal of Accounting Research*, *4*, 71–111.

Bishop, C. M. (1995). *Neural networks for pattern recognition*. Oxford: Oxford University Press.

Bishop, C. M. (2006). *Pattern recognition and machine learning. Information science and statistics*. New York: Springer.

Box, G. E., & Tiao, G. C. (1973). *Bayesian inference in statistical analysis. Wiley classics library, published 1992*. New York: Wiley.

Chen, S.-H. (Ed.) (2002). *Genetic algorithms and genetic programming in computational finance*. Dordrecht: Kluwer Academic.

Cortes, C., & Vapnik, V. V. (1995). Support vector networks. *Machine Learning*, *20*, 273–297.

Efron, B. (1979). Bootstrap methods: another look at the Jackknife. *The Annals of Statistics*, *7*, 1–26.

Estrella, A., Park, S., & Peristiani, S. (2000). Capital ratios as predictors of bank failure. *Federal reserve bank of New York economic policy review*, pp. 33–52, July 2000.

Fisher, R. A. (1936). The use of multiple measurements in taxonomic problems. *Annals of Eugenics*, *7*, 179.

Grimmett, G., & Stirzaker, D. (2004). *Probability and random processes* (3rd ed.). Oxford: Oxford University Press.

Joos, P., Vanhoof, K., Ooghe, H., & Sierens, N. (1998). Credit classification: a comparison of logit models and decision trees. In *10th European conference on machine learning. Proceedings notes of the workshop on application of machine learning and data mining in finance* (pp. 59–72). 24 April 1998, Chemnitz, Germany.

Credit Metrics—Technical Document (1997). JP Morgan. New York, April 1997.

Kimeldorf, G. S., & Wahba, G. (1970). A correspondence between Bayesian estimation on stochastic processes and smoothing by splines. *Annals of Mathematical Statistics*, *41*(2), 495–502.

Krige, D. G. (1996). Two-dimensional weighting moving average trend surfaces for ore evaluation. *Journal of the South African Institute of Mining and Metallurgy*.

Mackay, D. J. C. (1995). Probable networks and plausible predictions—a review of practical Bayesian methods for supervised neural networks. *Network: Computation in Neural Systems*, *6*(3), 469–505.

Mackay, D. J. C. (1998). Introduction to Gaussian processes. In C. M. Bishop (Ed.), *NATO ASI Series: Vol. 168. Neural networks and machine learning* (pp. 133–165). Berlin: Springer.

Mackay, D. J. C. (2003). *Information theory, learning and inference algorithms*. Cambridge: Cambridge University Press.

MacLachlan, G. J. (1991). *Discriminant analysis and pattern recognition*. New York: Wiley.

Minka, T. P. (2001). *A family of algorithms for approximate Bayesian inference*. PhD thesis, Massachusetts Institute of Technology.

Neal, R. M. (1996). *Bayesian learning for neural networks*. New York: Springer.

O'Hagan, A. (1978). Curve fitting and optimal design for prediction. *Journal of the Royal Statistical Society, Series B (Methodological)*, *40*(1), 1–42.

Park, C., & Han, I. (2002). A case-based reasoning with the feature weights derived by analytic hierarchy process for bankruptcy prediction. *Expert Systems with Applications*, *23*, 255–264.

Peña Centeno, T., & Lawrence, N. D. (2006). Optimising kernel parameters and regularisation coefficients for non-linear discriminant analysis. *Journal of Machine Learning Research*, *7*, 455–491.

Quintana, D., Saez, Y., Mochon, A., & Isasi, P. (2007). Early bankruptcy prediction using ENPC. *Journal of Applied Intelligence*, ISSN 0924-669X.

Rasmussen, C. E. (2004). Gaussian processes in machine learning. In O. Bousquet, U. von Luxburg, & G. Rätsch (Eds.), *Lecture notes in computer science/artificial intelligence: Vol. 3176. Advanced lectures on machine learning*. Berlin: Springer.

Rasmussen, C. E., & Williams, C. K. (2006). *Adaptive computation and machine learning. Gaussian processes for machine learning*. Cambridge: MIT Press. http://www.GaussianProcess.org/gpml.

Rätsch, G., Onoda, T., & Müller, K.-R. (1998) *Soft margins for AdaBoost* (Technical Report NC-TR-98-021). Royal Holloway College, University of London, London, UK.

Seeger, M. (2004). Gaussian processes for machine learning. *International Journal of Neural Systems*, *14*(2), 69–106.

Serrano-Cinca, C., Martin, C. B., & Gallizo, J. (1993). Artificial neural networks in financial statement analysis: ratios versus accounting data. In *16th annual congress of the European accounting association*, Turku, Finland, 28–30 Apr.

Shin, K.-S., & Lee, Y.-J. (2002). A genetic algorithm application in bankruptcy prediction modeling. *Expert Systems with Applications*, *23*, 321–328.

Snelson, E., Rasmussen, C. E., & Ghahramani, Z. (2003). Warped Gaussian processes. In S. Thrun, L. K. Saul, & B. Schölkopf (Eds.), *Advances in neural information processing systems 16*. Cambridge: MIT Press.

Stone, M. (1974). Cross-validatory choice and assessment of statistical predictions. *Journal of the Royal Statistical Society*, *36*, 111–147.

Suykens, J. A. & Vandewalle, J. (1999). Least squares support vector machines. *Neural Processing Letters*, *9*(3), 293–300.

Suykens, J. A., Van Gestel, T., Brabanter, J. D., Moor, B. D., & Vandewalle, J. (2002). *Least squares support vector machines*. Singapore: World Scientific.

Thiele, T. N. (1931). *Theory of observations*. London: Layton. Reprinted in *Annals of Mathematical Statistics, 2*, 165–308.

Tsang, E. P. K., & Martinez-Jaramillo, S. (2004). Computational finance. In *IEEE computational intelligence society newsletter* (pp. 3–8). New York: IEEE Press.

Varetto, F. (1998). Genetic algorithms applications in the analysis of insolvency risk. *Journal of Banking and Finance*, *22*, 1421–1439.

Wahba, G. (1990). *CBMS-NSF regional conference in applied mathematics: Vol. 59. Spline models for observational data*. Philadelphia: Society for Industrial and Applied Mathematics.

Williams, C. K. (1999). Prediction with Gaussian processes: from linear regression to linear prediction and beyond. In M. I. Jordan (Ed.), *Behavioural and social sciences: Vol. 11. Learning in graphical models, D*. Dordrecht: Kluwer Academic.

Williams, C. K., & Barber, D. (1998). Bayesian classification with Gaussian processes. *IEEE Transactions, Pattern Analysis and Machine Intelligence*, *20*(12), 1342–1351.

Yip, A. Y. N. (2003). *A hybrid case-based reasoning approach to business failure prediction* (pp. 371–378). Amsterdam: IOS Press. ISBN 1-58603-394-8.

Part II
Dynamic Policy Perspectives

Testing Institutional Arrangements via Agent-Based Modeling: A U.S. Electricity Market Application

Hongyan Li, Junjie Sun, and Leigh Tesfatsion

Abstract Many critical goods and services in modern-day economies are produced and distributed through complex institutional arrangements. Agent-based computational economics (ACE) modeling tools are capable of handling this degree of complexity. In concrete support of this claim, this study presents an ACE test bed designed to permit the exploratory study of restructured U.S. wholesale power markets with transmission grid congestion managed by locational marginal prices (LMPs). Illustrative findings are presented showing how spatial LMP cross-correlation patterns vary systematically in response to changes in the price responsiveness of wholesale power demand when wholesale power sellers have learning capabilities. These findings highlight several distinctive features of ACE modeling: namely, an emphasis on process rather than on equilibrium; an ability to capture complicated structural, institutional, and behavioral real-world aspects (micro-validation); and an ability to study the effects of changes in these aspects on spatial and temporal outcome distributions.

1 Introduction

Modern economies depend strongly on large-scale institutions for the production and distribution of critical goods and services, such as electric power, health care, credit, and education. The performance of these institutions in turn depends in complicated ways on the structural constraints restricting feasible activities, on the rules governing participation, operation, and oversight, and on the behavioral dispositions of human participants. To be useful and informative, institutional studies need to take proper account of all three elements.

Agent-based computational economics (*ACE*) modeling is well suited for undertaking institutional studies. ACE modeling begins with assumptions about "agents" and their interactions and then uses computer simulation to generate histories that reveal the dynamic consequences of these assumptions. The agents in ACE models can range from passive structural features with no cognitive function to individual

L. Tesfatsion (✉)
Economics Department, Iowa State University, Ames, IA 50011-1070, USA
e-mail: tesfatsi@iastate.edu

H. Dawid, W. Semmler (eds.), *Computational Methods in Economic Dynamics*, Dynamic Modeling and Econometrics in Economics and Finance 13,
DOI 10.1007/978-3-642-16943-4_7,

and group decision makers with sophisticated learning and communication capabilities. ACE researchers use controlled experimentation to investigate how large-scale effects arise from the micro-level interactions of dispersed agents, starting from variously specified initial conditions.

In particular, ACE researchers take a culture-dish approach to the study of institutional designs. The first step is to develop a computational world that incorporates the salient aspects of the institutional design, along with relevant structural constraints, and that is populated with cognitive agents endowed with realistic behavioral dispositions and learning capabilities. The second step is to specify initial conditions for the computational world. The final step is to permit the computational world to evolve over time driven solely by agent interactions, with no further intervention from the modeler. Two basic questions are typically addressed. First, does the institutional design promote efficient, fair, and orderly social outcomes over time, despite possible attempts by cognitive agents to game the design for their own advantage? Second, under what conditions might the design give rise to adverse unintended consequences?

Introductory discussions focusing on the applicability of ACE modeling for economic research in general can be found in Tesfatsion (2006, 2010a). Annotated pointers to extensive ACE institutional research can be found at the ACE homepage (Tesfation 2010b). The focus of this latter research runs the gamut from macroeconomic policy rules to the microeconomic procurement processes of individual firms.

In this study we apply the ACE approach to a meso-level institutional design problem: namely, exploration of the performance characteristics of wholesale power markets with transmission grid congestion managed by locational marginal prices (LMPs). Under this pricing system, electric power is priced at wholesale in accordance with the location and timing of its injection into, or withdrawal from, the transmission grid.

Our basic framework of analysis is an ACE wholesale power market test bed ("AMES") developed by a group of researchers at Iowa State University (AMES 2010). Illustrative findings are presented from AMES experiments showing how spatial LMP cross-correlation patterns vary systematically in response to changes in the price responsiveness of wholesale power demand when wholesale power sellers have learning capabilities. For example, it is shown how the strategic supply offers of the pivotal sellers whose supply is needed to meet total fixed (price-insensitive) demand strongly influence the LMPs at neighboring locations as well as the LMPs at their own locations. An important policy implication of this finding is that the exercise of market power at any one location can have substantial adverse spill-over effects on prices at other locations, particularly when total demand is largely fixed.

Section 2 provides a brief overview of restructuring efforts for the U.S. electric power industry that have led to the widespread adoption of LMP pricing. Section 3 describes the key features of AMES. An experimental design is outlined in Sect. 4 for testing the spatial cross-correlation patterns arising among LMPs under systematically varied demand conditions when wholesale power sellers have learning capabilities. Section 5 presents AMES-generated findings for this experimental design. These findings are compared with empirical LMP data for the U.S. Midwest wholesale power market in Sect. 6. Concluding remarks are provided in Sect. 7.

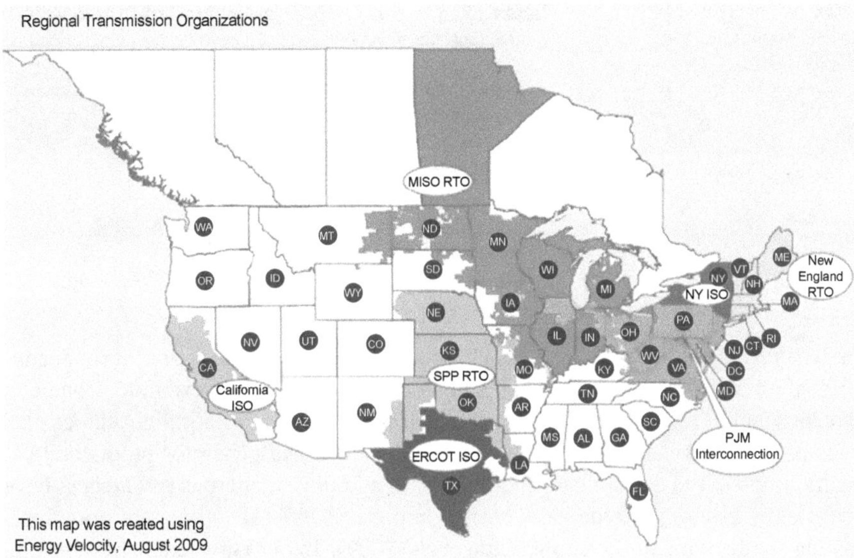

Fig. 1 U.S. energy regions that have adopted FERC's wholesale power market design. Source: www.ferc.gov/industries/electric/indus-act/rto/rto-map.asp

2 Study Context: U.S. Restructured Wholesale Power Markets

The U.S. electric power industry is currently undergoing substantial changes in both its *structure* (ownership and technology aspects) and its *architecture* (operational and oversight aspects). These changes involve attempts to move the industry away from highly regulated markets with administered cost-based pricing and towards competitive markets in which prices more fully reflect supply and demand forces.

The goal of these changes is to provide industry participants with better incentives to control costs and introduce innovations. The process of enacting and implementing policies and laws to bring about these changes has come to be known as *restructuring*.

In 2003 the U.S. Federal Energy Regulatory Commission (FERC) recommended the adoption of a common market design for U.S. wholesale power markets (FERC 2003). As indicated in Fig. 1, and elaborated in Joskow (2006), versions of this design have now been implemented in U.S. energy regions in the Midwest (MISO), New England (ISO-NE), New York (NYISO), the Mid-Atlantic states (PJM), California (CAISO), the Southwest (SPP), and Texas (ERCOT).

A core feature of FERC's design is a reliance on *locational marginal prices* (*LMPs*) to manage transmission grid congestion. Under this pricing system, the price (LMP) charged to wholesale buyers and received by wholesale sellers at a particular grid bus at a particular point in time is the least cost to the system of providing an additional increment of power at that bus at that time.

A key fact about LMPs is that congestion arising on any transmission grid branch necessarily results in separation between the LMPs at two or more grid buses. Pre-

Fig. 2 Architecture of the AMES Wholesale Power Market Test Bed

- **Traders**
  - LSEs (bulk-power buyers)
  - GenCos (bulk-power sellers with ***learning capabilities***)
- **Independent System Operator (ISO)**
  - Day-ahead hourly scheduling via ***bid/offer-based DC OPF***
  - System reliability assessments
- **Two-settlement process**
  - ***Day-ahead market*** (double auction, financial contracts)
  - ***Real-time market*** (settlement of differences)
- **AC transmission grid**
  - LSEs & GenCos located at user-specified buses across the transmission grid
  - Congestion managed via ***Locational Marginal Pricing (LMP)***.

vious studies have derived analytical expressions for LMPs at a point in time, conditional on given grid, demand, and supply conditions; see, for example, Conejo et al. (2005) and Orfanogianni and Gross (2007). These studies highlight the critical roles played by transmission grid branch constraints and generator production capacity limits in the determination of LMPs. In addition, numerous researchers have empirically investigated the autocorrelation patterns in LMPs as part of price forecasting studies; see, for example, Zhou et al. (2009). To our knowledge, however, no previous research has focused on the spatial cross-correlation patterns deliberately or inadvertently induced in LMPs by strategically learning power traders.

This study uses controlled experiments for a 5-bus test case to explore spatial cross-correlation patterns induced in LMPs under systematically varied conditions for the price-sensitivity of wholesale power demand when generation companies have learning capabilities. All experiments were conducted using Version 2.05 of the AMES Wholesale Power Market Test Bed (AMES 2010), a Java software package developed by H. Li, J. Sun, and L. Tesfatsion. The key features of AMES used in this study are explained in the following section.

3 AMES Wholesale Power Market Test Bed

AMES(V2.05) captures key features of wholesale power market operations in U.S. energy regions operating under FERC's wholesale power market design (FERC 2003). These key features are listed in Fig. 2 and briefly described below.[1]

The AMES(V2.05) wholesale power market operates over an AC transmission grid starting with hour H00 of day 1 and continuing through hour H23 of a user-specified maximum day. AMES includes an *Independent System Operator* (*ISO*) and a collection of energy traders consisting of *Load-Serving Entities* (*LSEs*) $j = 1, \ldots, J$ and *Generation Companies* (*GenCos*) $i = 1, \ldots, I$ distributed across the buses of the transmission grid.

---

[1]For a more detailed description of AMES, including pointers to tutorials, manuals, and downloadable code, see AMES (2010), Li and Tesfatsion (2009). AMES is an acronym for *A*gent-based *M*odeling of *E*lectricity *S*ystems. Annotated pointers to other agent-based electricity research can be accessed at Tesfatsion (2010c).

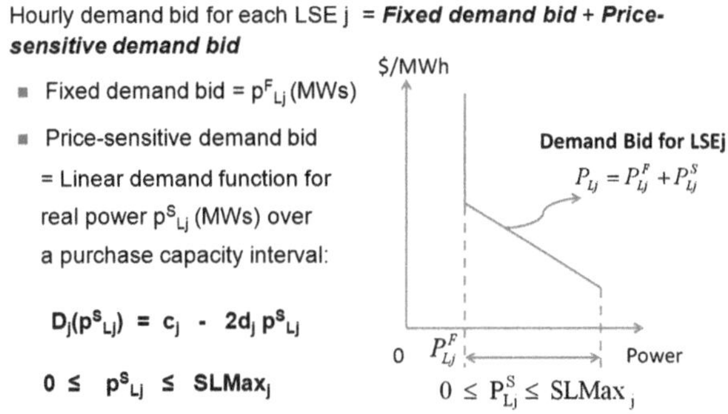

Fig. 3 AMES LSE demand bids consist of fixed and price-sensitive parts

The objective of the not-for-profit ISO is the maximization of *Total Net Surplus* (*TNS*) subject to transmission constraints and GenCo operating capacity limits. In an attempt to attain this objective, the ISO operates a day-ahead energy market settled by means of *locational marginal prices* (*LMPs*).

The objective of each LSE j is to secure for itself the highest possible daily net earnings through purchases of power in the day-ahead market and resale of this power to retail customers. During the morning of each day D, each LSE j reports a *demand bid* to the ISO for the day-ahead market for day $D+1$. Each demand bid consists of two parts: fixed demand (i.e., a 24-hour load profile) that can be sold downstream at a regulated rate to retail customers with flat-rate pricing contracts; and 24 price-sensitive inverse demand functions, one for each hour, reflecting price-sensitive demand (willingness to pay) by retail customers with real-time pricing contracts. Figure 3 illustrates the form of a demand bid for a particular hour H. LSEs have no learning capabilities; demand bids for LSEs are user-specified at the beginning of each simulation run.

The objective of each GenCo i is to secure for itself the highest possible daily net earnings through the sale of power in the day-ahead market. GenCos have learning capabilities.[2] During the morning of each day D, each GenCo i uses its current "action choice probabilities" to choose a supply offer from its action domain AD_i to report to the ISO for use in all 24 hours of the day-ahead market for day $D+1$. As depicted in Fig. 4, this *supply offer* consists of a reported marginal cost function $\mathrm{MC}_i^R(p_{Gi}) = a_i^R + 2b_i^R p_{Gi}$ defined over a reported operating capacity interval $[\mathrm{Cap}_i^L, \mathrm{Cap}_i^{RU}]$. GenCo i's ability to vary its choice of a supply offer from AD_i permits it to adjust the ordinate a_i^R, slope $2b_i^R$, and upper operating capacity limit Cap_i^{RU} for its reported marginal cost function in an attempt to increase its daily net earnings.

After receiving demand bids from LSEs and supply offers from GenCos during the morning of day D, the ISO determines and publicly posts hourly LMP and dispatch levels for the day-ahead market for day $D+1$. These hourly outcomes are determined via *Security-Constrained Economic Dispatch* (*SCED*) formulated as

[2]A detailed presentation of GenCo learning is given below in Sect. 4.2.1.

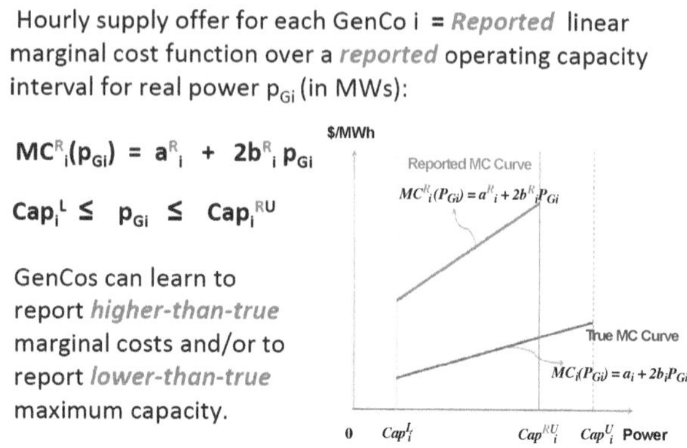

Fig. 4 AMES GenCos with learning capabilities report strategic supply offers to the ISO

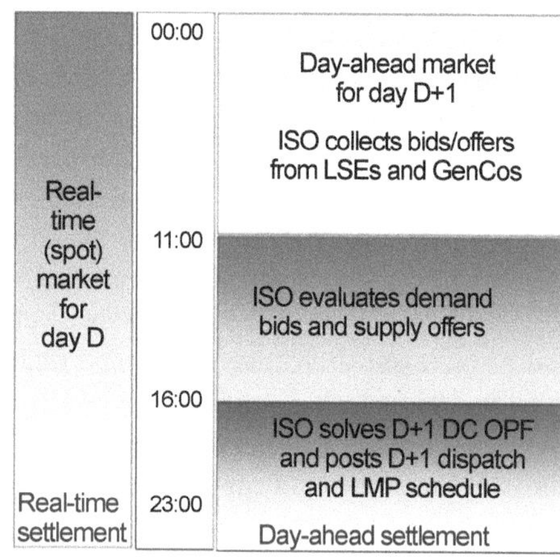

Fig. 5 AMES ISO activities during a typical day *D*

bid/offer-based DC optimal power flow (OPF) problems with approximated TNS objective functions based on reported rather than true GenCo costs. Grid congestion is managed by the inclusion of congestion cost components in LMPs. At the end of each day D the ISO settles the day-ahead market for day $D + 1$ by receiving all purchase payments from LSEs and making all sale payments to GenCos based on the LMPs for the day-ahead market for day $D + 1$, collecting the difference as *ISO net surplus*. The activities of the ISO on a typical day D are depicted in Fig. 5.

Each GenCo i at the end of each day D uses stochastic reinforcement learning to update the action choice probabilities currently assigned to the supply offers in its action domain AD_i, taking into account its day-D settlement payment ("reward"). In particular, if GenCo i's supply offer on day D results in a relatively good reward, GenCo i increases the probability it will choose to report this same supply offer on day $D + 1$, and conversely.

There are no system disturbances (e.g., weather changes) or shocks (e.g., line outages). Consequently, the dispatch levels determined on each day D for the day-

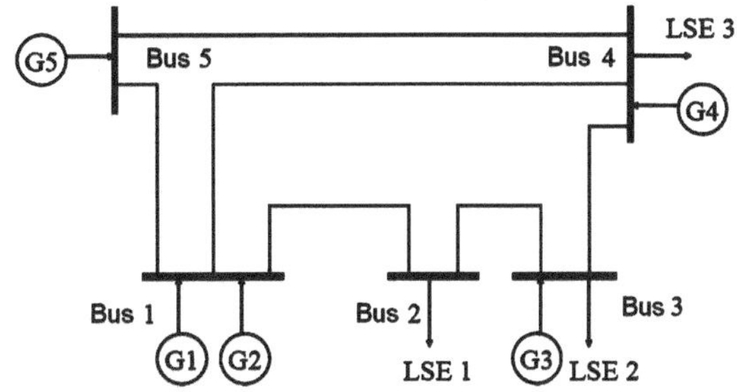

Fig. 6 Transmission grid for the benchmark dynamic 5-bus test case

ahead market for day $D + 1$ are carried out as planned without need for settlement of differences in the real-time market.

4 Experimental Design

As detailed below, our experimental design is based on a multi-period version of a static 5-bus test case commonly used in ISO business practices manuals and training programs to illustrate market operations. Two treatment factors are selected for the experimental design. The first treatment factor is the degree to which GenCos can learn to exercise *economic capacity withholding*, i.e., the reporting of higher-than-true marginal costs. The second treatment factor is the degree to which LSEs report fixed versus price-sensitive demand bids, an increasingly important issue as pressures increase for more demand response in wholesale power markets (Kiesling 2007; FERC 2008).

Three key issues are highlighted in this experimental design. First, given fixed demands, how are bus LMPs affected by the introduction of learning capabilities for the GenCos that permit them to strategically adjust their supply offers over time? Second, given fixed demands, how do network effects and the strategically reported supply offers of the learning GenCos affect the spatial cross-correlations exhibited by bus LMPs? Third, how do the spatial cross-correlations for bus LMPs change in response to systematic increases in demand-bid price sensitivity?

4.1 Benchmark Dynamic 5-Bus Test Case

Our experimental design is anchored by a *benchmark dynamic 5-bus test case* described in full detail in Li et al. (2009). This benchmark case is characterized by the following structural, institutional, and behavioral conditions:

- The wholesale power market operates over a 5-bus transmission grid as depicted in Fig. 6, with branch reactances, locations of LSEs and GenCos, and initial hour-0 LSE fixed demand levels adopted from a static 5-bus test case (Lally 2002) developed for ISO training purposes.

Fig. 7 GenCo true marginal cost functions and true capacity attributes for the benchmark dynamic 5-bus test case

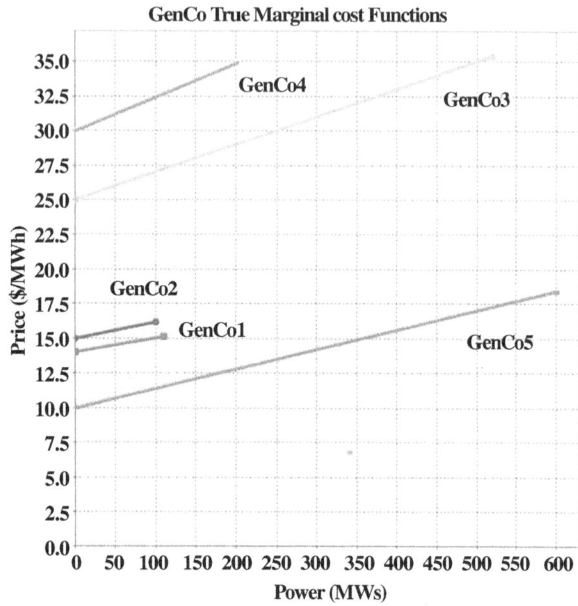

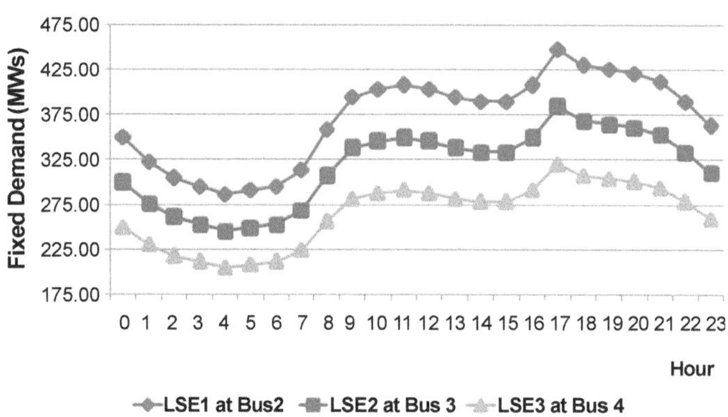

Fig. 8 Fixed demand (load profiles) for the benchmark dynamic 5-bus test case

- True GenCo cost and capacity attributes are as depicted in Fig. 7. GenCos range from GenCo 5, a relatively large coal-fired baseload unit with low marginal operating costs, to GenCo 4, a relatively small gas-fired peaking unit with relatively high marginal operating costs.
- Demand is 100% fixed (no price sensitivity) with LSE daily fixed-demand profiles adopted from a case study presented in Shahidehpour et al. (2002, pp. 296–297). As depicted in Fig. 8, hourly load varies from light (hour H04) to peak (hour H17).
- GenCos are non-learners, meaning they report supply offers to the ISO that convey their true marginal cost functions and true operating capacity limits.

4.2 Learning Treatments

Each GenCo i has available an *action domain* AD_i consisting of a finite number of possible supply offers. For the study at hand, a *supply offer* for any GenCo i takes the form of a reported marginal cost function $\mathrm{MC}_i^R(p_{Gi}) = a_i^R + 2b_i^R p_{Gi}$ that can be summarized by a vector $s_i^R = (a_i^R, b_i^R)$ determining its ordinate a_i^R and slope $2b_i^R$; see Fig. 4.[3]

The action domain AD_i is tailored to GenCo i's own particular true cost and capacity attributes. In particular, AD_i only contains reportable marginal cost functions $\mathrm{MC}_i^R(p_{Gi})$ lying on or above GenCo i's true marginal cost function $\mathrm{MC}_i(p_{Gi}) = a_i + 2b_i p_{Gi}$, and AD_i always contains this true marginal cost function. However, the action domains are constructed so as to ensure equal cardinalities and similar densities across all GenCos to avoid favoring some GenCos over others purely through action domain construction.[4]

In learning treatments, each GenCo makes daily use of stochastic reinforcement learning to adjust its supply offers in pursuit of increased daily net earnings. As detailed below in Sect. 4.2.1, GenCo learning is implemented by means of a variant of a stochastic reinforcement learning algorithm developed by Roth and Erev (1995, 1998) based on human-subject experiments, hereafter referred to as the *VRE learning algorithm.*

For experimental treatments with GenCo VRE learning, we use 30 pseudo-random number seed values to initialize 30 distinct runs, each 1000 simulated days in length.[5] To control for random effects, outcomes are then reported as mean values across all 30 runs.

4.2.1 VRE Learning Algorithm

This section describes how an arbitrary GenCo i goes about using the VRE learning algorithm to select supply offers s_i^R from its action domain AD_i to report to the ISO for the day-ahead market on successive days D, starting from an initial day $D = 1$. As will be seen below, the only relevant attribute of AD_i for implementation of VRE learning is that it has finite cardinality. Consequently, letting $M_i \geq 1$ denote the cardinality of AD_i, it suffices to index the supply offers ("actions") in AD_i by $m = 1, \ldots, M_i$.

---

[3]In the present study it is assumed for simplicity that GenCos only strategically report the ordinate and slope values for their marginal cost functions. They always truthfully report their upper operating capacity limits Cap^U.

[4]A detailed explanation of this action domain construction can be found in Li et al. (2009, Appendix B).

[5]These 30 seed values, together with all parameter value settings used for action domain construction and implementation of the VRE learning algorithm, are provided in the input data file for the 5-bus test case included with the AMES(V2.05) download (AMES 2010).

The *initial propensity* of GenCo i to choose action $m \in \text{AD}_i$ is given by $q_{im}(1)$ for $m = 1, \ldots, M_i$. AMES(V2.05) permits the user to set these initial propensity levels to any real numbers. However, the assumption used in this study is that GenCo i's initial propensity levels are all set equal to some common value $q_i(1)$, as follows:

$$q_{im}(1) = q_i(1) \quad \text{for all actions } m \in \text{AD}_i \tag{1}$$

Now consider the beginning of any day $D \geq 1$, and suppose the current propensity of GenCo i to choose action m in AD_i is given by $q_{im}(D)$. The *choice probabilities* that GenCo i uses to select an action for day D are then constructed from these propensities using the following commonly used Gibbs-Boltzmann transformation:

$$p_{im}(D) = \frac{\exp(q_{im}(D)/T_i)}{\sum_{j=1}^{M_i} \exp(q_{ij}(D)/T_i)}, \quad m \in \text{AD}_i \tag{2}$$

In (2), T_i is a *temperature parameter* that affects the degree to which GenCo i makes use of propensity values in determining its choice probabilities. As $T_i \to \infty$, then $p_{im}(D) \to 1/M_i$, so that in the limit GenCo i pays no attention to propensity values in forming its choice probabilities. On the other hand, as $T_i \to 0$, the choice probabilities (2) become increasingly peaked over the particular actions m having the highest propensity values $q_{im}(D)$, thereby increasing the probability that these actions will be chosen.

At the end of day D, the current propensity $q_{im}(D)$ that GenCo i associates with each action m in AD_i is updated in accordance with the following rule. Let m' denote the action *actually* selected and reported into the day-ahead market by GenCo i in day D. Also, let $\text{NE}_{im'}(D)$ denote the *actual* daily net earnings (revenues minus avoidable costs) attained by GenCo i at the end of day D as its settlement payment for all 24 hours of the day-ahead market for day $D+1$.[6]

Then, for each action m in AD_i,

$$q_{im}(D+1) = [1 - r_i]q_{im}(D) + \text{Response}_{im}(D), \tag{3}$$

where

$$\text{Response}_{im}(D) = \begin{cases} [1 - e_i] \cdot \text{NE}_{im'}(D) & \text{if } m = m' \\ e_i \cdot q_{im}(D)/[M_i - 1] & \text{if } m \neq m', \end{cases} \tag{4}$$

and $m \neq m'$ implies $M_i \geq 2$. The introduction of the *recency parameter* r_i in (3) acts as a damper on the growth of the propensities over time. The *experimentation parameter* e_i in (4) permits reinforcement to spill over to some extent from a chosen action to other actions to encourage continued experimentation with various actions in the early stages of the learning process.

---

[6] At the beginning of any planning period, a GenCo's *avoidable costs* refer to the costs it can avoid during the period by shutting down production and possibly taking other actions (e.g., asset re-use or re-sale). In order for production to proceed, revenues from production should at least cover avoidable costs. In the present study the GenCos do not incur start-up/shut-down or no-load costs, and all of their asset expenditures are assumed to be *sunk costs* (not recoverable by re-use or re-sale). Consequently, the *avoidable costs* $\text{VC}_i(p^*_{Gi})$ for each GenCo i associated with a real power production level p^*_{Gi} in any given hour H is the integral of its true marginal cost function $\text{MC}_i(p_{Gi}) = a_i + 2b_i p_{Gi}$ over the interval from 0 to p^*_{Gi}.

4.2.2 Calibration of VRE Learning Parameters

As a prelude to conducting experiments with GenCo VRE learning for the dynamic 5-bus test case, we calibrated each GenCo's VRE learning parameter settings to its particular choice environment. We first set common "sweet spot" values $(r, e) = (0.04, 0.96)$ across the GenCos for the recency and experimentation parameters r_i and e_i in (3) and (4) based on the dynamic 5-bus test case analysis conducted by Pentapalli (2008). Given this (r, e) setting, we then conducted intensive parameter sweeps to determine individual "sweet spot" settings for each GenCo i's initial propensity $q_i(1)$ in (1) and temperature parameter T_i in (2).

More precisely, regarding the latter step, we defined two derived VRE learning parameters (α_i, β_i) for each GenCo i as follows. We proxied GenCo i's daily net earnings aspirations in normalized form at the beginning of the initial day 1 by constructing the ratio

$$\alpha_i = \frac{q_i(1)}{\text{MaxDNE}_i} \tag{5}$$

of GenCo i's initial propensity $q_i(1)$ in (1) to an approximate valuation $\text{MaxDNE}_i = [24 \cdot \text{MC}_i(\text{Cap}_i^U) \cdot \text{Cap}_i^U]$ for GenCo i's maximum possible daily net earnings. We also defined the ratio

$$\beta_i = \frac{q_i(1)}{T_i} \tag{6}$$

of $q_i(1)$ in (1) to GenCo i's temperature parameter T_i in (2). We then conducted an intensive set of experiments for the dynamic 5-bus test case under alternative specifications for (α, β), set commonly across the GenCos, with LSE demand maintained at 100% fixed ($R = 0.0$).

Figure 9 displays a 3D visualization for the mean total GenCo daily net earnings on day 1000 resulting under the variously tested specifications for (α, β). Two interesting findings are immediately evident. First, the specification for (α, β) substantially affects GenCo net earnings outcomes. Second, the highest net earnings are associated with "sweet spot" (α, β) combinations that lie along a nonlinear ridge line ranging from $(\alpha, \beta) = (1, 100)$ in the northwest corner to $(\alpha, \beta) = (1/24, 2)$ in the south-central region.

The particular sweet-spot specification $(\alpha, \beta) = (1, 100)$ is used in all of the learning experiments reported below in Sect. 5.

4.3 Demand Treatments

The linearity of the LSEs' price-sensitive demand bids implies that price-elasticity of demand varies all along the plots of these functions. Hence, elasticity cannot easily be used to parameterize their sensitivity to price.

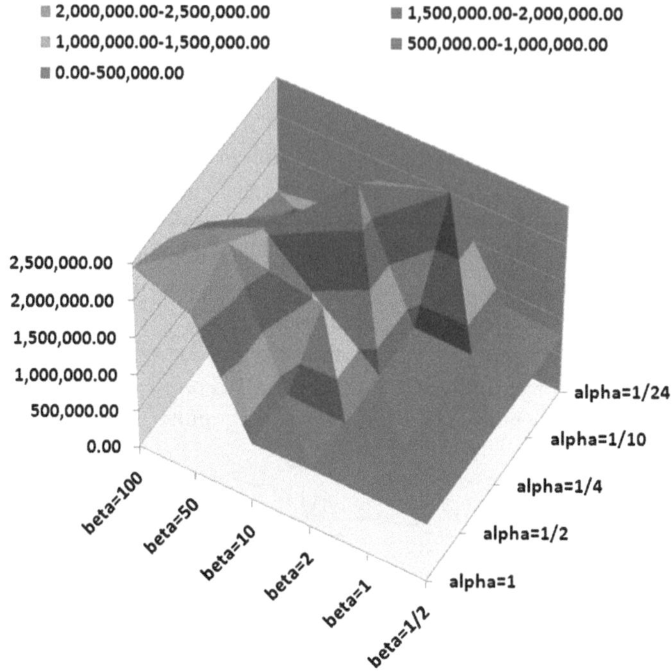

Fig. 9 A 3D depiction of mean outcomes for total GenCo daily net earnings on day 1000 for the dynamic 5-bus test case with GenCo VRE learning and 100% fixed LSE demand ($R = 0.0$) under alternative settings for the derived VRE learning parameters (α, β)

To investigate the effects of changes in LSE demand-bid price sensitivity both with and without GenCo VRE learning, we first defined the R-ratio

$$R_j(H, D) = \frac{\text{SLMax}_j(H, D)}{[p^F_{Lj}(H, D) + \text{SLMax}_j(H, D)]} \tag{7}$$

The numerator of (7) denotes LSE j's maximum potential price-sensitive demand $\text{SLMax}_j(H, D)$ for hour H of the day-ahead market in day $D + 1$; see Fig. 3. The denominator of (7) denotes LSE j's maximum potential total demand for hour H of the day-ahead market in day $D + 1$, i.e., the sum of its fixed demand and maximum potential price-sensitive demand. Figure 10 illustrates the construction of the R-ratio (7) for the special cases $R = 0.0$, $R = 0.5$, and $R = 1.0$.

We next set all of the LSE fixed demands $p^F_{Lj}(H, D)$ to their positive benchmark-case values $\text{BP}^F_{Lj}(H)$ (differing by hour but not by day) and all of the maximum potential price-sensitive demands $\text{SLMax}_j(H, D)$ to their benchmark-case value 0, thus obtaining a common R-ratio value of $R = 0.0$ across all LSEs j for each H and D. We then systematically varied the settings for $p^F_{Lj}(H, D)$ from their benchmark-case values to 0, and the settings for $\text{SLMax}_j(H, D)$ from 0 to the positive benchmark-case values $\text{BP}^F_{Lj}(H)$ for fixed demand, which resulted in a sequence of common R-ratio values for the LSEs ranging from $R = 0.0$ (100% fixed demand) to $R = 1.0$ (100% price-sensitive demand).

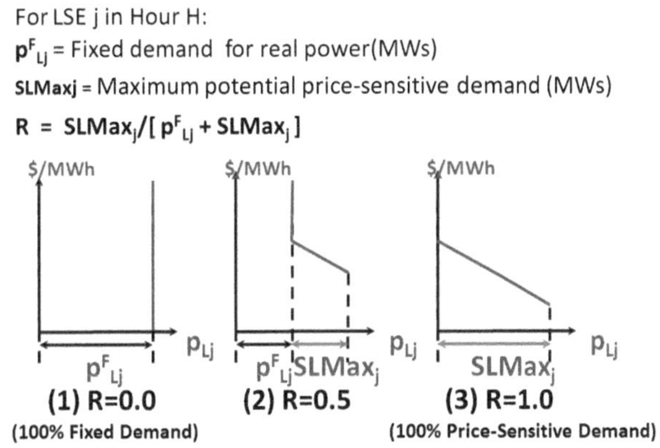

Fig. 10 Illustration of the R-ratio construction for the experimental control of relative demand-bid price sensitivity in each hour H

To prevent confounding effects arising from changes in the ordinate and slope values of the LSE price-sensitive demand bids, these ordinate and slope values were held fixed across all experiments. The specific settings for these fixed ordinate and slope values (along with all benchmark-case values $\mathrm{BP}^F_{Lj}(H)$ for LSE fixed demands) are provided in the input data file for the 5-bus test case included with the AMES(V2.05) download (AMES 2010).

5 Experimental Findings

As shown in Fig. 11, GenCo VRE learning and LSE demand-bid price sensitivity critically affect mean LMP outcomes for the dynamic 5-bus test case. In particular, relative to the benchmark (no learning) case, the mean LMP value on day 1000 increases for each given R-ratio value when GenCos are permitted to have VRE learning capabilities. This increase is particularly dramatic for small R-ratio values corresponding to low price-sensitivity of demand.

However, the mean LMP outcomes reported in Fig. 11 do not provide any information regarding the potentially correlated impact of learning and demand-bid price sensitivity on the spatial distribution of LMPs across buses. This section presents experimental findings showing how LMP spatial cross-correlation patterns are systematically affected by changes in GenCo learning capabilities and the price-sensitivity of LSE demand.[7]

5.1 Correlation Experiment Preliminaries

Two types of experimental findings are reported below: (a) pairwise cross-correlations between GenCo reported marginal costs and bus LMPs evaluated at

[7]For a fuller presentation of our correlation experiment findings, including detailed comparisons with the no-learning benchmark case, see Li et al. (2009).

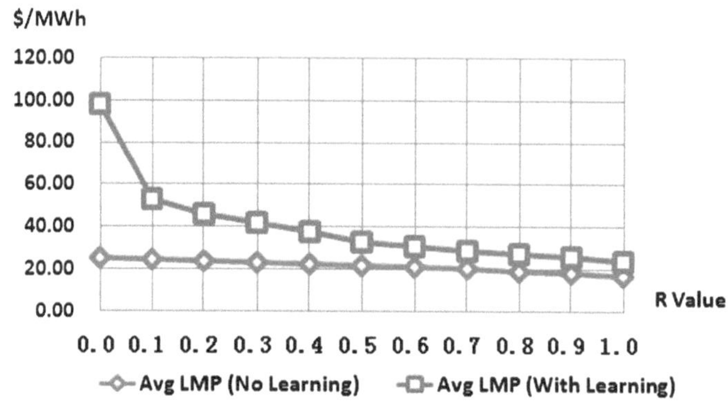

Fig. 11 Mean outcomes for average hourly LMP values on day 1000 for the dynamic 5-bus test case with GenCo VRE learning and LSE demand varying from $R = 0.0$ (100% fixed) to $R = 1.0$ (100% price sensitive)

dispatch operating points; and (b) pairwise cross-correlations between bus LMPs evaluated at dispatch operating points.

In each case the cross-correlations are reported at four representative hours from the LSE load profiles depicted in Fig. 8: the off-peak hour H04; the shoulder hour H11; the peak-demand hour H17; and the shoulder hour H20. Moreover, for each hour the two types of cross-correlations are reported for three different demand scenarios as characterized by three different settings for the R-ratio. In total, then, 24 distinct cross-correlation treatments ($2 \times 4 \times 3$) are reported below.

Illustrative findings are depicted using correlation diagrams as well as tables. Each correlation diagram uses shape, shape direction, and color to convey information about the sign and strength of the resulting pairwise cross-correlations.

The shapes and shape directions in the correlation diagrams are rough indicators of the patterns observed in the underlying scatter plots for the two random variables whose cross-correlation is under examination. Color is used to reinforce shape and shape direction information.

More precisely, if a scatter plot for two random variables X and Y roughly lies along a straight line, this suggests that X and Y are perfectly correlated. If the line is positively sloped, the indication is perfect positive correlation (1.0); if the line is negatively sloped, the indication is perfect negative correlation (-1.0). The correlation diagrams indicate these possible scatter-plot patterns by means of straight lines that are either forward or backward slanted to indicate positive or negative correlation respectively. Conversely, if the scatter plot for X and Y instead consists of a roughly rectangular cloud of points, this indicates that X and Y are independent of each other, implying zero correlation. The correlation diagrams indicate this scatter-plot pattern by means of full circles. Intermediate to this are scatter plots for X and Y that are roughly elliptical in shape, indicating moderate but not perfect correlation between X and Y. The correlation diagrams indicate this scatter-plot pattern by means of oval shapes that point to the right for positive correlation values and to the left for negative correlation values.

Table 1 Pairwise cross-correlations between GenCo reported marginal costs and bus LMPs at the peak-demand hour H17 of day 1000 for the dynamic 5-bus test case with GenCo VRE learning and 100% fixed LSE demand ($R = 0.0$)

	LMP 1	LMP 2	LMP 3	LMP 4	LMP 5
G1	0.3136	−0.2244	−0.2143	−0.0718	0.2879
G2	0.4150	0.1344	0.1591	0.4148	0.5042
G3	−0.1164	0.5147	0.5222	0.5363	0.0163
G4	−0.2711	0.4641	0.4625	0.3811	−0.1718
G5	0.9704	−0.3125	−0.2712	0.2293	1.0000

Red-colored shapes indicate positive correlation and blue-colored shapes indicate negative correlation. The intensity of the red (blue) color indicates the degree of the positive (negative) correlation.

5.2 GenCo-LMP Cross-Correlations

Table 1 presents pairwise cross-correlations between GenCo reported marginal costs and bus LMPs for the peak-demand hour H17 of day 1000 for the dynamic 5-bus test case with GenCo VRE learning and 100% fixed LSE demand ($R = 0.0$). These cross-correlations indicate positive correlation between GenCo 3 and the LMPs at buses 2–4, negative correlation between GenCo 4 and the LMPs at buses 1 and 5, and strong positive correlation between GenCo 5 and the LMPs at buses 1 and 5. What explains this correlation pattern?

One important explanatory factor is branch congestion and direction of branch power flows during hour H17. As detailed in Li et al. (2009), the branch 1–2 connecting bus 1 and bus 2 is typically congested in every hour under learning. Consequently, buses 2–4 constitute a demand pocket for GenCo 3 located at bus 3. It is therefore not surprising that GenCo 3's reported marginal costs are positively correlated with the LMPs at these demand-pocket buses during the peak-demand hour H17.

In addition, the persistent congestion on branch 1–2 results in a negative correlation between the reported marginal cost for GenCo 4 at bus 4 and the LMPs at buses 1 and 5 during the peak-demand hour H17. This happens because the power injected by GenCo 4 during hour H17 substitutes in part for the cheaper power of GenCos 1 and 5 in servicing demand at the demand-pocket buses 2–4. This substitution occurs because GenCos 1 and 5 are located at buses 1 and 5 and hence are semi-islanded behind the congested branch 1–2 during hour H17 as dictated by the directions of branch power flows.

A second important explanatory factor is limits on generation operating capacities during hour H17, which affect the marginal status of the different GenCos.[8] As is well known (see Orfanogianni and Gross 2007), the LMP at each bus with a

[8] A GenCo is said to be *marginal* if its minimum and maximum operating capacity limits are not binding at its dispatch point.

Table 2 Frequency of GenCo marginality across 30 runs measured at four different hours on day 1000 for the dynamic 5-bus test case with GenCo VRE learning and 100% fixed LSE demand ($R = 0.0$)

	G1	G2	G3	G4	G5
H04	13%	37%	100%	37%	100%
H11	10%	30%	100%	20%	100%
H17	10%	23%	87%	20%	100%
H20	10%	30%	100%	13%	100%

marginal GenCo is given by the reported marginal cost of this GenCo whereas the LMP at each bus without a marginal GenCo is given by a weighted linear combination of the reported marginal costs of the marginal GenCos.

As indicated in Table 2, GenCo 5 located at bus 5 is persistently marginal during the peak-demand hour H17, hence the LMP at bus 5 persistently coincides with GenCo 5's reported marginal cost. This explains the finding in Table 1 of a perfect positive correlation of 1.0 between GenCo 5's reported marginal cost and the LMP at bus 5 during hour H17.

Table 2 also indicates that no other GenCo is persistently marginal during hour H17. For example, GenCo 3 is dispatched at maximum operating capacity in 13% of the runs due either to a relatively low reported marginal cost by GenCo 3 or a relatively high reported marginal cost by GenCo 4. This non-marginality of GenCo 3 restrains the positive correlation between GenCo 3's reported marginal costs and the LMPs at the demand-pocket buses 2–4 as well as the extent to which power supplied by GenCo 3 can substitute for the power of GenCos 1 and 5 during H17.

The correlation diagram in Fig. 12 for the peak-demand hour H17 provides a visualization of the GenCo-LMP cross-correlation findings in Table 1. In particular, it helps to highlight the importance of GenCos 3 and 4 for the determination of LMPs at the demand-pocket buses 2–4, and the importance of GenCo 5 for the determination of LMPs at buses 1 and 5.

The remaining correlation diagrams in Fig. 12 depict the GenCo-LMP cross-correlations that arise in the off-peak hour H04, the shoulder hour H11, and the shoulder hour H20. Comparing these results to the results depicted in Fig. 12 for the peak-demand hour H17, note that GenCo 3's reported marginal cost is now perfectly positively correlated with the LMP at bus 3 and is strongly positively correlated with the LMPs at its neighboring buses 2 and 4. These changes arise because the substantially lower fixed demand in these three non-peak hours results in the persistent marginality of the relatively large GenCo 3; see Table 2.

Also, in contrast to the peak-demand hour H17, GenCo 4's reported marginal cost is negatively correlated with the LMPs at buses 2 and 3 in the three non-peak hours. This occurs because GenCo 4 is in direct rivalry with the marginal GenCo 3 to supply power to buses 2 and 3 during these non-peak hours. For example, GenCo 4 is dispatched at maximum capacity when its reported marginal cost is relatively low, which then permits GenCo 3 to service residual demand at buses 2 and 3 at a relatively high reported marginal cost.

Figures 13 and 14 report the effects on GenCo-LMP cross-correlations when the R-ratio for measuring relative price-sensitivity of LSE demand is systematically in-

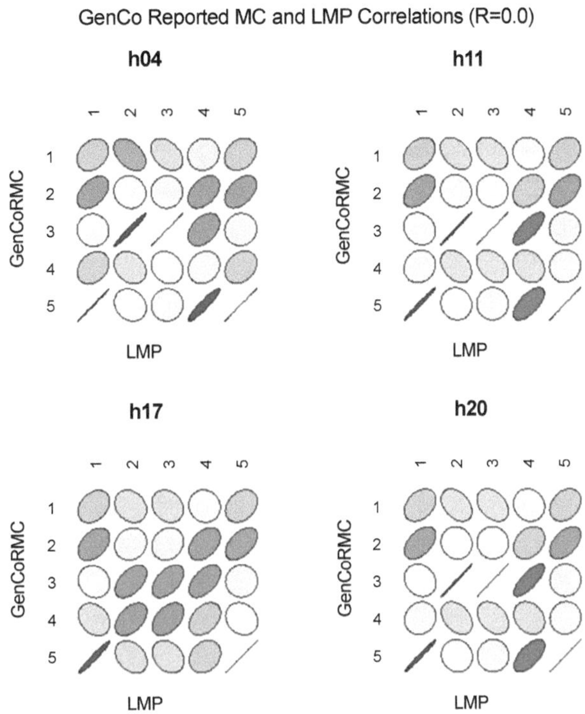

Fig. 12 Pairwise cross-correlations between GenCo reported marginal costs and bus LMPs for hours H04, H11, H17, and H20 on day 1000 for the dynamic 5-bus test case with GenCo VRE learning and 100% fixed LSE demand ($R = 0.0$)

creased first to $R = 0.5$ (50% potential price sensitivity) and then to $R = 1.0$ (100% price sensitivity). As demand becomes more price sensitive, the LSEs more strongly contract their demand in response to price increases and branch congestion becomes less frequent. This limits the GenCos' ability to profitably exercise economic withholding, i.e., to profitably report higher-than-true marginal costs.

In particular, as R increases, the GenCos with relatively low true marginal costs are advantaged and those with relatively high true marginal costs lose out. This can be seen by comparing the correlation diagrams in Figs. 12 through 14. As R increases from $R = 0.0$ to $R = 1.0$, the relatively cheap GenCo 5 gains increased influence over each bus LMP while the relatively expensive GenCo 3 loses influence over the demand-pocket buses 2 through 4.

5.3 *LMP Cross-Correlations*

Table 3 reports pairwise cross-correlations for the bus LMPs during the peak-demand hour H17 on day 1000 for the benchmark dynamic 5-bus test case extended to include GenCo VRE learning. Figures 15, 16, 17 depict the changes induced in these cross-correlations when the price-sensitivity of demand is systematically increased from $R = 0.0$ (100% fixed) to $R = 1.0$ (100% price sensitive).

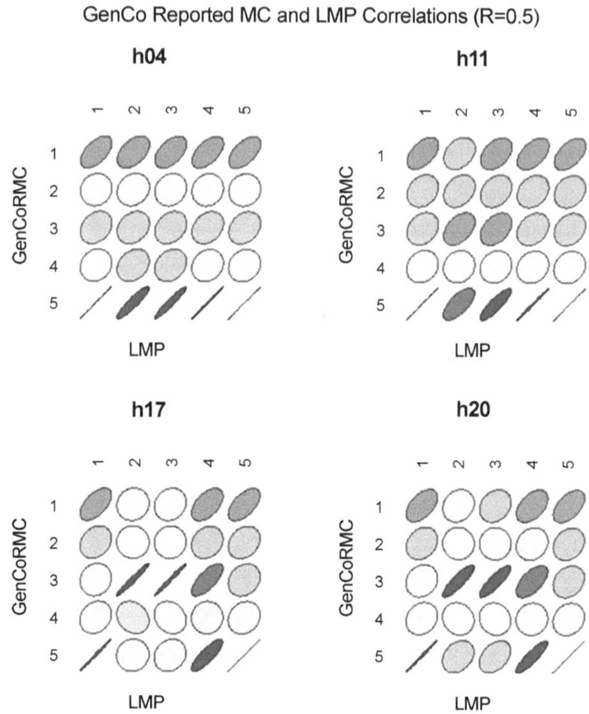

Fig. 13 Pairwise cross-correlations between GenCo reported marginal costs and bus LMPs for hours H04, H11, H17, and H20 on day 1000 for the dynamic 5-bus test case with GenCo VRE learning and 50% fixed LSE potential demand ($R = 0.5$)

Table 3 Pairwise cross-correlations between bus LMPs at the peak-demand hour H17 of day 1000 for the dynamic 5-bus test case with GenCo VRE learning and 100% fixed LSE demand ($R = 0.0$)

	LMP 1	LMP 2	LMP 3	LMP 4	LMP 5
LMP 1	1.0000	−0.5328	−0.4957	−0.0127	0.9704
LMP 2		1.0000	0.9991	0.8530	−0.3125
LMP 3			1.0000	0.8747	−0.2712
LMP 4				1.0000	0.2293
LMP 5					1.0000

The main regularity seen in Table 3 results is that all of the LMP cross-correlations become increasingly positive as R increases. This is particularly true for the non-peak hours H04, H11, and H20 with relatively lower LSE fixed demands.

As R increases, a larger portion of LSE total demand is price sensitive. Consequently, the LSEs are able to exercise more resistance to higher prices through demand contraction, which in turn reduces branch congestion. In the current context, bus LMPs are derived from bid/offer-based DC OPF solutions with zero losses assumed.[9] Consequently, as congestion diminishes, the LMPs exhibit less separation. In the limit, if all congestion were to disappear, the LMPs would converge to

[9]See Liu et al. (2009) for a rigorous presentation of this LMP derivation.

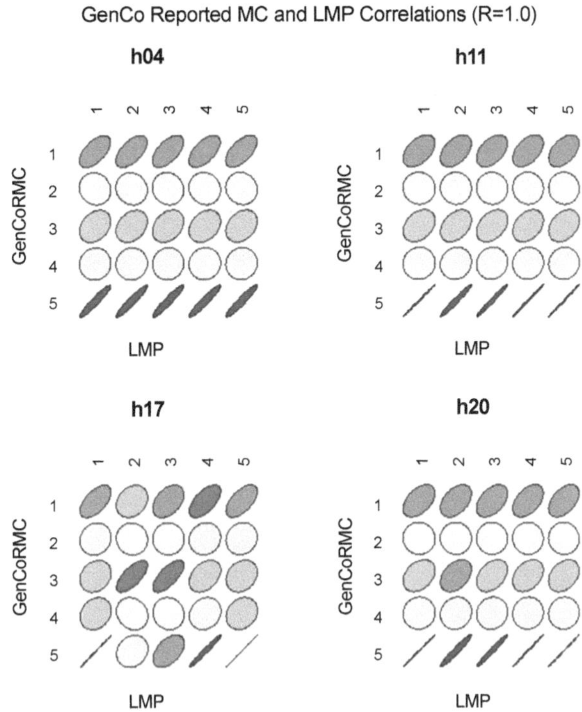

Fig. 14 Pairwise cross-correlations between GenCo reported marginal costs and bus LMPs for hours H04, H11, H17, and H20 on day 1000 for the dynamic 5-bus test case with GenCo VRE learning and 100% price-sensitive LSE demand ($R = 1.0$)

a single uniform price across the grid, which in turn would imply perfect positive correlation among all bus LMPs.

For the non-peak hours H04, H11, and H20, the typical result for the limiting case $R = 1.0$ is no branch congestion. Hence, the bus LMPs during these hours—particularly hour H04—are close to being perfectly positively correlated when $R = 1.0$. For the peak-demand hour H17, however, the branch 1–2 is typically congested even for $R = 1.0$. Consequently, LMP cross-correlations for hour H17 exhibit a strong but not perfect positive correlation.

Another regularity seen in Table 3, and graphically visualized in Figs. 15 through 17, is that the LMP at bus 2 is always strongly positively correlated with the LMP at bus 3. At high R levels, this reflects a lack of branch congestion and hence a lack of LMP separation. At low R levels, however, the branch 1–2 tends to be congested at all hours. The congestion on branch 1–2 means that the bulk of the demand at the load-only bus 2 must be supplied along branch 3-2 by the large and frequently marginal GenCo 3. This in turn means that the LMP at bus 2 is most strongly influenced by the LMP at bus 3.

6 Empirical Evidence on LMP Cross-Correlations

This section presents LMP cross-correlations calculated using real-world price data. In particular, we focus on LMP determination in a neighborhood of the *MidAmeri-*

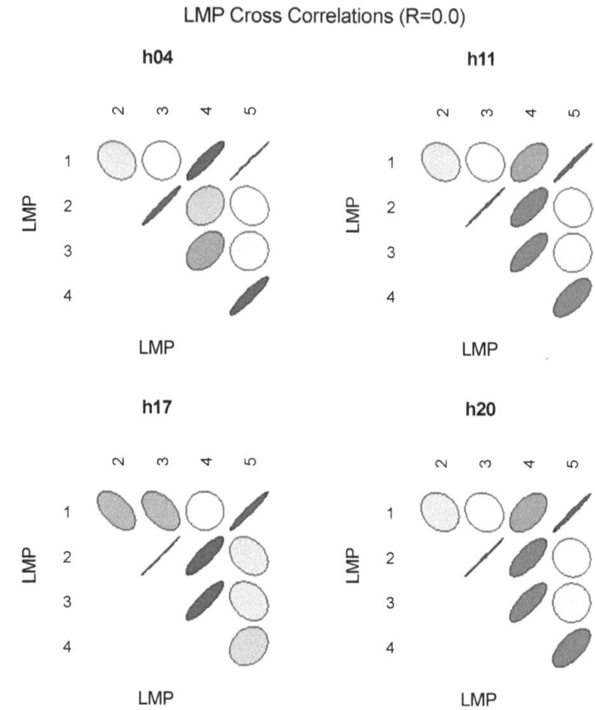

Fig. 15 Pairwise LMP cross-correlations for hours H04, H11, H17, and H20 on day 1000 for the dynamic 5-bus test case with GenCo VRE learning and 100% fixed LSE demand ($R = 0.0$)

can Energy Company (*MEC*), the largest utility in Iowa. Through April 2009, MEC was treated as a *Balancing Authority* (*BA*) in MISO.[10] A BA is responsible for maintaining load-interchange-generation balance and Interconnection frequency support.

From the geographical map depicted in Fig. 18, we picked four neighboring BAs of MEC in order to study MEC's effect on their LMPs. These BAs are *Alliant Energy Corporate Services, Inc.* (*ALTW*), *Muscatine Power and Water* (*MPW*), *Omaha Public Power District* (*OPPD*), and *Nebraska Public Power District* (*NPPD*). We obtained 24-hour historical data from MISO for the real-time market and day-ahead market LMPs determined for these BAs on August 1, August 3, and September 1 of 2008; see Li and Tesfatsion (2010). In particular, for ALTW we used the LMP for the loadzone ALTW.MECB, and for the remaining four BAs we used interface LMPs. We then used these data to calculate pairwise cross-correlations between the LMP reported for MEC and the LMPs reported for its four neighboring BAs.

Table 4 reports our LMP cross-correlation findings. All of the LMP cross-correlations are strongly positive. Since MEC is large, and presumably marginal, this suggests that the supply behavior of the MEC could be spilling over to affect the LMPs at neighboring BAs.

On the other hand, as always, care must be taken to recognize potentially confounding effects in real-world data. As noted above, the LMPs reported by MISO

[10]On May 1, 2009, MEC filed an application with the Iowa Utilities Board to become a transmission-owning member of MISO.

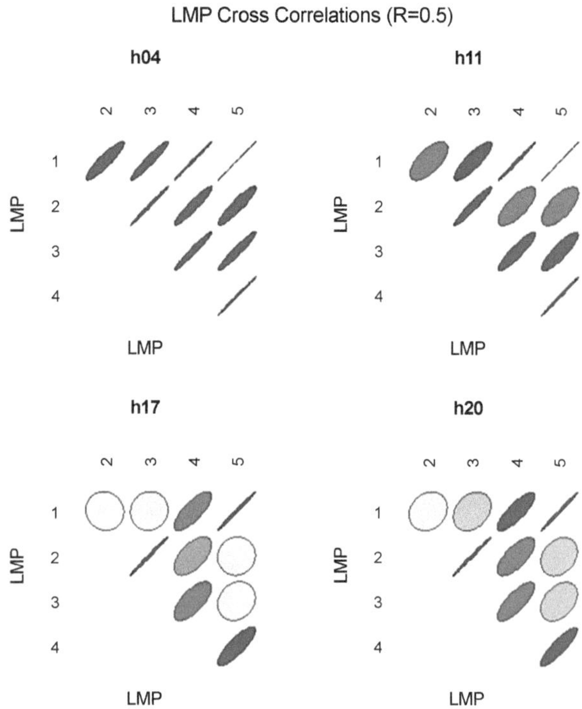

Fig. 16 Pairwise LMP cross-correlations for hours H04, H11, H17, and H20 on day 1000 for the dynamic 5-bus test case with GenCo VRE learning and 50% fixed LSE potential demand ($R = 0.5$)

Table 4 Pairwise cross-correlations between real-time market (RTM) and day-ahead market (DAM) LMPs for the MidAmerican Energy Company (MEC) and four neighboring Balancing Authorities ALTW, MPW, OPPD, and NPPD during three days in 2008

	DAM 8/1	DAM 8/3	DAM 9/1	RTM 8/1	RTM 8/3	RTM 9/1
MEC-ALTW	0.998	0.999	1.000	0.994	0.974	1.000
MEC-MPW	0.996	0.998	1.000	0.996	0.973	1.000
MEC-OPPD	1.000	0.999	1.000	0.996	0.973	1.000
MEC-NPPD	0.998	0.995	0.998	0.983	0.824	1.000

for MEC and its four neighboring BAs are load-weighted prices determined for a loadzone and interfaces and not for a single bus. The strong positive LMP cross-correlations in Table 4 could be a statistical artifact arising from the particular load-weighting method employed. Alternatively, they could indicate a lack of branch congestion during the selected days arising either through happenstance or through deliberate ISO planning.

To differentiate between these various potential explanations for the strong positive correlations in Table 4—GenCo spillover effects, statistical artifact, and lack of congestion—we would need to obtain data on MEC supply offers and branch congestion at an hourly level for the selected test days, as well as data giving individuated bus LMPs. These data are not currently publicly available.

Fig. 17 Pairwise LMP cross-correlations for hours H04, H11, H17, and H20 on day 1000 for the dynamic 5-bus test case with GenCo VRE learning and 100% price-sensitive LSE demand ($R = 1.0$)

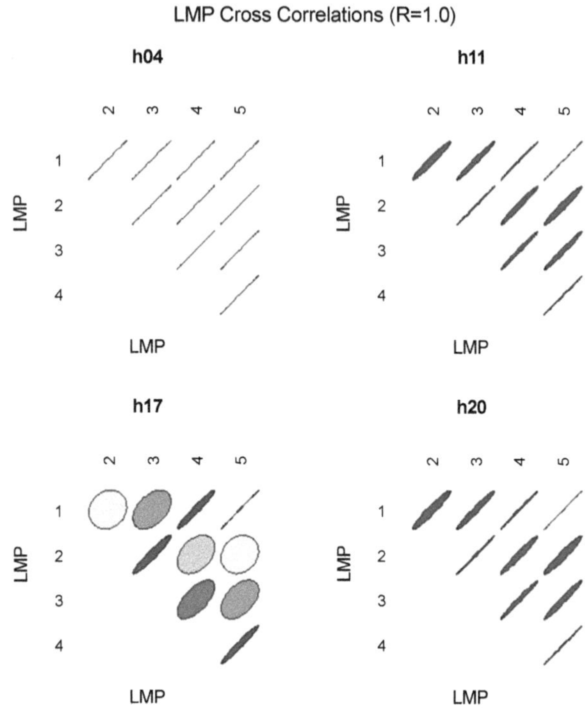

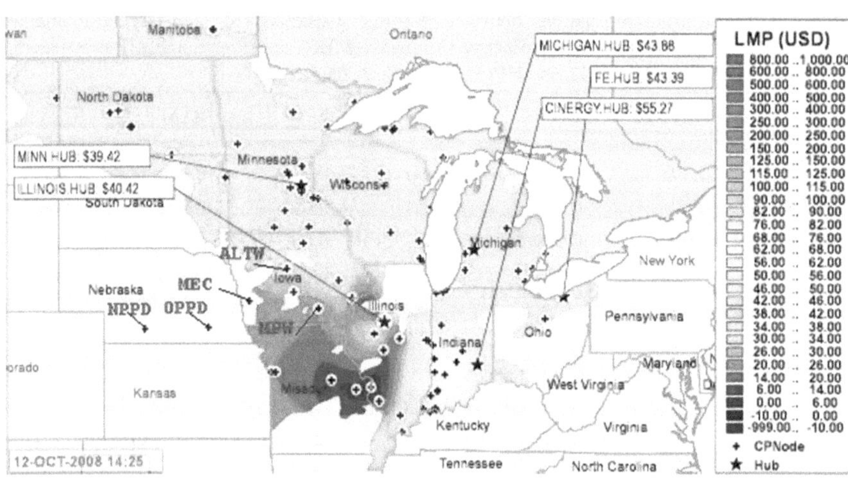

Fig. 18 MidAmerican Energy Company (MEC) Balancing Authority and four neighboring Balancing Authorities in relation to MISO

Although agent-based test beds such as AMES can be used to develop interesting hypotheses under simulated scenarios, the real payoff to such development will only come when these hypotheses can be tested more fully against empirical data.

7 Concluding Remarks

In this study we have used an ACE test bed to explore the performance characteristics of wholesale power markets operating under locational marginal pricing in accordance with a market design proposed by the U.S. Federal Energy Regulatory Commission (FERC 2003). In particular, we have focused on a novel issue, the extent to which economic capacity withholding by pivotal generation companies with learning capabilities at particular bus locations under variously specified LSE demand conditions has spill-over effects on the prices at neighboring bus locations.

As seen in Sect. 5, these spill-over effects can be substantial. These spill-over effects thus have practical policy consequences. For example, they greatly complicate efforts to develop and implement effective trigger rules and "reference curves" for the mitigation of market power in wholesale power markets. As surveyed in Isemonger (2007), many of these efforts have focused largely on local price effects.

Although our study focuses on a concrete ACE institutional design application, it illustrates more generally some of the more distinctive capabilities of ACE modeling. First, ACE modeling focuses on the playing out of processes over historical time rather than on the existence of equilibria. Second, the flexible nature of ACE modeling permits researchers to incorporate complicated structural, institutional, and behavioral aspects of actual real world situations. Third, ACE modeling permits researchers to study the effects of changes in these aspects on outcome distributions, both spatially and temporally.

Given these distinctive capabilities, ACE modeling would certainly appear to be a welcome addition to the economist's toolkit, complementing standard analytical and statistical modeling approaches.

Acknowledgements This work has been supported in part by the National Science Foundation under Grant NSF-0527460 and by grants from the ISU Electric Power Research Center.

References

AMES wholesale power market test bed homepage (2010). Website hosted by the ISU Economics Department, http://www.econ.iastate.edu/tesfatsi/AMESMarketHome.htm.

FERC (2003). *Notice of white paper*, U.S. Federal Energy Regulatory Commission, April 2003.

FERC (2008). *Assessment of demand response and advance metering* (Staff Report). Federal Energy Regulatory Commission, December 2008.

Conejo, A. J., Castillo, E., Minguez, R., & Milano, F. (2005). Locational marginal price sensitivities. *IEEE Transactions on Power Systems*, *20*(4), 2026–2033.

Erev, I., & Roth, A. E. (1998). Predicting how people play games with unique mixed-strategy equilibria. *American Economic Review*, *88*, 848–881.

Isemonger, A. (2007). Conduct and impact versus direct mitigation. *The Electricity Journal*, *20*(1), 53–62.

Joskow, P. (2006). Markets for power in the united states: an interim assessment. *The Energy Journal*, *27*(1), 1–36.

Kiesling, L.L. (2007). The role of retail pricing in electricity restructuring. In A. N. Kleit (Ed.), *Electric choices: deregulation and the future of electric power* (pp. 39–62). New York: Rowman & Littlefield.

Lally, J. (2002). Financial transmission rights: auction example. Section 6 in *Financial Transmission Rights Draft 01-10-02*, m-06 ed., ISO New England, Inc., January 2002.
Li, H., & Tesfatsion, L. (2009). The AMES wholesale power market test bed: a computational laboratory for research, teaching, and training. In *IEEE proceedings, power and energy society general meeting*, Calgary, Alberta, CA, July 2009.
Li, H., & Tesfatsion, L. (2010). *MISO energy project homepage*. Data section http://www.econ.iastate.edu/tesfatsi/MISOenergygroup.htm#Data.
Li, H., Sun, J., & Tesfatsion, L. (2009). *Separation and volatility of locational marginal prices in restructured wholesale power markets*. ISU Econ Working Paper No. 09009, June 2009. www.econ.iastate.edu/research/publications/viewabstract.asp?pid=13075.
Liu, H., Tesfatsion, L., & Chowdhury, A. A. (2009). Derivation of locational marginal prices for restructured wholesale power markets. *Journal of Energy Markets*, *2*(1), 3–27.
Orfanogianni, T., & Gross, G. (2007). A general formulation for LMP evaluation. *IEEE Transactions on Power Systems*, *22*(3), 1163–1173.
Pentapalli, M. (2008). *A comparative study of Roth-Erev and modified Roth-Erev reinforcement learning algorithms for uniform-price double auctions*. M.S. Thesis, Computer Science Department, March 2008.
Roth, A. E., & Ido, E. (1995). Learning in extensive form games: experimental data and simple dynamic models in the intermediate term. *Games and Econ. Behavior*, *8*, 164–212.
Shahidehpour, M., Yamin, H., & Li, Z. (2002). *Market operations in electric power systems*. New York: IEEE Press/Wiley–Interscience/Wiley.
Tesfatsion, L. (2006). Agent-based computational economics: a constructive approach to economic theory. In L. Tesfatsion & K. L. Judd (Eds.), *Handbook in economics series. Handbook of computational economics: Vol. 2. Agent-based computational economics* (pp. 831–880). Amsterdam: North-Holland/Elsevier.
Tesfatsion, L. (2010a). *Introductory materials: agent-based computational economics*, website hosted by the ISU Economics Department, http://www.econ.iastate.edu/tesfatsi/aintro.htm.
Tesfation, L. (2010b). *Agent-based computational economics homepage*, website hosted by the ISU Economics Department, www.econ.iastate.edu/tesfatsi/ace.htm.
Tesfatsion, L. (2010c). *Agent-based computational economics research area: restructured electricity markets*, website hosted by the ISU Economics Department, www.econ.iastate.edu/tesfatsi/aelect.htm.
Zhou, Q., Tesfatsion, L., & Liu, C. C. (2009). Scenario generation for price forecasting in restructured wholesale power markets. In *IEEE proceedings, power systems & exposition conference*, Seattle, WA, March 2009.

Energy Shocks and Macroeconomic Stabilization Policies in an Agent-Based Macro Model

Sander van der Hoog and Christophe Deissenberg

Abstract In this chapter we consider the effects of exogenous energy shocks on an agent-based macroeconomic system and study the out-of-equilibrium dynamics. We introduce automatic stabilizers that allow the artificial economy to absorbe the shocks. Two types of macroeconomic stabilization policies are implemented: a consumer subsidy scheme that compensates households for their loss in purchasing power, and a tax reduction scheme that affects both households and firms to support consumption and investments. Policy experiments are then carried out to evaluate the effectiveness of these macroeconomic policies. Finally, we are able to distinguish between short- and long-term effects of the policy measures.

1 Introduction

The variation of energy prices has substantial effects on the economic activity in a region affecting real output, economic growth and employment among other key variables. Rotemberg and Woodford (1996) for example estimate using U.S. data that a 10% increase in oil prices leads to an output decline of 2.5% after five or six quarters. Actual increases in energy prices, however substantially exceed such percentages as demonstrated in Fig. 1. The figure shows the real energy price behavior during the 2008 energy crisis. The price of Brent crude oil went up by 390% between 2002 and July 2008, which translates to a monthly increase of 2%. Then it went sharply down by −76% between July 2008 and Jan 2009, which implies a monthly decrease of −22%. When the crisis was over at the beginning of 2009 the price was basically back at its original level of 2002.

For an economy like the EU, which to a large extend depends on the supply of relevant factors like oil from the outside, variations in the price of energy can be

S. van der Hoog (✉)
Dept. of Business Administration and Economics, Bielefeld University, Universitätsstrasse 25, 33615 Bielefeld, Germany
e-mail: svdhoog@gmail.com

H. Dawid, W. Semmler (eds.), *Computational Methods in Economic Dynamics*, Dynamic Modeling and Econometrics in Economics and Finance 13,
DOI 10.1007/978-3-642-16943-4_8,

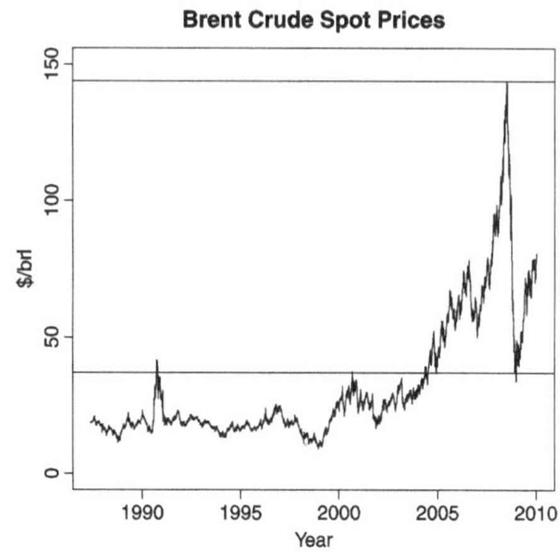

Fig. 1 May 1987–Jan 2010 daily Brent spot prices. Source: Energy Information Administration. *Horizontal lines* indicate the top in 2002 (36.87 USD) and the *top* in July 2008 (143.95 USD)

seen as exogeneous shocks affecting the economic dynamics within the EU. An important policy question in this respect is how the implications of such energy shocks can be alleviated by the appropriate choice of policy measures to be introduced in response to a shock.

Using the agent-based macroeconomic model that we have developed one can study such questions in relatively great detail. Since we have microscopic data at the level of individual households, firms and the government, the model provides us with a testbed, a computational laboratory, in which we can do 'What-if' analyses for such a policy measure and compare the effects between different scenarios.

In our computational experiments we focus on the use of two types of stabilization policies to mitigate the negative effects of energy shocks to the macroeconomy: (i) a consumer subsidy that only affects households, (ii) an income tax reduction that affects both households and firms (personal income and corporate income).

These policies are used to counteract the effects of energy shocks on the GDP growth rate, unemployment and inflation by directly stimulating consumption, employment and investment.

A direct motivation to study the tax reduction policy is that in many developed countries fuel taxes form a large part of the final fuel price, and the revenues from these taxes serve to finance public infrastructure (road maintenance for example). One measure used in the past to avoid the negative impacts of oil shocks is then to temporarily or permanently suspend these taxes as fuel costs are rising, as occurred in 2000, when France, Italy, and the Netherlands lowered fuel taxes in response to protests over high diesel and gasoline prices.

The remainder of the chapter is organized as follows. In Sect. 2 we describe the model, the agents and their behavioral repertoires. We also describe the stabilization policies and the setup of the computational experiments. Section 3 presents the simulation results and Sect. 4 concludes.

2 The Model

2.1 General Features

Here we can only briefly recapitulate the main features of the underlying model that was developed over a period of three years in the EURACE project.[1] For more details on its implementation, the interested reader is referred to the following papers.

A general overview of the model and a discussion of the computational issues can be found in Deissenberg et al. (2008). The core of the model is explained in Dawid et al. (2008, 2009), with formal descriptions of the production decisions in the consumption and investment goods sectors, the recruitment and wage setting mechanism on the labour market, and households' consumption and savings decisions.

A description of the financial market where households can trade firm stocks and government bonds is found in Raberto et al. (2008a, 2008b). Finally, the financial management of the firm describing the financing of production and linking the real side of the economy to the financial sphere is found in van der Hoog et al. (2008).

Putting all the pieces together, we obtain an agent-based model of a fully integrated macroeconomic system, consisting of two real sectors for consumption and investment goods and a financial sector consisting of a credit market and an asset market. The model also contains a public sector consisting of a government, a central bank, and a statistical office that collects microdata and generates macrodata.

The part of the model described here could be viewed as a *missing link* since it describes an exogenous energy market that constitutes a proxy for the link to the 'rest-of-the-world' by affecting the production costs of the investment goods producers. Using this exogeneous energy market we can study the out-of-equilibrium dynamics that follow from energy shocks.

2.2 The Agents

The model consists of 'active' agents and 'passive' agents, who provide auxiliary functions for information aggregation and dissemination such as data collection, intermediation between buyers and sellers, or they act as handles for affecting macroeconomic policy.

The active agents are: Households (1600), CGFirms (80 consumption goods producers), IGFirms (1, investment goods producers), Banks (2), and Governments (1). These agents all have a behavioral repertoire and interact, either directly or indirectly, on the various markets that make up the system.

The passive agents are: Malls (1, providing a local market for consumption), Eurostat (1, collecting data, distributing aggregate statistics), a Central Bank (1), and a Clearinghouse (1). The passive agents do not make any decisions.

Table 1 contains information on the types and numbers of agents in the artificial economy.

[1]For more information on the EURACE Project, see www.eurace.org.

Table 1 Agent population

Agent	Number
Households	1600
CGFirms	80
IGFirms	1
Banks	2
Government	1
Malls	1
Eurostat	1
Central Bank	1
Clearinghouse	1

2.2.1 Households

The main features of household behavior are summarized by these decisions:

- Employment decision: unemployed households/workers read vacancies from all firms, taking into account the wage offer and their own reservation wage.
- Consumption/savings decision: at the beginning of each month, households allocate a budget for consumption and savings (further divided between a savings account and an asset portfolio) that is modelled according to empirically-founded rules, as in Deaton (1991, 1992). The consumer k sets its consumption budget for the coming month by the rule:

$$B^{cons}_{k,t} = \begin{cases} Liq^{avail}_{k,t} - \kappa\Delta, & \Delta > 0, \\ Liq^{avail}_{k,t}, & \text{otherwise}, \end{cases} \qquad (1)$$

$$\Delta = (Liq^{avail}_{k,t} - \theta Inc^{Mean}_{k,t}).$$

  Here $Liq^{avail}_{k,t}$ is the available liquidity (called cash-on-hand in Deaton (1991, 1992), consisting of all liquid or near-liquid assets) and $Inc^{Mean}_{k,t}$ is the mean disposable income over the previous four months. Δ represents a buffer stock of liquidity in excess of the mean income, and the propensity to save satisfies $0 < \kappa < 1$. The parameter $0 < \theta \leq 1$ is a characteristic of the household, and represents the fraction of mean income that determines the size of the buffer stock. If the available cash-on-hand falls below the buffer stock ($Liq^{avail}_{k,t} < \theta Inc^{Mean}_{k,t}$), the household will not save anything and spend all cash-on-hand on consumption. If Δ is positive, there are positive savings as well.
- Selection of consumption goods: once a week a household visits a shopping mall located in its own region, where firms offer goods at local prices. The decision from which firm to buy (at the local mall) is based on a discrete-choice logit model, taking into account the prices offered by all firms that sell goods at the local mall.
- Financial decisions: households' asset portfolio allocation decisions are based on Prospect Theory (Kahneman and Tversky 1979), see Raberto et al. (2008a, 2008b) for further details.

2.2.2 Investment Goods Producers

In the basic setup of the model, there is only one single investment goods producer (IGFirm) who acts as a global supplier of investment goods (machinery). All firms producing consumption goods purchase their capital goods from this machine manufacturer. The profits of this single manufacturer are channelled back into the economy and distributed as dividends to the households. Each household is assumed to hold equal shares in the IGfirm.

The main features of the behavior of the investment goods producer are summarized by:

- Investment goods are produced on demand and without rationing and are produced using only energy as an input.
- Innovation process: Every period with probability $\gamma^{inv} \in (0, 1)$ an innovation leads to an increase in the quality of the capital good, and with probability $(1 - \gamma^{inv})$ there is no change in quality.
- Technological progress: The productivity of the investment good increases as a function of its quality. A successful innovation leads to an increase in productivity of newly produced capital goods by a fixed percentage Δq^{inv}.
- Pricing decision: The price of investment goods p^{inv} increases with the same rate as the quality level.

2.2.3 Consumption Goods Producers

The main features of the behavior of consumption goods producers are summarized by these decisions:

- Production decision: output is planned based on the current inventory levels at the malls, and a standard stock replenishment rule that can be found in the operations research and management literature (see e.g. Hillier and Lieberman 1986). In addition, there is production smoothing in order to prevent the output of the firm to fluctuate excessively.
- Employment decision: the planned labour force is directly related to the planned production quantity, and to the current technology of the capital stock. If additional workers are needed vacancies are opened, or workers are fired if the opposite is the case. The search and matching algorithm is described in detail in Dawid et al. (2009).
- Investment decision: The existing capital stock depreciates and needs to be upgraded if the firm wants to benefit from the productivity increase of newly produced capital goods. Investments follow from a planned or desired capital stock (expansion plus replacement of depreciated old stock).
- Financing decision: To finance the production plan, firms follow a hierarchical decision-making routine. The first least risky choice is to resort to internal financing. If internal liquidity is insufficient, firms apply for external funding. They first visit the credit market to apply for bank loans. If they experience credit constraints, the next step is to issue new equity (shares) on the asset market. If this

still does not suffice then the production plan is revised, and the planned investment, planned labour force, and planned output are all scaled down until it is possible to finance the new production plan. See van der Hoog et al. (2008) for details.

- Pricing decision: the price of consumption goods is determined using a mark-up pricing routine based on 'break-even analysis' (see Nagle 1987).
- Dividend payout decision: If the firm makes positive profits, it pays out dividends to its shareholders. The dividend decision is to maintain a constant dividend to earnings ratio. This choice of behavioral rule is based on survey data provided in Allen and Michaely (2004) and Brav et al. (2005).

2.3 Time Scales and Activation Regimes

Agents' actions are event-based or time-based, where the latter can follow either subjective or objective time schedules. Economic activities take place on a hierarchy of time-scales: yearly, monthly, weekly and daily activities all take place following calender-time or subjective agent-time. Agents are activated asynchronously according to their subjective time schedules that is anchored on an individual activation day. These activation days are uniformly randomly distributed among the agents at the start of the simulation, but may change endogenously (e.g., when a household gets re-employed, its subjective month gets synchronized with the activation day of its employer due to wage payments). Listing 1 provides a pseudocode of the economic activities taking place at various time-scales.

In the next section we explain how we include energy shocks into the basic model.

2.4 Capturing an Energy Shock in the Model

We now enrich the model by including the impact of increases in the price of energy on the production costs of the investment goods producers.

As was already briefly outlined in the introduction, the energy shocks enter the model through a multi-stage process. Investment goods are produced using energy as the only input. During an energy crisis the costs of energy increase, leading to an increase in the production costs of the producers of investment goods. This increase in production costs enters into the pricing of the investment goods through an energy price mark-up, and then enters into the production costs of the producers of consumption goods. At the final stage, the consumption goods producers incorporate the increase in their price for the consumption goods, again by using a mark-up pricing routine, which leads to an increase in the consumer prices.

We typically assume that an energy crisis consists of a succession of consecutive, identical (in length and intensity) energy price increases. Thus, an energy crisis is

Listing 1 Economic activities taking place on a hierarchy of time-scales with yearly, monthly, weekly and daily activities

```
On 1st day of calender year:
    Government:
        - announce new policies

On 1st day of calender month:
    IGFirm:
        - set new price for capital goods

On 1st day of subjective month:
    Firms:
        - decide production plan
        - determine input demand for capital and labour
        - determine external financial needs for production
        - visit credit market: ask for credit loans with banks
        - visit financial market: issue new shares
        - if credit rationed: rescale production
        - visit capital goods market
        - visit labour market
        - produce output
        - distribute output to malls
    Households:
        - if employed: receive wage
        - receive subsidy based on previous month consumption
        - determine consumption budget for upcoming month

On 1st day of subjective week:
    Households:
        - visit consumption goods market

Every day:
    Firms:
        - receive revenues from malls
    Households:
        - visit financial market: reallocate asset portfolio
        - if unemployed: visit labour market
        - receive dividends
    Banks:
        - receive loan requests, supply credit to firms
        - receive payment account updates
        - compute balance sheet (value-at-risk, total credit supply)
    Government:
        - receive tax revenues

On 20th (last) day of subjective month:
    Firms:
        - compute revenues, income statement and balance sheet
        - pay taxes, dividends
        - send data to Eurostat
    Households:
        - pay taxes

On 20th (last) day of calender month:
    Eurostat:
        - compute monthly aggregate macrodata and statistics

On last day of calender year:
    Eurostat:
        - compute yearly aggregate macrodata and statistics
    Government:
        - compute balance sheet
        - set new policies (tax rate, subsidy pct)
```

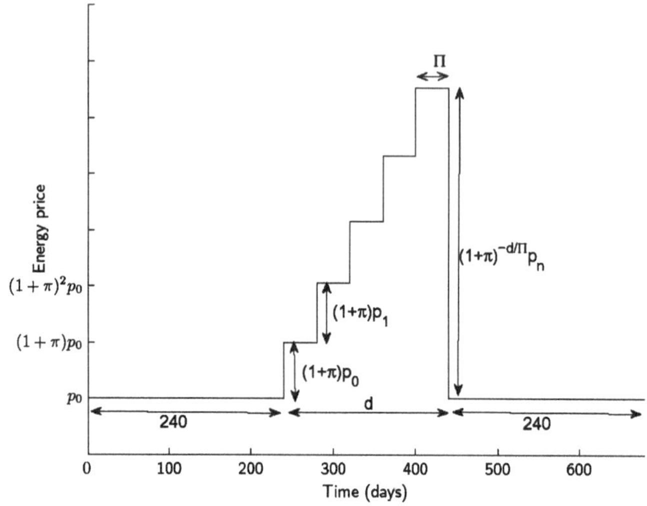

Fig. 2 The time profile of an energy shock experiment

captured by three parameters: the intensity of the single price increases (π), their periodicity Π (the number of days between two consecutive price increases), and the number of price increases (n). The total duration of the energy crisis (d) is then $d = \Pi n$. The price increase π is assumed to instantaneously disappear at the end of the total duration. The time profile of a typical energy crisis is illustrated in Fig. 2.

The energy costs of the investment goods producers are incorporated into the price of the capital good by an energy price mark-up that equals the intensity of the price shock (π):

$$p_{t+1} = (p_t + p_{t,c})(1+\pi), \tag{2}$$

where p_t is the price in period t and $p_{t,c}$ is the price update due to the stochastic process of productivity increases (technological innovations).

The additional revenues stemming from the technologically motivated price increase $p_{t,c}$ are partly paid out as taxes and partly paid out as dividends to households.

The revenues that accrue due to the energy costs mark-up (π) are not paid out in taxes or dividends. Instead, the money is stored in a variable that represents the total cumulative income of the owners of the energy source (the Sheik of Qatar, Dubai, Russian oligarchs), which does not play any role in the economic dynamics. In other words, it leaves the economic system.

2.5 The Consumer Subsidy Policy

The consumer subsidy is meant to compensate households for their loss in purchasing power. The objective is to support the demand side of the economy. Therefore

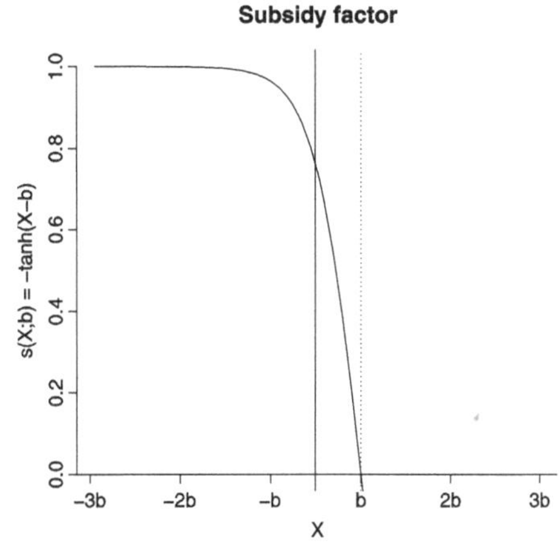

Fig. 3 Graph of the subsidy factor $s_t = -\tanh(X_t - b)$. To obtain the actual subsidy payment this should be multiplied by $|X_t - b|$ and the household's individual consumption C_t^h

each household receives a subsidy that is a percentage of its total monthly consumption expenditure. The subsidy percentage is determined at the end of each year. The individual subsidies are computed at the end of each month, after the household knows its total consumption expenditures. The Government thus acts with a yearly frequency, while households act on a monthly basis.

2.5.1 Policy Activation

The consumer subsidy is activated as a function of the GDP growth rate X_t (annualized growth, measured monthly) by using two trigger levels: an ON trigger a and an OFF trigger b, with typically $a < b$. The subsidy becomes active whenever the GDP growth rate *falls* below a ($X_t < a$), and is switched off again as soon as the growth rate is above b ($X_t > b$).

The magnitude S_t^h of the subsidy given to household h is determined by:

$$S_t^h = \begin{cases} -C_t^h |X_t - b| \tanh(X_t - b), & X_t < b \\ 0, & \text{otherwise.} \end{cases} \tag{3}$$

Figure 3 shows the graph of the subsidy factor $s_t : (-\infty, b] \to [0, 1)$, $s_t = -\tanh(X_t - b)$, which should still be multiplied by $|X_t - b|$ and the household's individual consumption C_t^h to obtain the total subsidy payment.

The first level a can be positive or negative. For example, an aggressive stabilization policy might be to set $a = 0.03$ implying that the subsidy regime becomes active if the GDP growth rate drops below $+3\%$. If instead $a = -0.01$, the subsidy takes effect only after the growth rate has fallen below -1%. In both cases, as already mentioned, the subsidy is awarded until X_t increases to b. A justification for the asymmetry between the on and off triggers is that the subsidy typically gets activated relatively late during a downturn because of recognition, decision, and implementation lags, but should remain active until strong growth is assured again.

2.6 The Tax Reduction Policy

The tax reduction policy has the objective to alleviate the tax burden of the private sector in general, so it applies to both firms and households. Therefore, in this policy we vary endogenously the income tax rate on both personal income and corporate income.

For the household this has the same effect as the subsidy scheme, except the stimulus is now based in income instead of consumption.

In the case of the firm, the tax reduction scheme is meant to compensate the firm for an increase in production costs. These costs consist of labour costs and the costs of acquiring new capital (investments).

We implement the tax reduction scheme using a similar approach as the one above for the consumer subsidy. We use the same on/off switches conditional on the GDP growth rate, and the reduction in the tax rate is given by almost the same formula (but note the reversed sign):

$$T_t = \begin{cases} \max\{0, \tau + |X_t - b| \tanh(X_t - b)\}, & X_t < b \\ \tau, & \text{otherwise.} \end{cases} \tag{4}$$

Here $\tau = 0.05$ is the default tax rate on households' personal income and firms' corporate income.[2] This results in an income tax rate $T_t \in (\tau - |X_t - b|, \tau)$, where X_t is the GDP growth rate.

2.7 Experimental Design

In this subsection we describe how we set up the computational experiments. In the model, one iteration represents one business day (1 week = 5 days, 1 month = 20 days, 1 year = 240 days). All our simulation runs have a length of 6000 iterations (300 months), consisting of an initial transient of 1000 iterations (50 months) that is ignored in the analysis of the experiment. Hence, all results are based on 250 months. Furthermore, all results are based on comparisons of distributional outcomes, since single runs will not provide generic results. To obtain statistically significant results we performed 10 batch runs for each scenario and then perform a Monte Carlo analysis. All plots show the Monte Carlo mean and the first and third quartile of the Monte Carlo distribution across the batch runs. Table 2 gives the default parameter values that are used in the computational experiments.

We consider an energy shock over a pre-determined time interval $[T_{start}, T_{end}]$. After the transient phase, we run the model for 12 more months before starting the energy shock at $T_{start} = 12$. After the energy crisis has ended, at $T_{end} = 24$, we run the model till $t = 250$ months in order to analyze the legacy of the shock.

[2] Note that the default tax rate of 5% is relatively low compared to empirical rates, but this should be seen in the model context where the tax rate refers to unemployment insurance contributions only, which in Germany are currently at 2.8%.

Table 2 Parameter values

Name	Symbol	Values	Description
Energy crisis duration	d	240	Duration of the energy crisis in days
Energy shock intensity	π	$\{0.01, 0.025, 0.05\}$	Percentage energy price change for a single shock
Periodicity of shocks	Π	20	Periodicity of the shock in days
Income tax rate	τ	0.05	Tax rate on personal and corporate income
Innovation probability	γ^{inv}	0.10	Probability that an innovation is successful
Technological progress		0.025	Increase in productivity in case of a successful innovation
Capital price mark-up	$p_{t,c}$	0.025	Price increase of capital goods in case a successful innovation occurs
Energy price mark-up	π	$\{0.01, 0.025, 0.05\}$	Price increase of capital goods in case of an energy price increase

Figure 2 shows the time profile of the energy shock experiment. The choice of the profile is motivated by the empirical evidence as shown in Fig. 1. There are n consecutive instantaneous price increases between T_{start} and T_{end}, at equidistant time intervals, and an instantaneous decrease of intensity $(1+\pi)^{-n}$ at $t = T_{end}$. This brings the price back to its pre-shock level, if no other influences would have affected the price in the meantime. However, over the course of the energy crisis, the process of technological innovation continues in the background so the capital goods price is updated as usual. Hence, the price level of the investment goods at the end of the crisis will typically differ from the price level at the beginning of the crisis.

3 Simulation Results

In this section we present simulation results for four scenarios:

1. Benchmark scenario: no energy shocks occur. This defines the default model behavior.
2. Energy shock only scenario: an energy crisis occurs, without any stabilization policy. This provides a baseline to compare the effectiveness of the stabilization policies.
3. Consumer subsidy scenario: an energy crisis occurs, and a stabilization policy is implemented by a consumer subsidy scheme.
4. Tax reduction scenario: an energy crisis occurs, and a stabilization policy is implemented by a tax reduction scheme.

Table 3 summarizes the computational settings in each scenario.

Table 3 Overview of the computational settings for the scenarios

Scenario	Parameter set
Benchmark	$\pi = 0, T = 0.05$
Energy shock	$\pi = 0.01, 0.025, 0.05, T = 0.05$
Consumer subsidy	$\pi = 0.025, T = 0.05, a = b = 0.03$
Tax reduction	$\pi = 0.025, a = b = 0.03$

3.1 Results per Scenario

Scenario 1: Simulations for the Benchmark Scenario

We recall the benchmark results in Fig. 4: GDP settles down to a stable growth path of 2.5% p.a., which equals the rate of technological progress. Total investments grow at the same rate. The price of capital goods shows a typical staircase pattern due to the incremental technological progress (see Fig. 4c). The budget deficit as a percentage of GDP is on average above the threshold of the Maastricht criterium (−0.03).

Scenario 2: Effects of Energy Shocks Without Countermeasures

We now consider a situation in which there are energy shocks but no active policy measures to counter the negative effects on the economy.

In Fig. 5a (column 1) we introduce a mild energy shock of 1% at $t = 12$. At $t = 24$ months there is a downward shock of 12%. Such low intensity shocks to the capital goods price hardly affects the economy.

A stronger energy crisis is shown in Fig. 5b (column 2), with multiple shocks of 2.5%. This results in a more pronounced energy spike with significant effects on key macroeconomic variables such as GDP, investments and the unemployment rate (not shown).

The final case is the one shown in Fig. 5c with multiple shocks of 5%, one per month. Here finally we have the signature of a true energy crisis, where at its peak capital goods cost twice as much as they did at the start of the crisis. The downward effect on GDP is considerable with a −20% decline. Investments also decline sharply during the crisis, but then rebound to original levels as soon as the energy prices return to normal levels.

Note that after the energy crisis there is an aftershock which is smaller than the main event. This is due to the overshooting that follows immediately after the crisis ends, when energy prices drop down to normal levels. This results in overconsumption and overinvestment, i.e. a build up of excess production capacity. After the secondary small correction, the economy settles down on its long-term growth path which is determined by the rate of technological progress (2.5% by default), see row 3.

In Tables 4 and 5 we quantify the relationship between the magnitude of the shocks and the mean and standard deviations of the GDP growth rate and the deficit/GDP fraction, respectively.

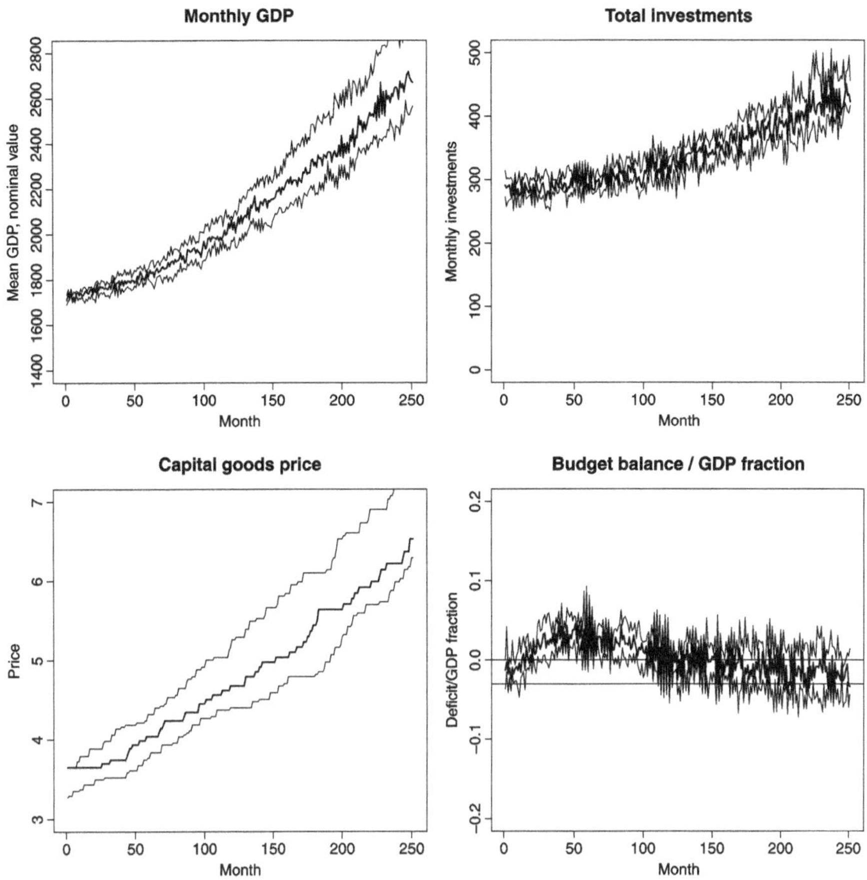

Fig. 4 Benchmark scenario. All results are Monte Carlo means across 10 runs. *Black line*: Monte–Carlo mean, *dotted lines*: 1st–3rd quartiles. (**a**) Monthly GDP in nominal values. (**b**) Total monthly investments. (**c**) Capital goods price. (**d**) Government finances: the budget deficit as a percentage of GDP (0.01 means 1%). The *horizontal line* at −0.03 is the Maastricht criterium

For increasing values of the shock intensity parameter ($\pi = 0.01, 0.025, 0.05$) the short-term fluctuations of GDP growth rates increase dramatically, displaying swings between −22% to +40% for a shock intensity of 5% (see Fig. 6). Another effect is that the budget deficit shows more volatility, with extreme deficits of −12% or surplusses of +25% of GDP.

Scenario 3: Energy Shock with the Consumer Subsidy

The results for the consumer subsidy scheme are shown in Fig. 7 (left panel). The on/off triggers are set to $a = b = 0.03$. The subsidy percentage increases during the energy crisis to average levels of 0.1–0.8% of the monthly consumption expenditure. Note that since the government only adjusts its policy once a year, at the end of the calendar year, the monthly data shown in the plot displays stepwise jumps with a yearly frequency.

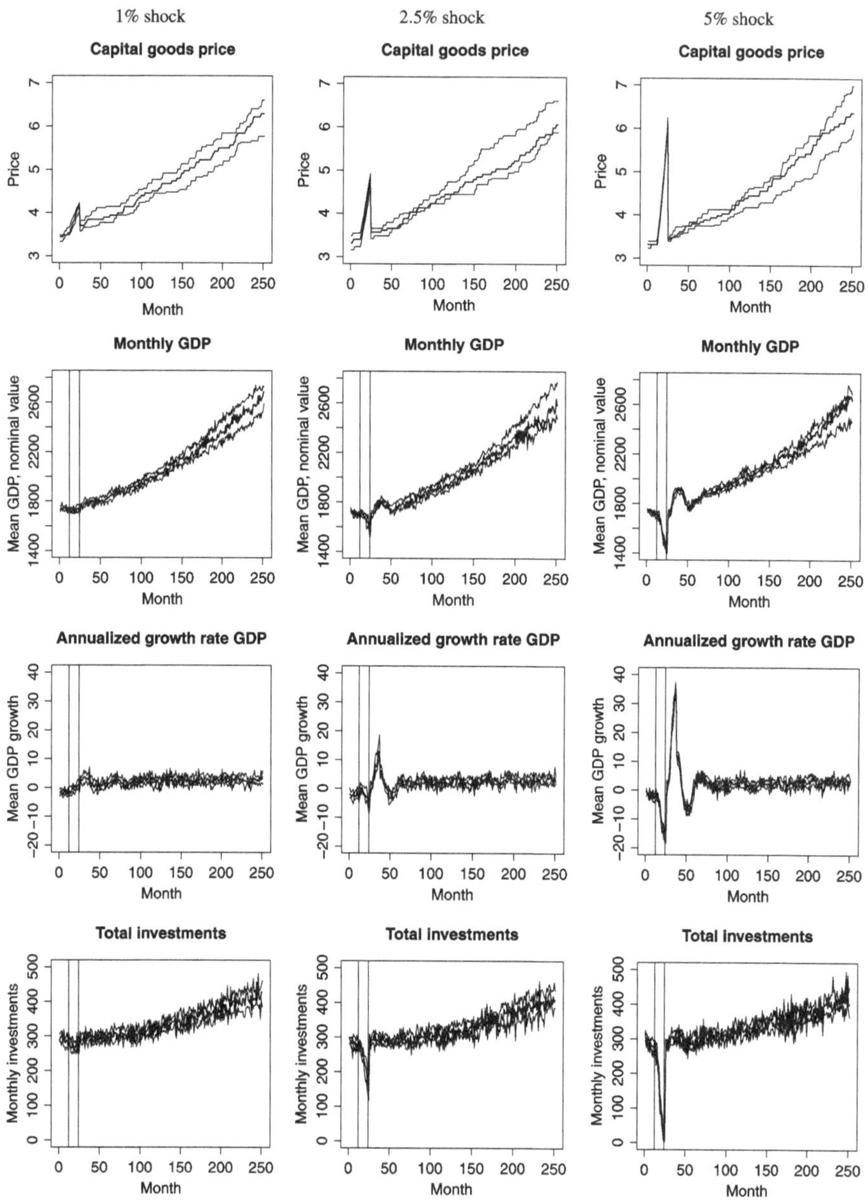

Fig. 5 Results for the energy shock scenario. *Vertical lines* indicate the energy crisis. *Parameters*: duration $d = 240$, periodicity $\Pi = 20$, intensity $\pi = 0.01, 0.025, 0.05$. *Row 1*: Capital goods price. *Row 2*: GDP nominal value. *Row 3*: GDP growth rate. *Row 4*: Total investments

Table 4 Summary statistics for short-term (months 0–75) and long-term (months 225–250) GDP growth factors

	Short-term		Long-term	
	Mean	Std.	Mean	Std.
Benchmark	−0.723	1.551	1.61	0.938
Energy shock:				
$\pi = 0.01$	−0.668	1.685	1.085	0.958
$\pi = 0.025$	−1.069	3.772	1.413	0.821
$\pi = 0.05$	−0.046	10.382	1.664	1.184
Subsidy	−0.646	3.718	1.17	0.976
Tax	−0.847	3.26	1.874	1.068

Table 5 Summary statistics for short-term (months 0–75) and long-term (months 225–250) deficit/GDP ratios (%)

	Short-term		Long-term	
	Mean	Std.	Mean	Std.
Benchmark	−0.130	1.904	−4.571	1.392
Energy shock:				
$\pi = 0.01$	−1.029	1.465	−4.362	1.228
$\pi = 0.025$	−1.043	2.482	−4.582	1.024
$\pi = 0.05$	−2.017	3.54	−3.933	1.167
Subsidy	−0.307	2.79	−4.064	1.743
Tax	−0.899	2.673	−4.473	1.601

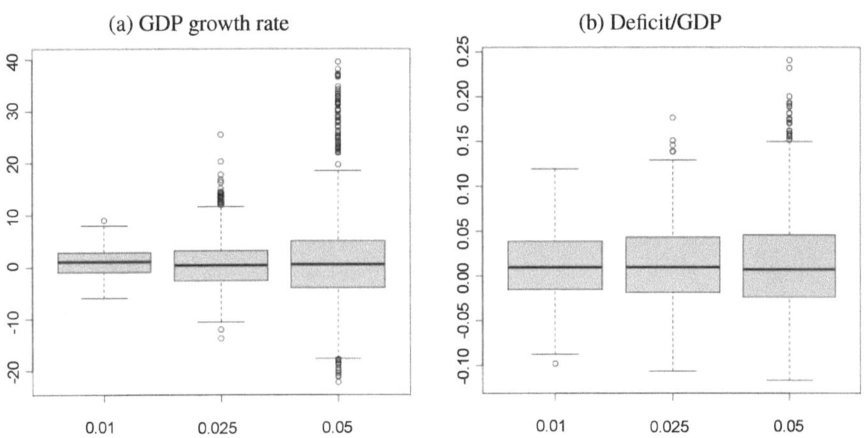

Fig. 6 Comparison for different values of the shock intensity: $\pi = 0.01, 0.025, 0.05$. (**a**) *Left panel*: annualized GDP growth rates in months 0–75 (includes the crisis and its aftershock). (**b**) *Right panel*: the effect on government finances due to the shock (monthly budget deficit as % of GDP)

Scenario 4: Energy Shock with the Tax Reduction

Figure 7(right panel) shows the results for the tax reduction stabilization scheme. The tax reduction results in a tax rate of 4.2–4.7% during the crisis, and 4.4–4.8% immediately afterwards (months 25–85, includes the aftershock), due to the persis-

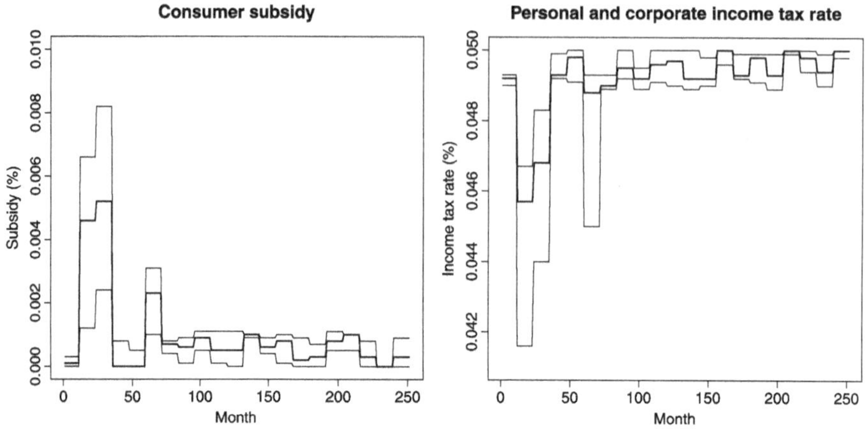

Fig. 7 Results for the energy shock scenario with the consumer subsidy scheme (*left panel*) and the tax reduction scheme (*right panel*). Parameters: $\pi = 0.025$, $a = b = 0.03$. The plot shows the stepwise yearly adjustments of the policy parameter

tence in the policy. Similar to the subsidy scenario, the tax reduction policy also has a yearly frequency, and there is a lag in the government response time.

3.2 Comparison Between Scenarios

In Fig. 8 we make a direct comparison between the energy shock-only scenario and the stabilization scenarios in terms of the ratio of nominal GDP and the ratio of total investments with respect to the energy shock-only results (all scenarios use $\pi = 0.025$). Three main results follow from these simulations.

Result 1

We consider the GDP ratios in Fig. 8 (row 1). The mean GDP levels in the stabilization scenarios are consistently higher than in the energy shock-only scenario (the mean is consistently above the 1.0 ratio). This shows that the demand stimulus of both stabilization policies results in an upward shift of the nominal value of GDP.

Result 2

We consider the investment ratios in Fig. 8 (row 2). During the energy crisis, the mean investments in both stabilization scenarios are higher than in the shock-only scenario. However, this is only true during the crisis, not before or after it. This means that the stabilization policies have their intended effect to stimulate consumption and investments, either directly or indirectly.

Result 3

The tax reduction policy yields slightly better results than the consumer subsidy policy with respect to stimulating investments, since the former affects both con-

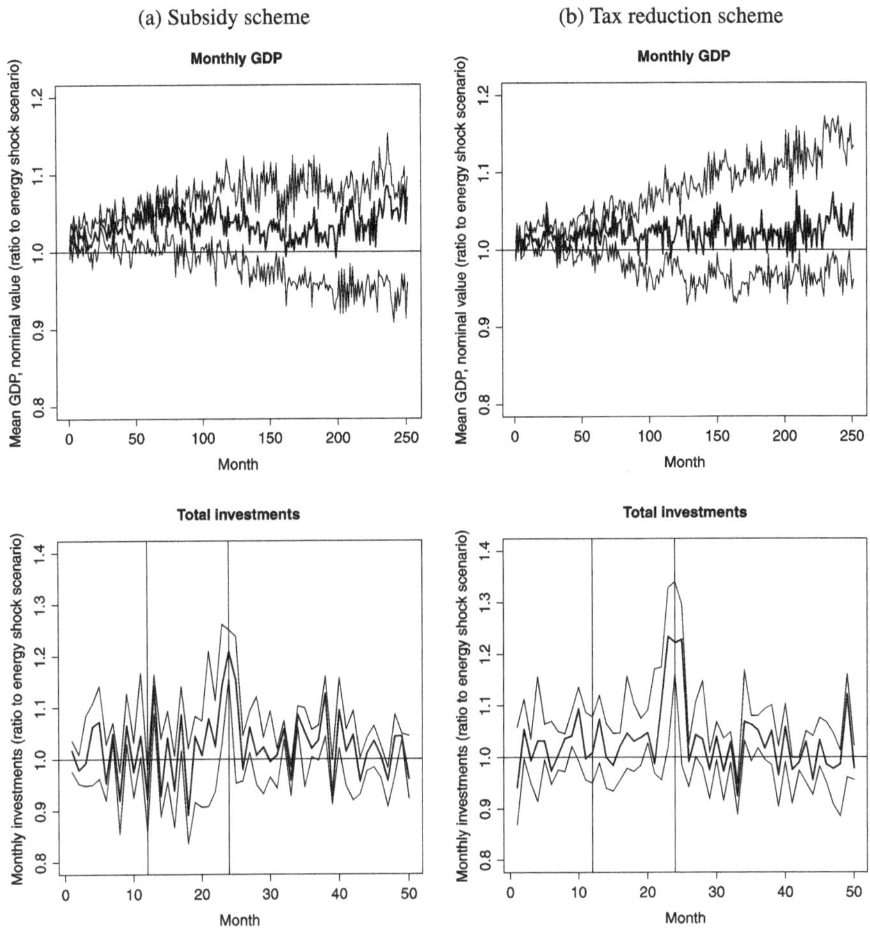

Fig. 8 Comparison of the stabilization scenarios to the energy shock scenario. Measured are the ratios of nominal GDP and total investments, resp. *Vertical lines* indicate the energy crisis. (**a**) *Top*: GDP in the subsidy scenario divided by GDP in the energy-shock-only scenario. (**a**) *Bottom*: Total investment in the subsidy scenario divided by investment in the energy-shock-only scenario. (**b**) *Top*: GDP in the tax reduction scenario divided by GDP in the energy-shock-only scenario. (**b**) *Bottom*: Total investment in the tax reduction scenario divided by investment in the energy-shock-only scenario

sumers and firms, while the latter only affects consumers. Thus, the tax reduction policy is in fact the more effective policy, if only due to the choice of having it apply to both personal income and corporate income taxes. Furthermore, the consumer subsidy only has an indirect stimulating effect on investments through the demand channel, while the tax reduction for firms has a more direct effect on stimulating investments.

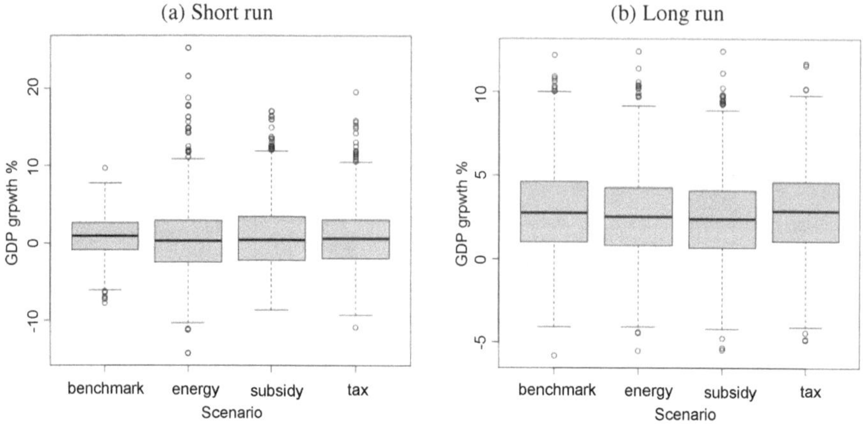

Fig. 9 Comparison of short- and long-run effects on GDP growth rates. *Left panel*: short run, months 0–75. *Right panel*: long run, months 100–250, 6 years after the crisis has ended

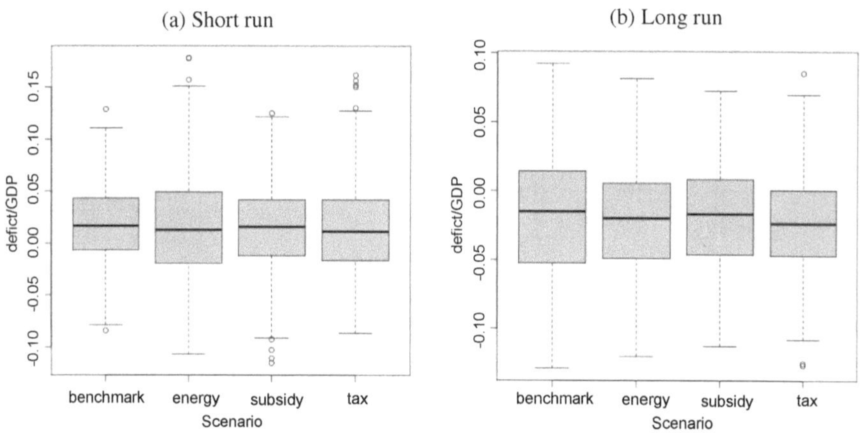

Fig. 10 Comparison of short- and long-run effects for Government monthly budget deficit across the four scenarios. *Left panel*: short run, months 0–75. *Right panel*: long run, months 225–250

3.3 Short-Term Versus Long-Term Effects of Energy Shocks

In this section we compare the four scenarios discussed above by analysing their short- and long-term effects.

3.3.1 Short-Term Effects

The short-run effects are calculated across months 0–75, which includes the crisis and its aftershock. The results are shown in the left panels of Figs. 9, 10 and Tables 4, 5 (see Appendix) report the summary statistics for resp. the distributions of the GDP growth rate and the Government deficit/GDP ratio, across all scenarios.

Result 4: GDP Growth

Figure 9 and Table 4(left panel) show an increase in short-run volatility of the GDP growth rate in the energy shock scenario ($\sigma = 3.772$ vs. 1.551), which is due to the overconsumption/overinvestment bubble in the short-run. Compared to the benchmark scenario the energy shock obviously causes increased fluctuations in the absence of any stabilization.

The subsidy policy however aggrevates the upswing after the crisis since the government provides easy money that enters the economy through the consumption of households and then leads to an overheating effect. Hence the higher standard deviation ($\sigma = 3.718$). The tax reduction policy results in smaller upswings and downswings than the subsidy regime, resulting in a lower short-run volatility ($\sigma = 3.26$).

Result 5: Deficit/GDP Ratio

In Fig. 10 and Table 5(left panel) we observe that in the energy shock-only scenario the short-run volatility of the deficit/GDP ratio increases ($\sigma = 2.482$ vs. 1.904). The subsidy policy raises the volatility of the budget deficit/GDP ratio somewhat more than the energy shock itself ($\sigma = 2.79$) while the tax reduction scheme also raises it ($\sigma = 2.673$), but somewhat less than in the subsidy scenario.

3.3.2 Long-Term Effects

The long-run effects are calculated across months 225–250, and shown in the right panels of Figs. 9, 10, with Tables 4, 5(right panels) reporting the summary statistics.

Result 6: GDP Growth

The energy shock and subsidy scenarios have lower average long-run growth rates than in the benchmark scenario (1.413 and 1.17 vs. 1.61), while the tax reduction scenario has a higher growth rate than the benchmark scenario (1.874). The difference in distribution between the tax and subsidy scenarios can be shown to be statistically significant.[3] Hence, there are long lasting effects of energy shocks in the case of a subsidy policy, but not in the case of a tax reduction policy, leading to a permanent loss in economic value in the long run.

[3]Results of Wilcoxon tests are shown in the Appendix.

Result 7: Deficit/GDP Ratio

The long-run values of the deficit-to-gdp ratio are all around $\mu = -4.5 \pm 1.5$. The long-run volatility in the energy shock scenario is lower than in the benchmark ($\sigma = 1.024$ vs. 1.392), while for the subsidy scenario it is slightly higher (1.743). The tax scenario is in between these two values (1.601). The high long-run volatility the subsidy scenario can be explained by the lower long-run average growth rates, as shown in result 6. The Government finances deteriorate more than in the tax reduction scenario.

3.4 Discussion

A tentative explanation for the long-term memory effect on the growth rates is that there exists a '*permanent loss of time*' effect. The argument can be sketched as follows. The employees' specific skill levels increase when using a new technology. If firms do not invest, the technological progress embodied in newly produced capital goods does not get incorporated into their existing capital stock and workers' specific skills do not get a chance to be augmented (there is no learning-by-doing). This delay in augmenting the specific skills reflects a permanent "loss in time", and has reverbating effects on the entire future development of the economy.

In the case of the subsidy scheme, firms are only indirectly stimulated to invest. Therefore, during the crisis period, firms reduce investments and despite the overshooting and overheating of the economy, this does not compensate for the structural loss in time. It is merely the burning of easy money provided by the government through the subsidy scheme to households, instead of money being used for structural investments in both physical capital and human capital.

Immediately following the crisis there is overinvestment and a corresponding build-up of excess production capacity, but without the employees' specific skill levels to work effectively with the new technology, the higher potential productivity of the physical capital cannot be turned into *effective* productivity due to the complementarity between labour and capital.

In the case of the tax reduction scheme, however, firms receive a more direct stimulus to invest. Hence, they reduce the investments in both physical and human capital less during the crisis and the resulting "loss of time" incurred by the economy is reduced.

A final conclusion of this argument would then be that in order to support long-run growth, policy measures are needed that directly stimulate investments, in both human and physical capital, instead of stimulating consumption and hoping that this will indirectly affect investments through the demand channel.

4 Conclusions

We have studied the out-of-equilibrium dynamic response of an artificial macroeconomy to external disturbances such as an energy crisis. A bubble can occur in the real sector when at the end of the crisis prices decrease drastically leading to overconsumption and overinvestment on the short-term. A stabilization policy can then dampen the magnitude of such fluctuations and reduce the overshooting effect.

We have made a direct comparison between two types of macroeconomic stabilization policies: a consumer subsidy that only affects households, and a tax reduction scheme that affects both households and firms.

The stabilization scenarios are compared to the baseline energy shock-only scenario in terms of the ratios of nominal GDP and total investments. Three main results follow from such a comparison.

First, over the entire length of the simulation, the mean GDP levels in the stabilization scenarios are consistently higher than in the energy shock-only scenario.

Second, during the energy crisis mean investments are higher in the stabilization scenarios than in the shock-only scenario. However, this only holds during the crisis, not before or after it, and means that the stabilization policies have their intended effect to stimulate consumption and investments, either directly or indirectly.

Third, the tax reduction policy yields slightly better results than the consumer subsidy policy with respect to stimulating investments. This can be explained by the observation that the tax reduction policy applies to both personal income and corporate income tax rates, so it affects both consumers and firms. Furthermore, the consumer subsidy only has an indirect stimulating effect on investments through the demand channel, while the tax reduction for firms has a more direct effect on investments.

Furthermore, we are able to distinguish between the short- and long-term effects of the stabilization policies. On the short run, the subsidy scheme aggrevates the upswing immediately following the crisis since the government provides easy money that enters the economy through the consumption of households and then leads to an overheating effect. The tax reduction scheme results in smaller fluctuations than the subsidy regime, with slightly lower variance in the short-run GDP growth rates.

On the long run, the subsidy scenario shows significantly lower average growth rates than the tax reduction scenario, while in the latter the growth rates do not significantly differ from those of the benchmark. Hence, there are long-lasting effects of energy shocks in the case of a subsidy policy but not in the case of a tax reduction policy.

A tentative explanation of this long-memory effect is that by postponing investment decisions during the crisis, firms are essentially foregoing the time to allow their workers to learn on-the-job so that when the crisis is over they are lagging behind in knowledge they could have potentially obtained, resulting in a lower effective productivity.

A final conclusion is that in order to support long-run growth, policy measures are needed that stimulate investments directly, both in human and physical capital, instead of stimulating consumption and hoping that this will indirectly affect the investments through the demand channel.

Acknowledgements This work was carried out in conjunction with the EURACE project (EU IST FP6 STREP grant 035086) which is a consortium lead by S. Cincotti (Università di Genova), H. Dawid (Universitaet Bielefeld), C. Deissenberg (Université de la Méditerranée), K. Erkan (TUBITAK National Research Institute of Electronics and Cryptology), M. Gallegati (Università Politecnica delle Marche), M. Holcombe (University of Sheffield), M. Marchesi (Università di Cagliari), C. Greenough (STFC—Rutherford Appleton Laboratory).

Appendix: Statistical Testing of the Long-Run Effects on GDP Growth Rates

In this appendix we test the hypothesis that the long-run GDP growth rate is lower in the energy shock and subsidy scenarios than in the benchmark scenario. More formally, we need to test the hypothesis that the sample mean of the GDP growth rates in one of the three alternative scenarios (energy shock only, energy shock with subsidy, energy shock with tax reduction) is lower than the sample mean in the benchmark scenario. We also have a fourth hypothesis which is that the mean long-term growth rate in the tax scenario is higher than the mean growth rate in the subsidy scenario.

More formally, we use the Wilcoxon test to test if the sample means of two distributions are equal, with these hypotheses:

H0 $x = y$, or $x - y = 0$,
H1 $x > y$, or $x - y > 0$,

where

x sample mean of long-run growth rates in the benchmark scenario (using observations 100–250).
y sample mean of long-run growth rates in the alternative scenario (using observations 100–250).

Table 6 gives p-values for each pairwise comparison of an alternative scenario to the benchmark scenario.[4] From this table we conclude the following.

Test 1 has a p-value $p = 0.2201$, so we cannot reject the hypothesis that the mean long-run growth rate in the energy shock scenario is equal to the mean long-run growth rate in the benchmark scenario. In test 2 the p-value is $p = 0.06563$, so for any significance level $\alpha > 6.6\%$ we can reject the null, and conclude that the mean growth rate in the subsidy scenario is lower than the mean growth rate in the benchmark scenario. However, for $\alpha = 5\%$ we cannot reject the null. Test 3 has a p-value $p = 0.6347$, so we cannot reject the hypothesis that the mean in the tax scenario is equal to the mean in the benchmark scenario. Test 4 has a p-value $p = 0.03828$, so for any significance level $\alpha > 3.9\%$ we can reject the null, and

[4]For a given significance level α, the null hypothesis is rejected if $p \leq \alpha$, for $p > \alpha$ we do not reject the null.

Table 6 Overview of Wilcoxon test results

Scenario	p-value
Energy shock only	0.2201
Consumer subsidy	0.06563
Tax reduction	0.6347
Tax vs. subsidy	0.03828

conclude that the mean in the tax scenario is higher than the mean in the subsidy scenario.

The overall conclusion is thus that the mean long-run growth rate in the subsidy scenario is significantly lower than in the benchmark and tax reduction scenarios. All other comparisons are not statistically significant at reasonable significance levels.

References

Allen, F., & Michaely, R. (2004). Payout policy. In *Corporate finance: handbook of the economics of finance* (pp. 337–429). Amsterdam: North-Holland.

Brav, A., Graham, J. R., Harvey, C. R., & Michaely, R. (2005). Payout policy in the 21st century. *Journal of Financial Economics*, *77*(3), 483–527.

Dawid, H., Gemkow, S., Harting, P., Kabus, K., Neugart, M., & Wersching, K. (2008). Skills, innovation, and growth: an agent-based policy analysis. *Journal of Economics and Statistics*, *228*, 251–275.

Dawid, H., Gemkow, S., Harting, P., & Neugart, M. (2009). On the effects of skill upgrading in the presence of spatial labor market frictions: an agent-based analysis of spatial policy design. *Journal of Artificial Societies and Social Simulation*, *12*(4), 5. http://jasss.soc.surrey.ac.uk/12/4/5.html.

Deaton, A. (1991). Saving and liquidity constraints. *Econometrica*, *59*, 1221–1248.

Deaton, A. (1992). Household saving in LDCs: credit markets, insurance and welfare. *Scandinavian journal of Economics*, *94*, 253–273.

Deissenberg, C., van der Hoog, S., & Dawid, H. (2008). Eurace: a massively parallel agent-based model of the European economy. *Applied Mathematics and Computation*, *204*, 541–552.

Hillier, F., & Lieberman, G. (1986). *Introduction to operations research*. Oakland: Holden–Day.

Kahneman, D., & Tversky, A. (1979). Prospect theory: an analysis of decision under risk. *Econometrica*, *47*(2), 263–292.

Nagle, T. (1987). *Strategy and tactics of pricing*. New York: Prentice Hall.

Raberto, M., Teglio, A., & Cincotti, S. (2008a). Integrating real and financial markets in an agent-based economic model: an application to monetary policy design. *Computational Economics*, *32*(1), 147–162.

Raberto, M., Teglio, A., & Cincotti, S. (2008b). Prospect theory behavioral assumptions in an artificial financial economy. In K. Schredelseker & F. Hauser (Eds.), *Lecture notes in economics and mathematical systems: Vol. 614. Complexity and artificial markets* (pp. 55–66). Berlin: Springer.

Rotemberg, J., & Woodford, M. (1996). Imperfect competition and the effects of energy price increases on economic activity. *Journal of Money, Credit and Banking*, *28*, 549–577.

van der Hoog, S., Deissenberg, C., & Dawid, H. (2008). Production and finance in EURACE. In K. Schredelseker & F. Hauser (Eds.), *Lecture notes in economics and mathematical systems: Vol. 614. Complexity and artificial markets* (pp. 147–158). Berlin: Springer.

The Impact of Migration on Origin Countries: A Numerical Analysis

Luca Marchiori, Patrice Pieretti, and Benteng Zou

Abstract The focus of this article is on the impact of high-skilled emigration on fertility and human capital of a sending country. The model shows that an increase in the intensity of the brain drain induces parents to provide higher education to a larger number of their children and to rear less low-skilled children. The impact on fertility and on human capital formation, however, remains unclear. This is why we run numerical simulations by calibrating our model to a developing country like the Philippines. Since, within our dynamic framework, parents' decisions depend on the expected earnings of their children, we employ a simulation method that is able to solve models with forward-looking variables. The calibration results show in particular that increased brain drain lowers fertility and boosts long-run human capital formation in the sending country.

1 Introduction

Recent empirical evidence indicates that migration becomes increasingly skill-biased, and that South to North human flows are gaining heightened importance. For example, the immigration rate in high income countries has tripled since 1960 and doubled since 1985 (IOM 2005; Docquier and Marfouk 2006). Remittances are an important by-product of emigration from poor countries. According to the Human Development Report (2009), the volume of officially recorded remittances to developing countries was in 2007 about four times the size of total official development aid.

The impact of skilled emigration on migrants' source countries remains an open question. The early theoretical literature, with foremost Bhagwati and Hamada (1974), perceived brain drain as having a negative impact on the source country's welfare. In recent years, economists took a new look and highlighted a range of positive side-effects of skilled emigration that may outweigh the negative ones (Mountford 1997; Beine et al. 2001; Stark and Wang 2002).

B. Zou (✉)
CREA, Université du Luxembourg, Luxembourg City, Luxembourg
e-mail: benteng.zou@uni.lu

H. Dawid, W. Semmler (eds.), *Computational Methods in Economic Dynamics*, Dynamic Modeling and Econometrics in Economics and Finance 13,
DOI 10.1007/978-3-642-16943-4_9, © Springer-Verlag Berlin Heidelberg 2011

Other benefits to the origin country induced by skills' emigration have been recognized by the recent literature. For example, brain drain may enable the transfer at home of knowledge acquired abroad (Dustmann and Kirchkamp 2002); and, by the creation of migrant networks, human outflows may also help to reduce informational barriers to FDIs and increase the attractiveness of the home country to foreign investors (Kugler and Rapoport 2007).

However, most of this economic literature on the brain drain takes population as a constant and does not analyze fertility decisions.[1] The objective of this article is to examine the implications of brain drain on fertility and human capital in migrants' countries of origin. To do so, we develop an overlapping generations model where parents choose to finance higher education for a certain number of their children. High- and low-skilled children emigrate with a certain probability when they reach adulthood and send remittances to their parents back home. We find that an increase in the intensity of the brain drain stimulates parents to finance higher education for a larger number of their children and to rear less low-skilled children. However, the impact on fertility and on the human capital formation remains unclear. In order to further investigate these issues, we calibrate our model to a developing country, the Philippines. The numerical analysis solves the system by using a method developed by Laffargue (1990) and Boucekkine (1995). This method is based on a Newton-Raphson relaxation algorithm dealing with nonlinear dynamic models with perfect foresight. As shown by Boucekkine (1995), it is no longer necessary to linearize the dynamic system and compute the eigenvalues of the linearized system to characterize the nature of the dynamics of the model. Furthermore, the originality of this method is that it is mathematically robust and that there is no need for a grid search procedure. This methodology is implemented with the Dynare software developed by Juillard (1996). The simulation results show, in particular, that increased brain drain lowers fertility and boosts long-run human capital formation in the sending country.

2 The Economic Model

Following de la Croix and Doepke (2003), we consider an overlapping generation economy where individuals live for three periods: childhood, adulthood and old age. Each individual has one parent, which creates the connection between generations. Individuals have either a low- (superscript l) or a high-educational level (superscript h). Higher education is costly while lower education is offered for free by the society. During their childhood, individuals who attend school do not work whether they obtain higher education or not. Also, agents work only in their adulthood and earn a wage that depends on their educational level. High-skilled adults earn a wage w^h, while low-skilled ones a wage w^l with $w^h > w^l$.

[1]Exceptions are Chen (2006), Mountford and Rapoport (2009) and Beine et al. (2008).

We consider a small open economy where capital is perfectly mobile which implies a fixed international interest factor R^*. Also, both high and low skilled wages are exogenous and constants. Both low- and high-skilled labor in this small open economy can emigrate to an advanced economy and earn a higher salary, w^{*i} ($i = h, l$), which is exogenously given with $w^{*i} > w^i$. Finally, we assume that emigration is not large enough to affect the economy of the destination country.

2.1 Individual Behavior

All decisions are made by the individual during her adulthood. Thus at time t, each adult with educational level i cares about her own old age consumption D^i_{t+1}. It is assumed that individuals consume only when old. Thus there is no arbitrage opportunity for consumption, which is purchased through savings and remittances. The individual also cares about the return from her "education investment," that is, the expected income of her children, V^i_{t+1}, which represents the altruistic component in the utility. Moreover, an adult chooses how many low- (n^i_t) and high-skilled children (m^i_t) she would like to have.

At the beginning of their adulthood, individuals with educational level i can emigrate with a probability of p^i, $i = h, l$ to a more advanced economy. Hence, the expected income of a child with education level $i = h, l$ is

$$\overline{w}^i = (1 - p^i)w^i + p^i w^{*i}, \quad i = h, l. \tag{1}$$

The probability to emigrate p^i is exogenous and will serve as a policy variable in the comparative statics as well as in the numerical example. A rise in p^i can either be associated with a more liberal immigration policy of a destination country such as, for example, a reduction of the entry barriers or with more liberal emigration policies in the origin country such as larger exit quotas.

Rearing one child takes a fraction $\phi \in (0, 1)$ of an adult's time, and high-skilled children induce an additional cost for their education x. Therefore, savings, S^i_{t+1}, result from an adult's labor earnings minus rearing and educational costs of her children, and parents' old age support,

$$S^i_{t+1} = R^*[w^i(1 - \phi(n^i_t + m^i_t) - \theta^i) - xm^i_t]. \tag{2}$$

It is assumed that all children care about their parents and remit a proportion $\theta^i \in (0, 1)$ of their incomes to their parents. Hence, parents' expected transfers, T^i_{t+1}, from her low- and high-skilled children are given by

$$T^i_{t+1} = \theta^h \overline{w}^h m^i_t + \theta^l \overline{w}^l n^i_t. \tag{3}$$

Therefore, lifetime consumption writes as follows:

$$D^i_{t+1} = S^i_{t+1} + T^i_{t+1}. \tag{4}$$

The utility function of an individual who is an adult with education level i at time t is then given by

$$U(D^i_{t+1}, V^i_{t+1}) = \ln(D^i_{t+1}) + \beta \ln(V^i_{t+1}) \tag{5}$$

and

$$V_{t+1}^i = (n^i)^\epsilon \overline{w}^l + (m^i)^\epsilon \overline{w}^h. \tag{6}$$

Apart from the fact that we explicitly introduce heterogeneity among the types of children, the non-linear term in V_{t+1}^i is similar to the idea of Becker and Barro (1988), Barro and Becker (1989), and Doepke (2005), with $\epsilon \in (0, 1)$ playing the role of the elasticity of the utility with respect to each type of children. As mentioned by Barro and Becker (1989), this form of the altruism term means that, for a given expected income per child $\overline{w}^i$, "parental utility $U(\cdot)$ increases but at a diminishing rate with the number of children" (here n^i and m^i).

Thus, combining the above information, each adult is facing the following problem:

$$\max_{n^i, m^i} U^i = \ln(D_{t+1}^i) + \beta \ln(V_{t+1}^i), \quad i = l, h, \tag{7}$$

subject to (4) with parameter $\beta \in (0, 1)$ the weight of the altruism term in the utility.

2.2 Solving the Individual Problem

It is possible to show[2] that the first order condition of maximizing U^i with respect to n_t^i is

$$\frac{R^* \phi w_t^i - \theta^l \overline{w}^l}{D_{t+1}^i} = \frac{\beta \epsilon \overline{w}^l (n_t^i)^{\epsilon - 1}}{V_{t+1}^i}, \tag{8}$$

which states that the net marginal cost of rearing a low-skilled child, $R^* \phi w_t^i - \theta^l \overline{w}^l$ (cost minus expected transfers), in terms of consumption, should equal the marginal utility gain from a low-skilled child's expected income in terms of the future value of total children V_{t+1}^i. If this equality does not hold, rearing children is either too costly (it is then optimal to have no children) or not costly enough (then individuals choose to have more and more children).

Similarly, the first order condition of maximizing U^i with respect to m_t^i yields

$$\frac{R^* (\phi w^i + x) - \theta^h \overline{w}^h}{D_{t+1}^i} = \frac{\beta \epsilon \overline{w}^h (m_t^i)^{\epsilon - 1}}{V_{t+1}^i}, \tag{9}$$

which means that the net marginal cost of educating one child in terms of consumption (left hand side) should be equal to the marginal benefit from educating a child.

The second order conditions of the agents' maximization problem are satisfied. It follows that the solutions from (8) and (9) are optimal for the households.

It is easy to see that in (8) and (9), the right hand sides are positive, implying that the left hand sides are positive too. In the following of this paper, we will assume that the necessary conditions for the existence of interior solutions are granted.

[2]The proofs of the results presented in this section are available on request.

Assumption 1 The following conditions are supposed to hold (for $i = l, h$ and $\forall t$),

$$R^*\phi w^i > \theta^l \overline{w}^l, \qquad R^*(\phi w^i + x) > \theta^h \overline{w}^h.$$

Assumption 1 guarantees that rearing children is expensive; otherwise parents will have as many children as they can. At the same time, educating children is also costly; otherwise all children will get higher education.

Combining these two equations leads to explicit solutions for m and n, which are given in the following proposition.

Proposition 1 *Under Assumption* 1, *we obtain*

$$m_t^i = \frac{\beta\epsilon\overline{w}^h R^* w^i (1-\theta^i)}{(1+\beta\epsilon)[R^*(\phi w^i + x) - \theta^h \overline{w}^h][\overline{w}^l \sigma_{n,m}^i + \overline{w}^h]} \tag{10}$$

and

$$n_t^i = (\sigma_{n,m}^i)^{\frac{1}{\epsilon}} m_t^i \tag{11}$$

where

$$\sigma_{n,m}^i = \left(\frac{B}{A^i}\right)^{\frac{\epsilon}{1-\epsilon}}, \quad \text{with } A^i = \frac{R^*\phi w^i - \theta^l \overline{w}^l}{R^*(\phi w^i + x) - \theta^h \overline{w}^h}, \; B = \frac{\overline{w}^l}{\overline{w}^h}. \tag{12}$$

The parameter A^i represents the ratio of net costs of rearing a low-educated child to a high-educated one (see (8) and (9)) while B is the ratio of the expected income of a low-educated child to a high-educated one. Since ϵ is the elasticity of the utility with respect to each children type, then $\sigma_{n,m}^i$ can be considered as the elasticity of substitution between high and low educated children in each type of household.

3 Numerical Analysis

In this section, we provide a numerical illustration to analyze the effects of a brain drain (skilled emigration) on fertility and human capital of the native country. Higher migration can be due to the fact that destination countries adopt more liberal immigration policies. Since immigration policies tend to be more and more skilled-biased, we focus on the effects of increased high-skilled emigration. Our model is calibrated to the Philippine economy, since this country is experiencing an important brain drain.

In order to run our simulation exercise, we assume that the year 2000 corresponds to a steady state. A migration shock moves the economy away from this initial state to a new long-run equilibrium. We, then, focus on the transitional dynamics. This analysis is conducted under three different variants: (i) one with a higher propensity to remit for low-skilled, which we consider as our benchmark (ii) one with equal remittance propensities between low- and high-skilled emigrants and (iii) finally one without remittances. In what follows, we cast a glance on the simulation method we use before turning to the calibrations.

3.1 Simulation Method

The dynamic model is characterized by a set of non-linear equations of the following form:[3]

$$f(y_{t-1}^A, y_t^A, y_t^B, y_{t+1}^B, z_t) = 0 \tag{13}$$

where y_t^i denotes an endogenous variable at time t. The subscript A stands for a predetermined variable and B for a forward-looking variable. The system also depends on a vector of exogenous variables and parameters denoted by z_t and accounts for leads or lags of one period corresponding to the lifetime of a an individual.[4] We finally assume initial conditions on the predetermined variables, which correspond to an initial steady state (in our case, reproducing the economic conditions of the Philippines in the year 2000) by the following equation

$$y_{-1}^A, y_0^A = y_{\text{initial}}^A.$$

Concerning the terminal conditions, we assume in the baseline that exogenous variables stay constant as in 2000. Thus, the initial and final steady states coincide in the baseline. In our simulation, we analyze the impact of increased skilled emigration, which translates into a permanent increase in one of the exogenous variables contained in vector z. Under such a scenario, the final steady state will obviously differ from the initial one. After this shock, the economy should converge to a new steady state if this latter is a saddle-point and as long as local stability is granted (if the distant between the initial and the final steady states is not too large).

Since f is non-linear, it is not possible to obtain an analytical solution of the model, especially when calibrating large-scale economies. The general problem consists in solving a system of finite difference equations with initial and terminal conditions. The infinite horizon of the model is approximated by a finite one, meaning that the steady state is reached at the end of the simulation limit (T). The complete system has as many equations as the number of equations at each period multiplied by the simulation horizon plus the initial and terminal conditions as the following system shows

$$(\Gamma) = \begin{cases} y_{-1}^A, y_0^A = y_{\text{initial}}^A \\ f(y_{-1}^A, y_1^A, y_1^B, y_2^B, z_t) = 0 \\ \vdots \\ f(y_{T-1}^A, y_T^A, y_T^B, y_{T+1}^B, z_T) = 0 \\ y_T^B, y_{T+1}^B = y_{\text{final}}^B \end{cases}$$

The simulation method solves the system (Γ) for y_t. It builds on a Newton-Raphson relaxation method put forward by Laffargue (1990) and Boucekkine (1995)

---

[3] A more extensive description of the simulation method can be found in de la Croix et al. (2007).

[4] Notice that the model would have a two-period lead or lag structure if the optimization problem was written from a child's perspective.

for solving dynamic nonlinear models with perfect foresight. This routine is implemented with the package Dynare of Juillard (1996).

3.2 Calibration

Our model is calibrated to depict a typical situation of South-North migration and, as such, the parameter of our model are adjusted to match the economy of the Philippines which is the migrants' origin country. This choice seems appropriate since emigration and large inflows of remittances have been notorious characteristics of the Philippine economy for several decades (see the IMF study of Burgess and Haksar 2005). The foreign country in the model is represented by a combination of OECD countries—the relative importance of which is weighted by the share of Filipino emigrants they host (see below). As mentioned above, the initial steady state is assumed to correspond to 2000 data.

3.2.1 Observed Parameters and Exogenous Variables

The values of observed parameters and exogenous variables are reported in Table 1 and chosen as follows. According to Haveman and Wolfe (1995), parents spend around 15% of their time rearing children which enables us to set the rearing cost parameter ϕ to 0.15. We further know that the wage of a high-skilled worker in the Philippines is 2.54 times larger than the one of a low-skilled.[5] Thus, if w^l is set to 1, w^h equals 2.54. Since one period is considered to be 20 years, the interest factor is set to $R^* = 1.806$ which corresponds to an annual interest rate of 3%.

Then, we try to quantify the probabilities to emigrate, p^h and p^l since they are not directly observable. Docquier and Marfouk (2006) indicate that 67% of the Filipinos living in OECD in 2000 are high-skilled, thus, we can set $p^h = 2p^l$. Since one period lasts 20 years, we consider that the number of migrants in the OECD in 2000 reported by the above authors represents the number of emigrants during one period in our model. This means that 1'678'735 Filipinos emigrated within one period.[6] If the number of migrants is written as $p^l N^l + p^h N^h$, then, taking N^l and N^h from Docquier and Marfouk, we obtain $p^l = 0.043094295$ and $p^h = 0.08618859$.

[5]The data is originally collected by the United Nations, *General Industrial Statistics* and corresponds to the skill premium in the manufacturing sector for the year 2000, see also Zhu (2005).

[6]This number is not exaggerated because, when considering also temporary residents (42%) and irregular migrants (21%) together with permanent residents (37%), the number of Filipinos living and working overseas was estimated to be around 7.58 million in 2002 with an increase of 1 million since 1996. This number is equivalent to almost one quarter of the domestic labor force (Burgess and Haksar 2005; Castro 2006).

Table 1 Parameter values for the Philippines

$\phi = 0.15$	$w^l = 1$	$w^h = 2.54$
$p^h = 0.086$	$p^l = 0.043$	$R^* = 1.806$

3.2.2 Unobserved Parameters and Exogenous Variables

For the remaining exogenous variables, no data are available. We start by equalling to 0.5 the parameter ϵ in the "altruistic" argument of the utility function.[7] Remaining variables are set in order to match four main characteristics of the Philippine economy. Let us describe this procedure, which is summarized in Table 2. First, we know from Docquier and Marfouk (2006), who themselves rely on the data of Barro and Lee (2001), that in 2000 the ratio of the low- to high-skilled labor force, $1/h$ $(= N^l/N^h)$, amounts to 3.5045. This value is obtained by fixing the educational costs of a low-skilled child to $x_t^l = 0.413033$ and by the plausible assumption that $x^h = x^l$. Second, annual population growth rate in the Philippines equals 1.98% during the period 1999–2004. If we consider one period to be 20 years, then the population growth rate in our model equals $g = 0.481$, implying that $\beta = 0.664238$. Moreover, we can consider the wage differential between the Philippines and the OECD to be similar to the per capita GDP differential. According to the World Development Indicators (WDI 2007), average per capita GDP between 1999–2004 was \$3'991 in the Philippines and \$34'268 in the OECD (PPP, constant 2000 international \$), thus 7.98 times higher in the OECD.[8] If the average domestic wage is defined as $\widehat{w} = (w^h + w^l/h)/(1 + 1/h)$ and the average foreign wage as $\widehat{w}^* = (w^{*h} + w^{*l}/h^*)/(1 + 1/h^*)$, the average wage difference $\omega = \widehat{w}^*/\widehat{w}$ equals 7.98. Relying on the same sources as for the domestic economy and applying the same weights to the distribution of migrants among OECD countries as for GDP per capita, the average ratio of low- to high-skilled labor force in the OECD, $1/h^*$ was 1.096703272 and the skill premium w^{*h}/w^{*l}, 1.96.[9] Then, to match the aforementioned average wage difference, the variable w^{*h} is required to be 14.3876 and w^{*l} is set equal to $w^{*h}/1.96$. Finally, we need to quantify the propensities to remit (θ^l and θ^h). While high-skilled migrants remit a larger amount than low educated migrants, recent research claims that their propensity to remit is lower than the one of low-skilled migrants, see Faini (2007) and Nimii et al. (2008). In our benchmark model it is assumed that the propensity to remit of the skilled equals 50% of the low-skilled propensity and thus $\theta^h = 0.5\theta^l$. This assumption will be

[7] It can be shown that our findings are qualitatively robust to alternative values of this parameter.

[8] According to Docquier and Marfouk, migrants from the Philippines living in the OECD in 2000 were distributed as follows: United States (69.31%), Canada (11.41%), Australia (4.65%), Japan (4.56%), Italy (2.44%), United Kingdom (2.07%), Germany (0.75%), Korea (0.72%), Spain (0.67%), New Zealand (0.51%), Austria (0.45%), Switzerland (0.43%), Netherlands (0.34%), Greece (0.29%), France (0.28%), Norway (0.25%), Sweden (0.23%), Ireland (0.21%), Denmark (0.15%), Belgium (0.13%), Iceland (0.04%), Mexico (0.04%), Finland (0.037%), Czech Republic (0.0014%), Hungary (0.001%), Slovakia (0.0001%).

[9] The same data source as for the skill premium in the Philippines is used.

Table 2 Calibration of unobserved exogenous variables

$N^l/N^h = 3.50$	$\Leftrightarrow$	$x^l = 0.413033$
$g = 0.481$	$\Leftrightarrow$	$\beta = 0.664238$
$\omega = 7.98$	$\Leftrightarrow$	$w^{*h} = 14.3876$
$\Lambda_t/Y_t = 0.094$	$\Leftrightarrow$	$\theta^l = 0.113158$

subject to robustness checks (see below). Based on Fund staff estimates and on the World Bank, Burgess and Haksar (2005) indicate that remittances in percentage of GDP amount to 9.4%. If we define GDP, Y, by the sum of total labor income and total capital income, then $Y_t = N_t^h w_t^h + N^l w_t^l + (R^* - 1)(N_{t-1}^h s_{t-1}^h + N_{t-1}^l s_{t-1}^l)$, where $s_t^i = [w_t^i 1 - \phi(n_t^i + m_t^i) - \theta^i) - xm_t^i]$. The total amount of remittances corresponding to one period, Λ, equals $\Lambda_t = N_{t-1}^h T_t^h + N_{t-1}^l T_t^l$. Then $\Lambda_t/Y_t = 0.094$ implies that $\theta^l = 0.113158$.[10]

We consider the case where low-skilled migrants have a higher propensity to remit as our benchmark model, labelled "Benchmark". As said above, we also calibrate two alternative specifications of our model, one where high- and low-skilled have the same propensity to remit ("*Variant 1*") and one without remittances ("*Variant 2*"). This implies that in both of these cases the values for the exogenous variables in Table 2 differ from those in the benchmark case. Notice that the case without remittances is extensively studied in Marchiori et al. (2010).

3.3 Results

We analyze the effects of a permanent increase of 10% in emigration flows, which means that more people leave the Philippines at each period with respect to the baseline. For instance, in the first period of the shock, the additional migrants amount to 164 thousand. To analyze the impact of permanent brain drain, we assume that all the additional migrants are high-skilled, which means that p^h rises from 0.086 to 0.109.

Theoretically, increased skilled emigration induces both types of parents to finance higher education for a larger number of children and to rear less low-skilled children. This is also confirmed by our numerical findings. However the impact of a brain drain on the total number of children is theoretically ambiguous.[11] The impact on human capital remains unclear as well. In fact, a brain drain induces a flight-out of high-skilled workers but at the same time stimulates parents to rear more high-skilled children. The purpose of the numerical exercise is to provide a

[10] According to aggregate data on remittances from the International Monetary Fund (IMF 2007), remittances amount to $7876 million in 2003. Moreover a more recent report of the World Bank (2006) indicates that the remittances share of GDP in the Philippines would even amount to 13.5% (see World Bank 2006, p. 90, Fig. 4.1).

[11] In the variant that entails no remittances, it can be theoretically shown that a brain drain reduces the number of children within a family, see Marchiori et al. (2010).

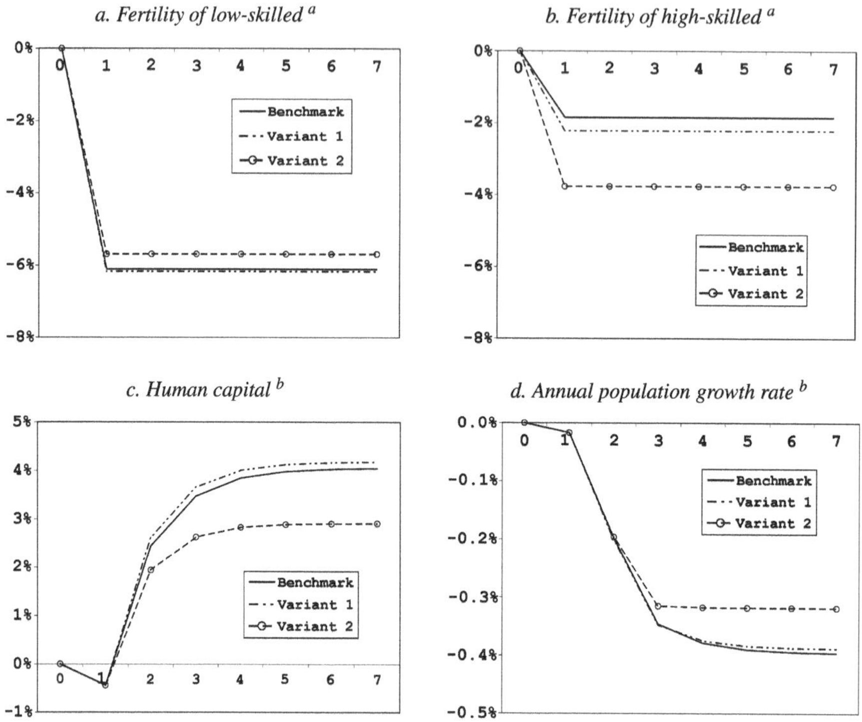

[a] Results are expressed in percentage changes with respect to the baseline.

[b] Percentage points deviations with respect to the baseline.

Benchmark stands for the case where high-skilled have a lower propensity to remit.

Variant 1 represents the case where high- and low-skilled have the same propensity to remit.

Variant 2 excludes remittances.

Fig. 1 Support ratio and labor income tax rate in the baseline

specific answer to the consequences of skilled emigration on fertility and human capital. Figure 1 depicts the effects of a brain drain on the number of children in a low- and high-skilled family, on human capital and on annual population growth under the three-model specifications.

Our findings indicate that both low- and high-skilled families choose to rear less children following a brain drain. The effect of a brain drain on human capital H (defined as the proportion of high educated workers in the total labor force) is negative in the short run when the policy is adopted.[12] The reason is that the shock is not anticipated in period 0 and more high-skilled individuals leave the country in period 1. However, in this first period parents already change their fertility decisions in favor of more high-skilled children. When these additional high-skilled children add to the high-skilled labor force in period 2, they will more than compensate the loss of

[12]Notice that the policy change arises from period 1 onwards.

Table 3 Long-run impact of an increase in p^h (5th period)

Impact on household decisions	Variables	Benchmark	$\gamma^h = \gamma^l$	$\Lambda = 0$
High-skilled children of high-skilled parents	m^h	4.75	5.51	4.02
High-skilled children of low-skilled parents	m^l	9.52	10.07	6.48
Low-skilled children of high-skilled parents	n^h	−11.88	−11.91	−10.27
Low-skilled children of low-skilled parents	n^l	−9.06	−9.32	−8.14
Total children of high-skilled parents	$m^h + n^h$	−1.84	−2.21	−3.76
Total children of low-skilled parents	$m^l + n^l$	−6.10	−6.17	−5.69
Human capital[a]	H	3.98	4.12	2.88
Annual population growth rate[a]	g_{annual}	−0.39	−0.38	−0.32

Note: Values display percentage changes compared to the baseline
[a]Percentage points deviations with respect to the baseline

the departing high-educated workers. A permanent 10% rise in emigration flows, where all additional emigrants are highly educated leads, in the long run (period 5), to a 4 percentage points increase in human capital (the proportion of high-skilled within a generation H rises from 22.20% to 26.18%). Due to diminished fertility choices in terms of the number of children, the annual population growth decreases by 0.4 percentage points and passes from 1.98% to 1.59%.

How to explain the differences across the different variants? First, it should be noted that since the baselines differ across the three specifications; any comparison between them should be taken with caution. Nevertheless, while it can be observed that the results are qualitatively similar across variants, differences in the response of the main variables of interest (human capital and population growth) are apparent. When high-skilled remit in the same propensity as low-skilled (*dashed line*), more remittances are sent back and, thus, the incentives to send more children to get education are higher (see Table 3, column "$\theta^l = \theta^h$"). It results that the impact on human capital is more intense than in the benchmark specification (*solid line*). Furthermore, human capital augments even in the absence of remittances (*line with circles*) because parents are altruistic and prefer having more high-skilled children who are expected to earn a higher wage.

In terms of population growth, the scenario in which both high- and low-skilled remit in the same way has a less reducing impact than in the benchmark case. The reason is that, since high-skilled migrants remit more, the number of high-skilled children is further stimulated and the decrease in population growth is dampened (see Table 3). In the absence of remittances, the purpose to rear high-skilled children to obtain additional remittances vanishes and low-skilled children are then relatively more "valuable" than in the other variants. Consequently, the decline in the number of low-skilled children is less important and the effect on population growth is reduced.

4 Conclusion

In this contribution, we analyze the impact of high- and low-skilled emigration on parents' fertility choices and on human capital formation in the country of origin. For that purpose, we develop an endogenous fertility model with overlapping generations in which parents decide upon the number of children to provide with higher education. This implies that families are composed of low- and high- educated children.

Though our theoretical analysis does not give unambiguous results on the central issues we address, it provides an interesting framework for running numerical simulations. We, therefore, decide to calibrate the model on the Philippines to provide specific quantitative results. More precisely, we analyze the effects of a permanent increase of 10% in emigration flows where all additional migrants are high-skilled. In the long-run we observe increasing formation of human capital (the share of high-skilled individuals rises from 22.20% to 26.18%). Finally, it appears that due to diminished fertility choices, the annual population growth decreases by 0.4 percentage points and passes thus from 1.98% to 1.59%.

References

Barro, R. J., & Becker, G. S. (1989). Fertility choice in a model of economic growth. *Econometrica, 57*(2), 481–501.

Barro, R. J., & Lee, J. W. (2001). International data on educational attainment: updates and implications. *Oxford Economic Papers, 53*(3), 541–563.

Becker, G. S., & Barro, R. J. (1988). A reformulation of the economic theory of fertility. *The Quarterly Journal of Economics, 103*(1), 1–25.

Beine, M., Docquier, F., & Rapoport, H. (2001). Brain drain and economic growth: theory and evidence. *Journal of Development Economics, 64*(1), 275–289.

Beine, M., Docquier, F., & Schiff, M. (2008). *International migration, transfers of norms and home country fertility*. IZA Discussion Papers No. 3912.

Bhagwati, J., & Hamada, K. (1974). The brain drain, international integration of markets for professionals and unemployment: a theoretical analysis. *Journal of Development Economics, 1*(1), 19–42.

Boucekkine, R. (1995). An alternative methodology for solving nonlinear forward-looking models. *Journal of Economic Dynamics and Control, 19*(4), 711–734.

Burgess, R., & Haksar, V. (2005). *Migration and foreign remittances in the Philippines*. IMF Working Paper, 05/111.

Castro, L. V. (2006). Measuring international migration in the Philippines. United Nations Expert Group Meeting on measuring international migration: concepts and methods, December 2006, United Nations, New York.

Chen, H.-J. (2006). International migration and economic growth: a source country perspective. *Journal of Population Economics, 19*(4), 725–748.

de la Croix, D., & Doepke, M. (2003). Inequality and growth: why differential fertility matters. *American Economic Review, 93*(4), 1091–1113.

de la Croix, D., Docquier, F., & Liégeois, P. (2007). Income growth in the 21st century: forecasts with an overlapping generations model. *International Journal of Forecasting, 23*(4), 621–635.

Docquier, F., & Marfouk, A. (2006). International migration by educational attainment (1990–2000)—release 1.1. In C. Ozden & M. Schiff (Eds.), *International migration, remittances and development*. New York: McMillan and Palgrave.

Doepke, M. (2005). Child mortality and fertility decline: does the Barro-Becker model fit the facts? *Journal of Population Economics*, *18*(2), 337–366.
Dustmann, C., & Kirchkamp, O. (2002). The optimal migration duration and activity choice after re-migration. *Journal of Development Economics*, *67*(2), 351–372.
Faini, R. (2007). Remittances and the brain drain: do more skilled migrants remit more? *World Bank Economic Review*, *21*(2).
Haveman, R., & Wolfe, B. (1995). The determinants of children's attainments: a review of methods and findings. *Journal of Economic Literature*, *33*, 1829–1878.
Human Development Report (2009). Overcoming barriers: human mobility and development. United Nations Development Programme (UNDP).
IOM (2005). International migration data and statistics. International Organisation for Migration.
Juillard, M. (1996). *Dynare: a program for the resolution and simulation of dynamic models with forward variables through the use of a relaxation algorithm*. CEPREMAP Working Papers (Couverture Orange), 9602.
Kugler, M., & Rapoport, H. (2007). International labor and capital flows: complements or substitutes? *Economics Letters*, *94*(2), 155–162.
Laffargue, J.-P. (1990). Résolution d'un modèle macroéconomique à anticipations rationnelles. *Annales d'Economie et de Statistique*, *17*, 97–119. (Solution of a macroeconomic model with rational expectations. With English summary.)
Marchiori, L., Pieretti, P., & Zou, B. (2010, in press). Migration and human capital in an endogenous fertility model. *Annales d'Economie et de Statistique*.
Mountford, A. (1997). Can a brain drain be good for growth in the source economy? *Journal of Development Economics*, *53*(2), 287–303.
Mountford, A., & Rapoport, H. (2011, in press). The brain drain and the world distribution of income and population. *Journal of Development Economics*.
Nimii, Y., Ozden, C., & Schiff, M. (2008). *Remittances and the brain drain: skilled migrants do remit less*. Paper presented at the conference "Migration and Development", Lille, June 2008.
Stark, O., & Wang, Y. (2002). Inducing human capital formation: migration as a substitute for subsidies. *Journal of Public Economics*, *86*(1), 29–46.
WDI (2007). *World development indicators online*. Development Data Group, World Bank, Washington, D.C.
World Bank (2006). *Global economic prospects 2006: economic implications of remittances and migration*. World Bank, Washington.
Zhu, S. C. (2005). Can product cycles explain skill upgrading? *Journal of International Economics*, *66*, 131–155.

An Algorithmic Equilibrium Solution for n-Person Dynamic Stackelberg Difference Games with Open-Loop Information Pattern

Philipp Hungerländer and Reinhard Neck

Abstract In this paper, extensions are presented for the open-loop Stackelberg equilibrium solution of n-person discrete-time affine-quadratic dynamic games of prespecified fixed duration to allow for an arbitrary number of followers and the possibility of algorithmic implementation. First we prove a general result about the existence of a Stackelberg equilibrium solution with one leader and arbitrarily many followers in n-person discrete-time deterministic infinite dynamic games of prespecified fixed duration with open-loop information pattern. Then this result is applied to affine-quadratic games. Thereby we get a system of equilibrium equations that can easily be used for an algorithmic solution of the given Stackelberg game.

1 Introduction

The goal of this paper is to present extensions for the open-loop Stackelberg equilibrium solution of n-person discrete-time affine-quadratic dynamic games of prespecified fixed duration and to provide an algorithm for computing such solutions. The results extend the results for one leader and one follower given by Başar and Olsder (1999).

Affine-quadratic dynamic games of prespecified fixed duration belong to one of the few classes of dynamic games that can be solved analytically. That is why they are used in numerical algorithms to approximate general dynamic games. In particular, time-varying linear systems and objective functions can be used to approximate nonlinear time-invariant systems and non-quadratic objective functions, respectively; see e.g., Behrens et al. (2003).

In the Stackelberg equilibrium solution concept, the set of players is divided into a "leader" and one or more "followers", where the "followers" act after the "leaders"

An earlier version of this paper was presented at the 14th Annual SCE Conference on Computing in Econometrics and Finance in Paris, France, June 26–28, 2008. Financial support by the Jubilaeumsfonds der Oesterreichischen Nationalbank (project no. 12166) and by the EU Commission (project no. MRTN-CT-2006-034270 COMISEF) is gratefully acknowledged.

R. Neck (✉)
Department of Economics, Klagenfurt University, Universitaetsstrasse 65-67, 9020 Klagenfurt, Austria
e-mail: reinhard.neck@uni-klu.ac.at

H. Dawid, W. Semmler (eds.), *Computational Methods in Economic Dynamics*, Dynamic Modeling and Econometrics in Economics and Finance 13,
DOI 10.1007/978-3-642-16943-4_10,

at each stage of the game. Under the open-loop information pattern considered here, each player can be imagined to commit himself a priori at the start of the game to all future actions he will take; therefore the strategies of the players depend only on the initial state of the dynamic system.

A frequent objection against the open-loop Stackelberg equilibrium solution consists in the fact that its strategies are not (not even weakly) time consistent. In fact, the famous Kydland and Prescott (1977) result of time inconsistency of optimal policies when private agents have forward-looking expectations is a direct application of the discrete-time analogue of the respective results by Simaan and Cruz (1973a, 1973b); cf. Kydland (1975). If one wants to know how time-consistent outcomes compare to the (possibly "ideal") outcome of an overall optimum without the time consistency constraint, which is based on commitment or reputation of the policy-maker, computation of the open-loop Stackelberg equilibrium solution as a benchmark is required. Therefore, it seems desirable to have a possibility of determining numerically the strategies and the resulting losses under that solution at hand. This may serve to assess the loss occurring due to a lack of credibility on the hand of the government in a numerical model of a dynamic game between the government and the private sector, for instance. The present paper is meant to provide a step towards that aim.

The present paper is structured as follows. In Sect. 2 a general result about the existence of a Stackelberg equilibrium solution with one leader and arbitrarily many followers in n-person discrete-time deterministic infinite dynamic games of prespecified fixed duration with open-loop information pattern is given. Then this result is applied to affine-quadratic games in Sects. 3 and 4. Section 5 provides a sketch of an algorithm and a result for a special case, and Sect. 6 concludes the paper.

2 Open-Loop Stackelberg Equilibrium Conditions for General Dynamic Games

First, we consider general discrete-time dynamic systems of the form

$$x_k = f_{k-1}(x_{k-1}, u_k^1, \ldots, u_k^n), \quad x_0 = x_0, \tag{1}$$

where $N := \{1, \ldots, n\}$ is an index set defining the number of players, $K := \{1, \ldots, T\}$ is an index set denoting the stages of the game, where T is the maximum possible number of moves a player is allowed to make in the game, $x_k \in \mathbf{R}^p$ is the state vector at stage k, and $u_k^i \in U_k^i = \mathbf{R}^{m_i}$ is the control vector of player i at stage k.

Each decision-maker (player) is assumed to have an objective function (a loss function, to be minimized) of the form

$$J^i(u^1, \ldots, u^n) = \sum_{k=1}^{T} g_k^i(x_k, u_k^1, \ldots, u_k^n, x_{k-1}). \tag{2}$$

This situation may describe the interaction between oligopolists in a market for a particular good or, in macroeconomic models, between an economic policy-maker and private-sector agents or between different policy-making institutions (e.g., the European Central Bank and the governments of the Euro Area). For applications of the former type, see Dockner et al. (2000), of the latter type, Holly and Hughes Hallet (1989) or Petit (1990), among others.

The following theorem gives sufficient conditions for the existence of an open-loop Stackelberg equilibrium solution with one leader and arbitrarily many followers and provides equations for state, control, costate and cocontrol vectors to be satisfied on the equilibrium path.

Theorem 1 *For an n-person discrete-time deterministic infinite dynamic game of prespecified fixed duration with open-loop information pattern, let*

- $f_k(x_{k-1}, \cdot, u_k^2, \ldots, u_k^n)$ *be continuously differentiable on* $\mathbf{R}^{m_1}$ *for* $k \in K$,
- $f_k(\cdot, u_k^1, \cdot, \ldots, \cdot)$ *be twice continuously differentiable on* $\mathbf{R}^p \times \mathbf{R}^{m_2} \times \cdots \times \mathbf{R}^{m_n}$ *for* $k \in K$,
- $g_k^1(\cdot, \cdot, \ldots, \cdot, \cdot)$ *be continuously differentiable on* $\mathbf{R}^p \times \mathbf{R}^{m_1} \times \cdots \times \mathbf{R}^{m_n} \times \mathbf{R}^p$ *for* $k \in K$,
- $g_k^i(x_k, \cdot, u_k^2, \ldots, u_k^n, x_{k-1})$ *be continuously differentiable on* $\mathbf{R}^{m_1}$ *for* $k \in K$, $i \in \{2, \ldots, n\}$,
- $g_k^i(\cdot, u_k^1, \cdot, \ldots, \cdot, \cdot)$ *be twice continuously differentiable on* $\mathbf{R}^p \times \mathbf{R}^{m_2} \times \cdots \times \mathbf{R}^{m_n} \times \mathbf{R}^p$ *for* $k \in K$, $i \in \{2, \ldots, n\}$,
- $f_k(\cdot, \cdot, \ldots, \cdot)$ *be convex on* $\mathbf{R}^p \times \mathbf{R}^{m_1} \times \cdots \times \mathbf{R}^{m_n}$ *for* $k \in K$,
- $g_k^i(\cdot, \cdot, \ldots, \cdot, \cdot)$ *be strictly convex on* $\mathbf{R}^p \times \mathbf{R}^{m_1} \times \cdots \times \mathbf{R}^{m_n} \times \mathbf{R}^p$ *for* $k \in K$, $i \in N$,
- *the cost functionals be stage-additive.*

Then the strategies $\{u_k^{i*}, i \in N, k \in K\}$ *provide a unique* open-loop Stackelberg equilibrium solution *with player* **P**1 *as the leader and players* **P**2, ..., **P**n *as followers. Furthermore, the corresponding state trajectory* $\{x_k^*; k \in K\}$, *the m-dimensional cocontrol vectors of the leader* $\{\nu_1^i, \ldots, \nu_{T-1}^i\,; i \in \{2, \ldots, n\}\}$ *and the p-dimensional costate vectors* $\{\lambda_1, \ldots, \lambda_T, \mu_1^i, \ldots, \mu_T^i, p_1^{i*}, \ldots, p_T^{i*}\}$ *(defined for* $i \in \{2, \ldots, n\}$*) exist such that the following relations are satisfied:*

$$x_k^* = f_{k-1}(x_{k-1}^*, u_k^{1*}, \ldots, u_k^{n*}), \quad x_0^* = x_0, \tag{3}$$

$$\nabla_{u_k^1} H_k^1(\lambda_k, \mu_{k-1}^2, \ldots, \mu_{k-1}^n, \nu_{k-1}^2, \ldots, \nu_{k-1}^n, p_k^{2*}, \ldots, p_k^{n*}, u_k^{1*}, \ldots, u_k^{n*}, x_{k-1}^*) = 0, \tag{4}$$

$$\nabla_{u_k^i} H_k^1(\lambda_k, \mu_k^2, \ldots, \mu_{k-1}^2, \ldots, \mu_{k-1}^n, \nu_{k-1}^2, \ldots, \nu_{k-1}^n, p_k^{2*}, \ldots, p_k^{n*}, u_k^{1*}, u_k^{2*}, \ldots, u_k^{n*}, x_{k-1}^*) = 0, \quad i \in \{2, \ldots, n\}, \tag{5}$$

$$\lambda_{k-1}' = \frac{\partial}{\partial x_{k-1}} H_k^1(\lambda_k, \mu_{k-1}^2, \ldots, \mu_{k-1}^n, \nu_{k-1}^2, \ldots, \nu_{k-1}^n, p_k^{2*}, \ldots, p_k^{n*}, u_k^{1*}, \ldots, u_k^{n*}, x_{k-1}^*), \quad \lambda_T^i = 0, \tag{6}$$

$$\mu_k^{i'} = \frac{\partial}{\partial p_k} H_k^1(\lambda_k, \mu_{k-1}^2, \ldots, \mu_{k-1}^n, \nu_{k-1}^2, \ldots, \nu_{k-1}^n, p_k^{2*}, \ldots, p_k^{n*},$$

$$u_k^{1*}, \ldots, u_k^{n*}, x_{k-1}^*), \quad \mu_0^i = 0, i \in \{2, \ldots, n\}, \tag{7}$$

$$\nabla_{u_k^i} H_k^i(p_k^{i*}, u_k^{1*}, \ldots, u_k^{n*}, x_{k-1}^*) = 0, \quad i \in \{2, \ldots, n\}, \tag{8}$$

$$p_{k-1}^{i*} = F_{k-1}^i(x_{k-1}^*, u_k^{1*}, \ldots, u_k^{n*}, p_k^i), \quad p_T^{i*} = 0, i \in \{2, \ldots, n\}, \tag{9}$$

where

$$\begin{aligned} &H_k^1(\lambda_k, \mu_{k-1}^2, \ldots, \mu_{k-1}^n, \nu_{k-1}^2, \ldots, \nu_{k-1}^n, p_k^2, \ldots, p_k^n, u_k^{1*}, \ldots, u_k^{n*}, x_{k-1}^*) \\ &\quad \widehat{=} g_k^1(f_k(x_{k-1}, u_k^1, \ldots, u_k^n), u_k^1, \ldots, u_k^n, x_{k-1}) + \lambda_k' f_k(x_{k-1}, u_k^1, \ldots, u_k^n) \\ &\quad + \sum_{j \in \{2,\ldots,n\}} \mu_{k-1}^{j'} F_{k-1}^j(x_{k-1}, u_k^1, \ldots, u_k^n, p_k^j) \\ &\quad + \sum_{j \in \{2,\ldots,n\}} \nu_{k-1}^{j'}(\nabla_{u_k^j} H_k^j(p_k^j, u_k^{1*}, \ldots, u_k^{n*}, x_{k-1}^*)), \end{aligned} \tag{10}$$

$$\begin{aligned} &F_k^i(x_k, u_{k+1}^1, \ldots, u_{k+1}^n, p_{k+1}^i) \\ &\quad \widehat{=} \frac{\partial}{\partial x_k} f_k(x_k, u_{k+1}^1, \ldots, u_{k+1}^n)' \Bigg[p_{k+1}^i \\ &\quad + \left(\frac{\partial}{\partial x_{k+1}} g_{k+1}^i(x_{k+1}, u_{k+1}^1, \ldots, u_{k+1}^n, x_k) \right)' \Bigg] \\ &\quad + \left[\frac{\partial}{\partial x_k} g_{k+1}^i(x_{k+1}, u_{k+1}^1, \ldots, u_{k+1}^n, x_k) \right]', \quad i \in \{2, \ldots, n\}, \end{aligned} \tag{11}$$

$$\begin{aligned} &H_k^i(p_k^i, u_k^1, \ldots, u_k^n, x_{k-1}) \\ &\quad \widehat{=} g_k^i(f_{k-1}(x_{k-1}, u_k^1, \ldots, u_k^n), u_k^1, \ldots, u_k^n, x_{k-1}) \\ &\quad + p_k^{i'} f_{k-1}(x_{k-1}, u_k^1, \ldots, u_k^n), \quad i \in \{2, \ldots, n\}. \end{aligned} \tag{12}$$

Proof Theorem 1 is a straightforward generalization of Theorem 7.1 in Başar and Olsder (1999, pp. 368–370) using well-known nonlinear programming results. Here we make stronger assumptions on the state and cost functions than their Theorem 7.1 to get a result about the existence of a unique open-loop Stackelberg equilibrium solution. □

3 Equilibrium Conditions for Affine-Quadratic Games

Definition 1 An n-person discrete-time deterministic infinite dynamic game of prespecified fixed duration is of *affine-quadratic* type if

$$f_{k-1}(x_{k-1}, u_k^1, \ldots, u_k^n) = A_k x_{k-1} + \sum_{j \in N} B_k^j u_k^j + s_k, \tag{13}$$

$$\begin{aligned} &g_k^i(x_k, u_k^1, \ldots, u_k^n, x_{k-1}) \\ &= \frac{1}{2}\Big(x_k' Q_k^i x_k + \sum_{j \in N} u_k^{j'} R_k^{ij} u_k^j\Big) + \frac{1}{2}\Big(\tilde{x}_k^{i'} Q_k^i \tilde{x}_k^i + \sum_{j \in N} \tilde{u}_k^{ij'} R_k^{ij} \tilde{u}_k^{ij}\Big) - \tilde{x}_k^{i'} Q_k^i x_k \\ &- \sum_{j \in N} \tilde{u}_k^{ij'} R_k^{ij} u_k^j, \end{aligned} \tag{14}$$

with $N = \{1, \ldots, n\}$, $K = \{1, \ldots, T\}$, $x_k \in \mathbf{R}^p$, and $u_k^i \in U_k^i = \mathbf{R}^{m_i}$. A_k, B_k^i, Q_k^i, R_k^{ij}, $\tilde{u}_k^{ij}$, $\tilde{x}_k^i$ (defined for $k \in K$, $i \in N$, $j \in N$) are fixed sequences of matrices or vectors of appropriate dimensions. Q_k^i and R_k^{ij} are symmetric. An affine-quadratic game is of the *linear-quadratic* type if $s_k \equiv 0$.

The cost function of player i at stage k $[g_k^i(x_k, u_k^1, \ldots, u_k^n, x_{k-1})]$ can also be written in the following way

$$\frac{1}{2}\Big((x_k^{i'} - \tilde{x}_k^{i'}) Q_k^i (x_k^i - \tilde{x}_k^i) + \sum_{j \in N} (u_k^{ij'} - \tilde{u}_k^{ij'}) R_k^{ij} (u_k^{ij} - \tilde{u}_k^{ij})\Big). \tag{15}$$

Therefore $\tilde{x}_k^i$ and $\tilde{u}_k^{ij}$ can be interpreted as desired (target) values of each player for all variables of the game.

It is possible to apply the results of Theorem 1 directly to affine-quadratic dynamic games with one leader and arbitrarily many followers by generalizing Corollary 7.1 in Başar and Olsder (1999, p. 371) for the more general state equation and more general cost functions under consideration and for arbitrarily many followers. As in Başar and Olsder (1999, p. 372), in this case two induction arguments are interwoven: The induction for μ_k^i, $i \in \{2, \ldots, n\}$, the costate vectors of the leader associated with the costate vectors of the followers, runs forward in time from $k = 0$ to $k = T - 1$, and the induction for p_k^i and λ_k, $i \in \{2, \ldots, n\}$, the costate vectors of the followers and the costate vectors of the leader, runs backward in time from $k = T$ to $k = 1$. In the inductive step, the induction hypotheses of the two inductions are used together. But this causes severe problems if we want to use the obtained equilibrium conditions for an algorithmic solution of the game. In this case the evolution of the system of difference equations cannot be decomposed into one subsystem with initial conditions and another one with terminal conditions. Therefore, the two-point boundary problem cannot be solved numerically except for extremely simple special cases; see Hungerländer and Neck (2009) for details.

Hence, another proof is used to solve the dynamic, affine-quadratic Stackelberg game. We show that p_k^i and λ_k ($i \in \{2, \ldots, n\}$) can be determined as linear functions x_k and μ_k^i ($i \in \{2, \ldots, n\}$). This yields equilibrium equations that can easily be used for an algorithm solving that game. So the results of Theorem 1 are applied to affine-quadratic dynamic games with one leader and arbitrarily many ($n-1$) followers. Theorem 2 presents our main result.

Theorem 2 *An n-person affine-quadratic dynamic game admits a* unique open-loop Stackelberg equilibrium solution with one leader and $n-1$ followers *if*

- $Q_k^i \geq 0$, $R_k^{ii} > 0$ *for all* $k \in K$, $i \in N$,
- $(I - B_{k+1}^1 W_{k+1}^x - \sum_{j \in \{2,\ldots,n\}} B_{k+1}^j T_{k+1}^{jx})^{-1}$ *exist for all* $k \in K$,
- (32), (33) *and* (34) *admit unique solutions for* N_k^{ix}, $N_k^{ij\mu}$ *and* n_k^i, *respectively, for all* $k \in K$, $i, j \in \{2, \ldots, n\}$.

If these conditions are satisfied, the unique equilibrium strategies are given by

$$\gamma_{k+1}^{i*}(x_0) = u_{k+1}^{i*} = P_{k+1}^{ix} x_k^* + \sum_{j \in \{2,\ldots,n\}} P_{k+1}^{ij\mu} \mu_k^j + \alpha_{k+1}^i, \tag{16}$$

where the associated state trajectory x_{k+1}^* *is given by*[1]

$$x_{k+1}^* = \Phi_k^x x_k^* + \sum_{j \in \{2,\ldots,n\}} \Phi_k^{j\mu} \mu_k^j + \phi_k, \quad x_0^* = x_0, \tag{17}$$

with

$$\mu_{k+1}^i = \Psi_k^{ix} x_k^* + \sum_{j \in \{2,\ldots,n\}} \Psi_k^{ij\mu} \mu_k^j + \psi_k^i, \quad \mu_0^i = 0, i \in \{2, \ldots, n\}, \tag{18}$$

where

$$\Phi_k^x = \left(I - B_{k+1}^1 W_{k+1}^x - \sum_{j \in \{2,\ldots,n\}} B_{k+1}^j T_{k+1}^{jx} \right)^{-1} A_{k+1}, \tag{19}$$

$$\begin{aligned} \Phi_k^{i\mu} = &\left(I - B_{k+1}^1 W_{k+1}^x - \sum_{j \in \{2,\ldots,n\}} B_{k+1}^j T_{k+1}^{jx} \right)^{-1} \\ &\times \left(B_{k+1}^1 W_{k+1}^{i\mu} + \sum_{j \in \{2,\ldots,n\}} B_{k+1}^j T_{k+1}^{ji\mu} \right), \quad i \in \{2, \ldots, n\}, \end{aligned} \tag{20}$$

$$\phi_k = \left(I - B_{k+1}^1 W_{k+1}^x - \sum_{j \in \{2,\ldots,n\}} B_{k+1}^j T_{k+1}^{jx} \right)^{-1}$$

[1]For all equations belonging to this theorem and its proof, $i \in N$ and $k \in \{0, \ldots, T-1\}$ unless otherwise indicated.

$$\times \left(B^1_{k+1} w_{k+1} + \sum_{j\in\{2,\dots,n\}} B^j_{k+1} t^j_{k+1} + s_{k+1} \right), \tag{21}$$

$$\Psi^{ix}_k = B^i_{k+1} N^{ix}_k \Phi^x_k, \quad i \in \{2,\dots,n\}, \tag{22}$$

$$\Psi^{ii\mu}_k = A_{k+1} + B^i_{k+1}(N^{ix}_k \Phi^{i\mu}_k + N^{ii\mu}_k), \quad i \in \{2,\dots,n\}, \tag{23}$$

$$\Psi^{im\mu}_k = B^i_{k+1}(N^{ix}_k \Phi^{m\mu}_k + N^{im\mu}_k), \quad i,m \in \{2,\dots,n\}, m \neq i, \tag{24}$$

$$\psi^i_k = B^i_{k+1}(N^{ix}_k \phi_k + n^i_k), \quad i \in \{2,\dots,n\}, \tag{25}$$

$$W^x_{k+1} = -(R^{11}_{k+1})^{-1} \left(B^{1'}_{k+1} \left(L^x_{k+1} + \sum_{j\in\{2,\dots,n\}} L^{j\mu}_{k+1} B^j_{k+1} N^{jx}_k \right) + \sum_{j\in\{2,\dots,n\}} B^{1'}_{k+1} Q^j_{k+1} B^j_{k+1} N^{jx}_k \right), \tag{26}$$

$$W^{m\mu}_{k+1} = -(R^{11}_{k+1})^{-1} \left(B^{1'}_{k+1} \left(L^{m\mu}_{k+1} A_{k+1} + \sum_{j\in\{2,\dots,n\}} L^{j\mu}_{k+1} B^j_{k+1} N^{jm\mu}_k \right) + B^{1'}_{k+1} Q^m_{k+1} A_{k+1} + \sum_{j\in\{2,\dots,n\}} B^{1'}_{k+1} Q^j_{k+1} B^j_{k+1} N^{jm\mu}_k \right), \quad m \in \{2,\dots,n\}, \tag{27}$$

$$w_{k+1} = -(R^{11}_{k+1})^{-1} \left(-B^{1'}_{k+1} Q^1_{k+1} \tilde{x}^i_{k+1} + B^{1'}_{k+1} \left(\sum_{j\in\{2,\dots,n\}} L^{j\mu}_{k+1} B^j_{k+1} n^j_k + l_{k+1} \right) + \sum_{j\in\{2,\dots,n\}} B^{1'}_{k+1} Q^j_{k+1} B^j_{k+1} n^j_k \right) + \tilde{u}^{11}_{k+1}, \tag{28}$$

$$T^{ix}_{k+1} = -(R^{ii}_{k+1})^{-1} B^{i'}_{k+1} \left(M^{ix}_{k+1} + \sum_{j\in\{2,\dots,n\}} M^{ij\mu}_{k+1} B^j_{k+1} N^{jx}_k \right), \quad i \in \{2,\dots,n\}, \tag{29}$$

$$T^{im\mu}_{k+1} = -(R^{ii}_{k+1})^{-1} B^{i'}_{k+1} \left(M^{im\mu}_{k+1} A_{k+1} + \sum_{j\in\{2,\dots,n\}} M^{ij\mu}_{k+1} B^j_{k+1} N^{jm\mu}_k \right), \quad i,m \in \{2,\dots,n\}, \tag{30}$$

$$t^i_{k+1} = -(R^{ii}_{k+1})^{-1} B^{i'}_{k+1} \left(\sum_{j\in\{2,\dots,n\}} M^{ij\mu}_{k+1} B^j_{k+1} n^j_k + m^i_{k+1} - Q^i_{k+1} \tilde{x}^{i'}_{k+1} \right) + \tilde{u}^{ii}_{k+1}, \quad i \in \{2,\dots,n\}, \tag{31}$$

$$-R^{1i}_{k+1}(R^{ii}_{k+1})^{-1}B^{i'}_{k+1}M^{ix}_{k+1}+B^{i'}_{k+1}L^{x}_{k+1}+(B^{i'}_{k+1}(Q^{i}_{k+1}+L^{i\mu}_{k+1})B^{i}_{k+1}+R^{ii}_{k+1}$$
$$-R^{1i}_{k+1}(R^{ii}_{k+1})^{-1}B^{i'}_{k+1}M^{ii\mu}_{k+1}B^{i}_{k+1})N^{ix}_{k}$$
$$+\sum_{j\in\{2,\dots,n\},j\neq i}(B^{i'}_{k+1}(Q^{j}_{k+1}+L^{j\mu}_{k+1})B^{j}_{k+1}-R^{1i}_{k+1}(R^{ii}_{k+1})^{-1}B^{i'}_{k+1}M^{ij\mu}_{k+1}B^{j}_{k+1})$$
$$\times N^{jx}_{k}=0,\quad i\in\{2,\dots,n\}, \tag{32}$$

$$-R^{1i}_{k+1}(R^{ii}_{k+1})^{-1}B^{i'}_{k+1}M^{im\mu}_{k+1}A_{k+1}+B^{i'}_{k+1}L^{m\mu}_{k+1}A_{k+1}+B^{i'}_{k+1}Q^{m}_{k+1}A_{k+1}$$
$$+(B^{i'}_{k+1}(Q^{i}_{k+1}+L^{i\mu}_{k+1})B^{i}_{k+1}+R^{ii}_{k+1}-R^{1i}_{k+1}(R^{ii}_{k+1})^{-1}B^{i'}_{k+1}M^{ii\mu}_{k+1}B^{i}_{k+1})N^{im\mu}_{k}$$
$$+\sum_{j\in\{2,\dots,n\},j\neq i}(B^{i'}_{k+1}(Q^{j}_{k+1}+L^{j\mu}_{k+1})B^{j}_{k+1}$$
$$-R^{1i}_{k+1}(R^{ii}_{k+1})^{-1}B^{i'}_{k+1}M^{ij\mu}_{k+1}B^{j}_{k+1})N^{jm\mu}_{k}=0,\quad i,m\in\{2,\dots,n\}, \tag{33}$$

$$-B^{i'}_{k+1}Q^{1}_{k+1}\tilde{x}^{i}_{k+1}+R^{1i}_{k+1}(-(R^{ii}_{k+1})^{-1}B^{i'}_{k+1}(m^{i}_{k+1}-Q^{i}_{k+1}\tilde{x}^{i}_{k+1})+\tilde{u}^{ii}_{k+1}-\tilde{u}^{1i}_{k+1})$$
$$+B^{i'}_{k+1}l_{k+1}+(B^{i'}_{k+1}(Q^{i}_{k+1}+L^{i\mu}_{k+1})B^{i}_{k+1}+R^{ii}_{k+1}$$
$$-R^{1i}_{k+1}(R^{ii}_{k+1})^{-1}B^{i'}_{k+1}M^{ii\mu}_{k+1}B^{i}_{k+1})n^{i}_{k}+\sum_{j\in\{2,\dots,n\},j\neq i}(B^{i'}_{k+1}(Q^{j}_{k+1}+L^{j\mu}_{k+1})B^{j}_{k+1}$$
$$-R^{1i}_{k+1}(R^{ii}_{k+1})^{-1}B^{i'}_{k+1}M^{ij\mu}_{k+1}B^{j}_{k+1})n^{j}_{k}=0,\quad i\in\{2,\dots,n\}, \tag{34}$$

$$M^{ix}_{k}=Q^{i}_{k}+A'_{k+1}\left[M^{ix}_{k+1}\Phi^{x}_{k}+\sum_{j\in\{2,\dots,n\}}M^{ij\mu}_{k+1}\Psi^{jx}_{k}\right],\quad M^{ix}_{T}=Q^{i}_{T},i\in\{2,\dots,n\}, \tag{35}$$

$$M^{im\mu}_{k}=A'_{k+1}\left[M^{ix}_{k+1}\Phi^{m\mu}_{k}+\sum_{j\in\{2,\dots,n\}}M^{ij\mu}_{k+1}\Psi^{jm\mu}_{k}\right],\quad M^{im\mu}_{T}=0,$$
$$i,m\in\{2,\dots,n\}, \tag{36}$$

$$m^{i}_{k}=A'_{k+1}\left[M^{ix}_{k+1}\phi_{k}+\sum_{j\in\{2,\dots,n\}}M^{ij\mu}_{k+1}\psi^{j}_{k}+m^{i}_{k+1}-Q^{i}_{k+1}\tilde{x}^{i}_{k+1}\right],\quad m^{i}_{T}=0,$$
$$i\in\{2,\dots,n\}, \tag{37}$$

$$L^{x}_{k}=Q^{1}_{k}+A'_{k+1}\left[L^{x}_{k+1}\Phi^{x}_{k}+\sum_{j\in\{2,\dots,n\}}L^{j\mu}_{k+1}\Psi^{jx}_{k}+\sum_{j\in\{2,\dots,n\}}Q^{j}_{k+1}B^{j}_{k+1}N^{jx}_{k}\Phi^{x}_{k}\right],$$
$$L^{x}_{T}=Q^{1}_{T}, \tag{38}$$

$$L_k^{i\mu} = A'_{k+1}\Bigg[L_{k+1}^x \Phi_k^{i\mu} + \sum_{j\in\{2,\dots,n\}} L_{k+1}^{j\mu}\Psi_k^{ji\mu} + Q_{k+1}^i A_{k+1} + \sum_{j\in\{2,\dots,n\}} Q_{k+1}^j B_{k+1}^j (N_k^{jx}\Phi_k^{i\mu} + N_k^{ji\mu})\Bigg], \quad L_T^{j\mu} = 0, i \in \{2,\dots,n\}, \tag{39}$$

$$l_k = A'_{k+1}\Bigg[L_{k+1}^x \phi_k + \sum_{j\in\{2,\dots,n\}} L_{k+1}^{j\mu}\psi_k^j + l_{k+1} - Q_{k+1}^1 \tilde{x}_{k+1}^1 + \sum_{j\in\{2,\dots,n\}} Q_{k+1}^j B_{k+1}^j (N_k^{jx}\phi_k + n_k^j)\Bigg], \quad l_T = 0, \tag{40}$$

$$P_{k+1}^{1x} = W_{k+1}^x \Phi_k^x, \tag{41}$$

$$P_{k+1}^{1i\mu} = W_{k+1}^x \Phi_k^{i\mu} + W_{k+1}^{i\mu}, \quad i \in \{2,\dots,n\}, \tag{42}$$

$$\alpha_{k+1}^1 = W_{k+1}^x \phi_k + w_{k+1}, \tag{43}$$

$$P_{k+1}^{ix} = T_{k+1}^{ix}\Phi_k^x, \quad i \in \{2,\dots,n\}, \tag{44}$$

$$P_{k+1}^{im\mu} = T_{k+1}^{ix}\Phi_k^{m\mu} + T_{k+1}^{im\mu}, \quad i, m \in \{2,\dots,n\}, \tag{45}$$

$$\alpha_{k+1}^i = T_{k+1}^{ix}\phi_k + t_{k+1}^i, \quad i \in \{2,\dots,n\}. \tag{46}$$

4 Proof of Theorem 2

Theorem 1 can be directly applied to the given affine-quadratic game because all conditions are satisfied for the state equation (13) and the cost functions (14). Note in particular that g_k^i is strictly convex in u_k^i, since the Hamiltonian of $g_k^i(x_k, u_k^1, \dots, u_k^n, x_{k-1})$ over $u_k^i \in R^{m_i}$ is positive definite due to the assumptions made on Q_k^i and R_k^{ii}:

$$\frac{\partial^2}{\partial u_k^{i2}} g_k^i(x_k, u_k^1, \dots, u_k^n, x_{k-1}) = B_k^{i'} Q_k^i B_k^i + R_k^{ii}. \tag{47}$$

To obtain relations which satisfy this unique solution we apply (3)–(12) to the state equation and cost functions. This yields for the Hamiltonian of the leader

$$H_k^1 = \frac{1}{2}\Big(x_k' Q_k^1 x_k + \sum_{j\in N} u_k^{j'} R_k^{1j} u_k^j\Big) + \frac{1}{2}\Big(\tilde{x}_k^{1'} Q_k^1 \tilde{x}_k^1 + \sum_{j\in N} \tilde{u}_k^{1j'} R_k^{1j}\tilde{u}_k^{1j}\Big) - \tilde{x}_k^{1'} Q_k^1 x_k - \sum_{j\in N} \tilde{u}_k^{1j'} R_k^{1j} u_k^j + \lambda_k'\Big(A_k x_{k-1} + \sum_{j\in N} B_k^j u_k^j + s_k\Big)$$

$$
\begin{aligned}
&+ \sum_{j\in\{2,\ldots,n\}} \mu_{k-1}^{j'} A_k' [p_k^i + Q_k^j (x_k - \tilde{x}_k^j)] \\
&+ \sum_{j\in\{2,\ldots,n\}} \nu_{k-1}^{j'} (B_k^{j'} Q_k^{jx_k} + R_k^{jj} u_k^j - B_k^{j'} Q_k^j \tilde{x}_k^j - R_k^{jj} \tilde{u}_k^{jj} + B_k^{j'} p_k^j) \qquad (48)
\end{aligned}
$$

and for the Hamiltonians of the followers

$$
\begin{aligned}
H_k^i &= \frac{1}{2}\left(x_k' Q_k^i x_k + \sum_{j\in N} u_k^{j'} R_k^{ij} u_k^j \right) \\
&+ \frac{1}{2}\left(\tilde{x}_k^{i'} Q_k^i \tilde{x}_k^i + \sum_{j\in N} \tilde{u}_k^{ij'} R_k^{ij} \tilde{u}_k^{ij} \right) - \tilde{x}_k^{i'} Q_k^i x_k - \sum_{j\in N} \tilde{u}_k^{ij'} R_k^{ij} u_k^j \\
&+ p_k^{i'} \left(A_k x_{k-1} + \sum_{j\in N} B_k^j u_k^j + s_k \right), \quad i \in \{2,\ldots,n\}. \qquad (49)
\end{aligned}
$$

$$
\begin{aligned}
\frac{\partial}{\partial u_k^1} H_k^1 = 0 \quad \Rightarrow \quad & B_k^{1'} Q_k^1 (x_k^* - \tilde{x}_k^i) + R_k^{11} (u_k^{1*} - \tilde{u}_k^{11}) + B_k^{1'} \lambda_k \\
&+ \sum_{j\in\{2,\ldots,n\}} B_k^{1'} Q_k^j A_k \mu_{k-1}^j + \sum_{j\in\{2,\ldots,n\}} B_k^{1'} Q_k^j B_k^j \nu_{k-1}^j = 0, \qquad (50)
\end{aligned}
$$

$$
\begin{aligned}
u_k^{1*} &= -(R_k^{11})^{-1} \Bigg(B_k^{1'} Q_k^1 (x_k^* - \tilde{x}_k^i) + B_k^{1'} \lambda_k \\
&+ \sum_{j\in\{2,\ldots,n\}} B_k^{1'} Q_k^j A_k \mu_{k-1}^j + \sum_{j\in\{2,\ldots,n\}} B_k^{1'} Q_k^j B_k^j \nu_{k-1}^j \Bigg) + \tilde{u}_k^{11}, \qquad (51)
\end{aligned}
$$

$$
\begin{aligned}
\frac{\partial}{\partial u_k^i} H_k^1 = 0 \quad \Rightarrow \quad & B_k^{i'} Q_k^1 (x_k^* - \tilde{x}_k^i) + R_k^{1i} (u_k^{i*} - \tilde{u}_k^{1i}) + B_k^{i'} \lambda_k \\
&+ \sum_{j\in\{2,\ldots,n\}} B_k^{i'} Q_k^j A_k \mu_{k-1}^j + (B_k^{i'} Q_k^i B_k^i + R_k^{ii}) \nu_{k-1}^i \\
&+ \sum_{j\in\{2,\ldots,n\}, j\neq i} B_k^{i'} Q_k^j B_k^j \nu_{k-1}^j = 0, \quad i \in \{2,\ldots,n\}, \qquad (52)
\end{aligned}
$$

$$
\begin{aligned}
\lambda_{k-1} &= A_k' Q_k^1 (x_k^* - \tilde{x}_k^1) + A_k' \lambda_k \\
&+ \sum_{j\in\{2,\ldots,n\}} A_k' Q_k^j A_k \mu_{k-1}^j + \sum_{j\in\{2,\ldots,n\}} A_k' Q_k^j B_k^j \nu_{k-1}^j, \quad \lambda_T = 0, \qquad (53)
\end{aligned}
$$

$$
\mu_k^i = A_k \mu_{k-1}^i + B_k^i \nu_{k-1}^i, \quad \mu_0^i = 0, i \in \{2,\ldots,n\}, \qquad (54)
$$

$$
u_k^{i*} = -(R_k^{ii})^{-1} B_k^{i'} (Q_k^i (x_k^* - \tilde{x}_k^i) + p_k^i) + \tilde{u}_k^{ii}, \quad i \in \{2,\ldots,n\}, \qquad (55)
$$

$$p_{k-1}^{i*} = A_k'[p_k^i + Q_k^i(x_k^* - \tilde{x}_k^i)], \quad p_T^i = 0, i \in \{2, \dots, n\}, \tag{56}$$

$$x_k^* = A_k x_{k-1}^* + \sum_{j \in N} B_k^j u_k^{j*} + s_k, \quad x_0^* = x_0. \tag{57}$$

Now we use these optimality conditions in an induction argument. We will show that (58) and (59) are valid and the recursive relations for M_k^{ix}, $M_k^{ij\mu}$, m_k^i, L_k^x, $L_k^{i\mu}$ and l_k ($i, j \in \{2, \dots, n\}$) as stated in Theorem 2 hold.

$$p_k^i = (M_k^{ix} - Q_k^i)x_k^* + \sum_{j \in \{2,\dots,n\}} M_k^{ij\mu}\mu_k^j + m_k^i, \quad i \in \{2, \dots, n\}, \tag{58}$$

$$\lambda_k = (L_k^x - Q_k^1)x_k^* + \sum_{j \in \{2,\dots n\}} L_k^{j\mu}\mu_k^j + l_k. \tag{59}$$

Induction Basis:

The induction starts at $k = T$. By making use of the general optimality conditions for p_k^i and λ_k at stage T, we get the transversality conditions for M_k^{ix}, $M_k^{ij\mu}$, m_k^i, L_k^x, $L_k^{i\mu}$ and l_k ($i, j \in \{2, \dots, n\}$).

Inductive Step:

As induction hypotheses, the system of (58) and (59) are assumed to hold at stage $l + 2$. Then we have to prove that these equations are fulfilled at stage $l + 1$ and determine the corresponding recursive relations for M_l^{ix}, $M_l^{ij\mu}$, m_l^i, L_l^x, $L_l^{i\mu}$ and l_l ($i, j \in \{2, \dots, n\}$). First the induction hypotheses are used in the optimality conditions for p_k^i (56) and λ_k (53) at stage $l + 1$:

$$p_l^{i*} = A_{l+1}'\left[M_{l+1}^{ix}x_{l+1}^* + \sum_{j \in \{2,\dots,n\}} M_{l+1}^{ij\mu}\mu_{l+1}^j + m_{l+1}^i - Q_{l+1}^i\tilde{x}_{l+1}^i\right],$$

$$i \in \{2, \dots, n\}, \tag{60}$$

$$\lambda_l = A_{l+1}'\left(L_{l+1}^x x_{l+1}^* + \sum_{j \in \{2,\dots,n\}} L_{l+1}^{j\mu}\mu_{l+1}^j + l_{l+1}\right) - A_{l+1}'Q_{l+1}^1\tilde{x}_{l+1}^1$$
$$+ \sum_{j \in \{2,\dots,n\}} A_{l+1}'Q_{l+1}^j A_{l+1}\mu_l^j + \sum_{j \in \{2,\dots,n\}} A_{l+1}'Q_{l+1}^j B_{l+1}^j \nu_l^j. \tag{61}$$

To complete the inductive step, we have to show that the p_l^i and λ_l can be written as affine functions of the variables $(x_l^*, \mu_l^2, \dots, \mu_l^n)$. Therefore, relations between x_{l+1}^* and $(x_l^*, \mu_l^2, \dots, \mu_l^n)$ and between μ_{l+1}^i and $(x_l^*, \mu_l^2, \dots, \mu_l^n)$ ($i \in \{2, \dots, n\}$) that do not depend on the controls of the players nor on costate $(p_{l+1}^i, \lambda_{l+1}^i)$ or cocontrol (ν_l^i) variables have to be derived. To do so, we first substitute for $u_{l+1}^{1*}, \dots, u_{l+1}^{n*}$ in the equation stated below for the evolution of the optimal state vector x^*_{l+1} by terms that are affine in $(x^*_l, x^*_{l+1}, \mu^2_l, \ldots, \mu^n_l)$ and contain only M^{ix}_{l+1}, $M^{ij\mu}_{l+1}$, m^i_{l+1}, L^x_{l+1}, $L^{i\mu}_{l+1}$, l_{l+1} and matrices and vectors given by the description of the game. The optimality condition for u^{i*}_{l+1} $(i \in \{2, \ldots, n\})$ can be rewritten using $(58)_{k=l+1}$ and the optimality conditions for μ^i_{l+1}:

$$u^{i*}_{l+1} = -(R^{ii}_{l+1})^{-1} B^{i'}_{l+1} \Bigg(M^{ix}_{l+1} x^*_{l+1} + \sum_{j \in \{2,\ldots,n\}} M^{ij\mu}_{l+1} (A_{l+1} \mu^j_l + B^j_{l+1} \nu^j_l) + m^i_{l+1} - Q^i_{l+1} \tilde{x}^i_{l+1} \Bigg) + \tilde{u}^{ii}_{l+1}, \quad i \in \{2, \ldots, n\}. \tag{62}$$

Moreover, we have to substitute for the ν^j_l $(j \in \{2, \ldots, n\})$. For that purpose, ν^j_l has to be determined from $(52)_{l+1}$. As a start, u^{i*}_{l+1} is replaced by (62) and λ_{l+1} is substituted from $(59)_{k=l+1}$. Then the μ^i_{l+1} are replaced using $(54)_{k=l+1}$ and the ν^j_l $(j \in \{2, \ldots, n\})$ are collected in one term:

$$\begin{aligned} &-B^{i'}_{l+1} Q^1_{l+1} \tilde{x}^i_{l+1} + R^{1i}_{l+1} \Bigg(-(R^{ii}_{l+1})^{-1} B^{i'}_{l+1} \Bigg(M^{ix}_{l+1} x^*_{l+1} \\ &+ \sum_{j \in \{2,\ldots,n\}} M^{ij\mu}_{l+1} A_{l+1} \mu^j_l + m^i_{l+1} - Q^i_{l+1} \tilde{x}^{i'}_{l+1} \Bigg) + \tilde{u}^{ii}_{l+1} - \tilde{u}^{1i}_{l+1} \Bigg) \\ &+ B^{i'}_{l+1} \Bigg(L^x_{l+1} x^*_{l+1} + \sum_{j \in \{2,\ldots,n\}} L^{j\mu}_{l+1} A_{l+1} \mu^j_l + l_{l+1} \Bigg) \\ &+ \sum_{j \in \{2,\ldots,n\}} B^{i'}_{l+1} Q^j_{l+1} A_{l+1} \mu^j_l + (B^{i'}_{l+1} (Q^i_{l+1} + L^{i\mu}_{l+1}) B^i_{l+1} + R^{ii}_{l+1} \\ &- R^{1i}_{l+1} (R^{ii}_{l+1})^{-1} B^{i'}_{l+1} M^{ii\mu}_{l+1} B^i_{l+1}) \nu^i_l + \sum_{j \in \{2,\ldots,n\}, j \neq i} (B^{i'}_{l+1} (Q^j_{l+1} + L^{j\mu}_{l+1}) B^j_{l+1} \\ &- R^{1i}_{l+1} (R^{ii}_{l+1})^{-1} B^{i'}_{l+1} M^{ij\mu}_{l+1} B^j_{l+1}) \nu^j_l = 0, i \in \{2, \ldots, n\}. \end{aligned} \tag{63}$$

The above equations contain only constant expressions and terms linear in x_{l+1} or μ^j_l $(j \in \{2, \ldots, n\})$. This fact justifies substitutions for the ν^i_l by $N^{ix}_l x^*_{l+1} + \sum_{j \in \{2,\ldots,n\}} N^{ij\mu}_l \mu^j_l + n^i_l$ $(i \in \{2, \ldots, n\})$. Then we get $(32)_{k=l}$, $(33)_{k=l}$ and $(34)_{k=l}$ by comparing coefficients. These systems of equations are assumed to admit unique solutions N^{ix}_l, $N^{im\mu}_l$ and n^i_l $(i, m \in \{2, \ldots, n\})$. Using the above relations for the ν^j_l $(j \in \{2, \ldots, n\})$ in (62), substituting for u^{i*}_{l+1} by $T^{ix}_{l+1} x^*_{l+1} + \sum_{j \in \{2,\ldots,n\}} T^{ij\mu}_{l+1} \mu^j_l + t^i_{l+1}$ $(i \in \{2 \ldots n\})$ and comparing coefficients gives $(29)_{k=l}$, $(30)_{k=l}$ and $(31)_{k=l}$. The optimality condition for u^{1*}_{l+1} can be rewritten with the help of $(59)_{k=l+1}$ and

$(54)_{k=l+1}$:

$$u_{l+1}^{1*} = -(R_{l+1}^{11})^{-1}\Bigg(-B_{l+1}^{1'}Q_{l+1}^{1}\tilde{x}_{l+1}^{i} + B_{l+1}^{1'}\Bigg(L_{l+1}^{x}x_{l+1}^{*} + \sum_{j\in\{2,\dots,n\}} L_{l+1}^{j\mu}(A_{l+1}\mu_l^j + B_{l+1}^j v_l^j) + l_{l+1}\Bigg) + \sum_{j\in\{2,\dots,n\}} B_{l+1}^{1'}Q_{l+1}^{j}A_{l+1}\mu_l^j + \sum_{j\in\{2,\dots,n\}} B_{l+1}^{1'}Q_{l+1}^{j}B_{l+1}^{j}v_l^j\Bigg) + \tilde{u}_{l+1}^{11}. \quad (64)$$

Now the v_l^i $(i \in \{2,\dots,n\})$ can be replaced by $N_l^{ix}x_{l+1}^* + \sum_{j\in\{2,\dots,n\}} N_l^{ij\mu}\mu_l^j + n_l^i$ using the relations derived above. Finally we substitute u_{l+1}^{1*} by $W_{l+1}^{x}x_{l+1}^* + \sum_{j\in\{2,\dots,n\}} W_{l+1}^{j\mu}\mu_l^j + w_{l+1}$ and compare coefficients to get $(26)_{k=l}$, $(27)_{k=l}$ and $(28)_{k=l}$. At this point it is possible to replace the control variables in the optimal state equation at stage $l+1$ by terms affine in $(x_{l+1}^*, \mu_l^2, \dots, \mu_l^n)$:

$$x_{l+1}^* = A_{l+1}x_l^* + B_{l+1}^1\Bigg(W_{l+1}^x x_{l+1}^* + \sum_{j\in\{2,\dots,n\}} W_{l+1}^{j\mu}\mu_l^j + w_{l+1}\Bigg) + \sum_{j\in\{2,\dots,n\}} B_{l+1}^j\Bigg(T_{l+1}^{jx}x_{l+1}^* + \sum_{m\in\{2,\dots,n\}} T_{l+1}^{jm\mu}\mu_l^m + t_{l+1}^j\Bigg) + s_{l+1}. \quad (65)$$

Replacing x_{l+1}^* by $\Phi_l^x x_l^* + \sum_{j\in\{2,\dots,n\}} \Phi_l^{j\mu}\mu_l^j + \phi_l$ and comparing coefficients gives $(19)_{k=l}$, $(20)_{k=l}$ and $(21)_{k=l}$. As a next step, affine relations between $(x_l^*, \mu_{l+1}^i, \mu_l^2, \dots, \mu_l^n)$ $(i \in \{2,\dots,n\})$ are derived. v_l^i is substituted in $(54)_{k=l+1}$:

$$\mu_{l+1}^i = A_{l+1}\mu_l^i + B_{l+1}^i\Bigg(N_l^{ix}x_{l+1}^* + \sum_{j\in\{2,\dots,n\}} N_l^{ij\mu}\mu_l^j + n_l^i\Bigg), \quad i \in \{2,\dots,n\}. \quad (66)$$

Using $(17)_{k=l}$, replacing μ_{l+1}^i by $\Psi_l^{ix}x_l^* + \sum_{j\in\{2,\dots,n\}} \Psi_l^{ij\mu}\mu_l^j + \psi_l^i$ $(i \in \{2,\dots,n\})$ and comparing coefficients yields $(22)_{k=l}$, $(23)_{k=l}$, $(24)_{k=l}$ and $(25)_{k=l}$. Now it is possible to finish the inductive step for p_l^i and λ_l. First, $(17)_{k=l}$ and $(18)_{k=l}$ are used to derive

$$p_l^{i*} = A_{l+1}'\Bigg[M_{l+1}^{ix}\Bigg(\Phi_l^x x_l^* + \sum_{j\in\{2,\dots,n\}} \Phi_l^{j\mu}\mu_l^j + \phi_l\Bigg) + \sum_{j\in\{2,\dots,n\}} M_{l+1}^{ij\mu}\Bigg(\Psi_l^{jx}x_l^* + \sum_{m\in\{2,\dots,n\}} \Psi_l^{jm\mu}\mu_l^m + \psi_l^j\Bigg) + m_{l+1}^i - Q_{l+1}^i\tilde{x}_{l+1}^i\Bigg], \quad i \in \{2,\dots,n\}. \quad (67)$$

Replacing p_l^i by $(M_l^{ix} - Q_l^i)x_l^* + \sum_{j\in\{2,\dots,n\}} M_l^{ij\mu}\mu_l^j + m_l^i$ $(i \in \{2,\dots,n\})$ and comparing coefficients gives $(35)_{k=l}$, $(36)_{k=l}$ and $(37)_{k=l}$. Next, $(17)_{k=l}$, $(18)_{k=l}$

and $v_l^i = N_l^{ix} x_{l+1}^* + \sum_{j\in\{2,\dots,n\}} N_l^{ij\mu} \mu_l^j + n_l^i$ ($i \in \{2,\dots,n\}$) are applied to derive λ_l:

$$\lambda_l = A'_{l+1}\Bigg(L_{l+1}^x\Bigg(\Phi_l^x x_l^* + \sum_{j\in\{2,\dots,n\}} \Phi_l^{j\mu}\mu_l^j + \phi_l\Bigg) + \sum_{j\in\{2,\dots,n\}} L_{l+1}^{j\mu}\Bigg(\Psi_l^{jx} x_l^*$$

$$+ \sum_{m\in\{2,\dots,n\}} \Psi_l^{jm\mu}\mu_l^m + \psi_l^j\Bigg) + l_{l+1}\Bigg) - A'_{l+1} Q_{l+1}^1 \tilde{x}_{l+1}^1$$

$$+ \sum_{j\in\{2,\dots,n\}} A'_{l+1} Q_{l+1}^j A_{l+1}\mu_l^j + \sum_{j\in\{2,\dots,n\}} A'_{l+1} Q_{l+1}^j B_{l+1}^j\Bigg(N_l^{jx}\Bigg(\Phi_l^x x_l^*$$

$$+ \sum_{m\in\{2,\dots,n\}} \Phi_l^{m\mu}\mu_l^m + \phi_l\Bigg) + \sum_{m\in\{2,\dots,n\}} N_l^{jm\mu}\mu_l^m + n_l^j\Bigg). \tag{68}$$

Replacing λ_l by $(L_l^x - Q_l^1)x_l^* + \sum_{j\in\{2,\dots,n\}} L_l^{j\mu}\mu_l^j + l_l$ and comparing coefficients gives $(38)_{k=l}$, $(39)_{k=l}$ and $(40)_{k=l}$. At this point the inductive step and hence the induction argument is completed. But we also transform $u_{l+1}^{1*}, \dots, u_{l+1}^{n*}$ such that their evolution depends affinely on $(x_l^*, \mu_l^2, \dots, \mu_l^n)$ and therefore their algorithmic computation is straightforward. Let us start with u_{l+1}^{1*} by applying $(17)_{k=l}$ to the relation $u_{l+1}^{1*} = W_{l+1}^x x_{l+1}^* + \sum_{j\in\{2,\dots,n\}} W_{l+1}^{j\mu}\mu_l^j + w_{l+1}$. We get:

$$u_{l+1}^{1*} = W_{l+1}^x\Bigg(\Phi_l^x x_l^* + \sum_{j\in\{2,\dots,n\}} \Phi_l^{j\mu}\mu_l^j + \phi_l\Bigg) + \sum_{j\in\{2,\dots,n\}} W_{l+1}^{j\mu}\mu_l^j + w_{l+1}. \tag{69}$$

Replacing u_{l+1}^{1*} by $P_{l+1}^{1x} x_l + \sum_{j\in\{2,\dots,n\}} P_{l+1}^{1j\mu}\mu_l^j + \alpha_{l+1}^1$ and comparing coefficients gives $(41)_{k=l}$, $(42)_{k=l}$ and $(43)_{k=l}$. Finally, $(17)_{k=l}$ is used in the above relations $u_{l+1}^{i*} = T_{l+1}^{ix} x_{l+1}^* + \sum_{j\in\{2,\dots,n\}} T_{l+1}^{ij\mu}\mu_l^j + t_{l+1}^i$ ($i \in \{2,\dots,n\}$) to give

$$u_{l+1}^{i*} = T_{l+1}^{ix}\Bigg(\Phi_l^x x_l^* + \sum_{j\in\{2,\dots,n\}} \Phi_l^{j\mu}\mu_l^j + \phi_l\Bigg)$$

$$+ \sum_{j\in\{2,\dots,n\}} T_{l+1}^{ij\mu}\mu_l^j + t_{l+1}^i, \quad i \in \{2,\dots,n\}. \tag{70}$$

Replacing u_{l+1}^{i*} by $P_{l+1}^{ix} x_l + \sum_{j\in\{2,\dots,n\}} P_{l+1}^{ij\mu}\mu_l^j + \alpha_{l+1}^i$ ($i \in \{2,\dots,n\}$) and comparing coefficients gives $(44)_{k=l}$, $(45)_{k=l}$ and $(46)_{k=l}$. □

5 Some Additional Results

To obtain the open-loop Stackelberg equilibrium solution of the game algorithmically, the following procedure applying the results of Theorem 2 can be carried out ($i, j \in \{2,\dots,n\}$):

1. Determine M_T^{ix}, $M_T^{ij\mu}$, m_T^i from the terminal conditions in (35)–(37).
2. Determine L_T^x, $L_T^{i\mu}$, l_T from the terminal conditions in (38)–(40).
3. For k running backward from $T-1$ to 0, determine alternating:
   a. N_k^{ix}, $N_k^{ij\mu}$ and n_k^i using (32)–(34),
   b. T_{k+1}^{ix}, $T_{k+1}^{ij\mu}$, t_{k+1}^i using (29)–(31),
   c. W_{k+1}^x, $W_{k+1}^{i\mu}$, w_{k+1} using (26)–(28),
   d. Φ_k^x, $\Phi_k^{i\mu}$, ϕ_k using (19)–(21),
   e. Ψ_k^{ix}, $\Psi_k^{ij\mu}$, ψ_k^i using (22)–(25),
   f. M_k^{ix}, $M_k^{ij\mu}$, m_k^i using (35)–(37),
   g. L_k^x, $L_k^{i\mu}$, l_k using (38)–(40).
4. x_0^* (given).
5. For k running forward from 0 to $T-1$, determine:
   a. μ_{k+1}^i from (18),
   b. P_{k+1}^{1x}, $P_{k+1}^{1i\mu}$, α_{k+1}^1 from (41)–(43),
   c. P_{k+1}^{ix}, $P_{k+1}^{ij\mu}$, α_{k+1}^i from (44)–(46),
   d. u_{k+1}^{1*}, u_{k+1}^{i*} from (16),
   e. x_{k+1}^* from (17).
6. Calculate $J^1(x_0, u^1, \ldots, u^n)$, $J^i(x_0, u^1, \ldots, u^n)$ from (2), (14).

Finally we specialize the results of Theorem 2 to a linear-quadratic 2-person game to allow for comparisons with Corollary 7.1 of Başar and Olsder (1999). This shows that the number and length of the equations of the game grow rapidly with the number of followers and the consideration of constant terms.

Corollary 1 *A 2-person linear-quadratic dynamic game admits a* unique open-loop Stackelberg equilibrium solution with one leader and one follower *if*

- $Q_k^i \geq 0$, $R_k^{ii} > 0$ *for* $k \in K$, $i \in N$,
- $(I - B_{k+1}^1 W_{k+1}^x - B_{k+1}^2 T_{k+1}^x)^{-1}$ *and* $(B_{k+1}^{2'}(Q_{k+1}^2 + L_{k+1}^\mu)B_{k+1}^2 + I - R_{k+1}^{12} B_{k+1}^{2'} M_{k+1}^\mu B_{k+1}^2)^{-1}$ *exist for* $k \in K$.

If these conditions are satisfied, the unique open-loop Stackelberg equilibrium strategies u_{k+1}^{i*} *are given by*

$$u_{k+1}^{i*} = P_{k+1}^{ix} x_k^* + P_{k+1}^{i\mu} \mu_k, \quad i \in \{1, 2\}, \tag{71}$$

where the associated state trajectory x_{k+1}^* *is given by*[2]

$$x_{k+1}^* = \Phi_k^x x_k^* + \Phi_k^\mu \mu_k, \quad x_0^* = x_0, \tag{72}$$

where

$$f_{k-1}(x_{k-1}, u_k^1, u_k^2) = A_k x_{k-1} + B_k^1 u_k^1 + B_k^2 u_k^2, \quad k \in K, \tag{73}$$

[2]For all equations belonging to this corollary $k \in \{0, \ldots, T-1\}$ unless otherwise stated.

$$L^i(x_0, u^1, u^2) = \sum_{k=1}^{T} g_k^i(x_k, u_k^1, u_k^2, x_{k-1}), \tag{74}$$

$$g_k^i(x_k, u_k^1, \ldots, u_k^n, x_{k-1}) = \frac{1}{2}(x_k' Q_k^i x_k + u_k^{i'} u_k^i + u_k^{j'} R_k^{ij} u_k^j),$$
$$k \in K, i, j \in \{1, 2\}, i \neq j, \tag{75}$$

$$\Phi_k^x = (I - B_{k+1}^1 W_{k+1}^x - B_{k+1}^2 T_{k+1}^x)^{-1} A_{k+1}, \tag{76}$$

$$\Phi_k^\mu = (I - B_{k+1}^1 W_{k+1}^x - B_{k+1}^2 T_{k+1}^x)^{-1}(B_{k+1}^1 W_{k+1}^\mu + B_{k+1}^2 T_{k+1}^\mu), \tag{77}$$

$$\mu_{k+1} = \Psi_k^x x_k^* + \Psi_k^\mu \mu_k, \quad \mu_0 = 0, \tag{78}$$

$$\Psi_k^x = B_{k+1}^2 N_k^x \Phi_k^x, \tag{79}$$

$$\Psi_k^\mu = A_{k+1} + B_{k+1}^2(N_k^x \Phi_k^\mu + N_k^\mu), \tag{80}$$

$$W_{k+1}^x = -B_{k+1}^{1'} L_{k+1}^x - B_{k+1}^{1'} L_{k+1}^\mu N_k^x - B_{k+1}^{1'} Q_{k+1}^2 B_{k+1}^2 N_k^x, \tag{81}$$

$$W_{k+1}^\mu = -B_{k+1}^{1'} L_{k+1}^\mu (A_{k+1} + B_{k+1}^2 N_k^\mu) - B_{k+1}^{1'} Q_{k+1}^2 A_{k+1}$$
$$- B_{k+1}^{1'} Q_{k+1}^2 B_{k+1}^2 N_k^\mu, \tag{82}$$

$$T_{k+1}^x = -B_{k+1}^{2'}(M_{k+1}^x + M_{k+1}^\mu B_{k+1}^2 N_k^x), \tag{83}$$

$$T_{k+1}^\mu = -B_{k+1}^{2'} M_{k+1}^\mu (A_{k+1} + B_{k+1}^2 N_k^\mu), \tag{84}$$

$$N_k^x = -(B_{k+1}^{2'}(Q_{k+1}^2 + L_{k+1}^\mu) B_{k+1}^2 + I - R_{k+1}^{12} B_{k+1}^{2'} M_{k+1}^\mu B_{k+1}^2)^{-1}$$
$$\times (B_{k+1}^{2'} L_{k+1}^x - R_{k+1}^{12} B_{k+1}^{2'} M_{k+1}^x), \tag{85}$$

$$N_k^\mu = -(B_{k+1}^{2'}(Q_{k+1}^2 + L_{k+1}^\mu) B_{k+1}^2 + I - R_{k+1}^{12} B_{k+1}^{2'} M_{k+1}^\mu B_{k+1}^2)^{-1}$$
$$\times (B_{k+1}^{2'}(Q_{k+1}^2 + L_{k+1}^\mu) - R_{k+1}^{12} B_{k+1}^{2'} M_{k+1}^\mu) A_{k+1}, \tag{86}$$

$$M_k^x = Q_k^2 + A_{k+1}'[M_{k+1}^x \Phi_k^x + M_{k+1}^\mu \Psi_k^x], \quad M_T^x = Q_T^2, \tag{87}$$

$$M_k^\mu = A_{k+1}'[M_{k+1}^x \Phi_k^\mu + M_{k+1}^\mu \Psi_k^\mu], \quad M_T^\mu = 0, \tag{88}$$

$$L_k^x = Q_k^1 + A_{k+1}' L_{k+1}^x \Psi_k^x + A_{k+1}' L_{k+1}^\mu \Psi_k^x + A_{k+1}' Q_{k+1}^2 B_{k+1}^2 N_k^x \Psi_k^x,$$
$$L_T^x = Q_T^1, \tag{89}$$

$$L_k^\mu = A_{k+1}' L_{k+1}^x \Psi_k^\mu + A_{k+1}' L_{k+1}^\mu \Psi_k^\mu + A_{k+1}' Q_{k+1}^2 A_{k+1} \mu_k$$
$$+ A_{k+1}' Q_{k+1}^2 B_{k+1}^2 (N_k^x \Psi_k^\mu + N_k^\mu), \quad L_T^\mu = 0, \tag{90}$$

$$P_{k+1}^{1x} = W_{k+1}^x \Phi_k^x, \tag{91}$$

$$P_{k+1}^{1\mu} = W_{k+1}^x \Phi_k^\mu + W_{k+1}^\mu, \tag{92}$$

$$P_{k+1}^{2x} = T_{k+1}^x \Phi_k^x, \tag{93}$$

$$P_{k+1}^{2\mu} = T_{k+1}^{x}\Phi_k^{\mu} + T_{k+1}^{\mu}. \tag{94}$$

Proof Corollary 1 is proven in the same way as Theorem 2 taking into consideration simplifications resulting from the different number of followers and the modified state equation and cost functions. It can also be obtained directly by specializing Theorem 2 to $n = 2$. □

Note that the assumption about the existence of unique solutions of the systems of equations (32), (33) and (34) in Theorem 2 is equivalent to assuming the existence of $(B_{k+1}^{2'}(Q_{k+1}^{2} + L_{k+1}^{\mu})B_{k+1}^{2} + I - R_{k+1}^{12}B_{k+1}^{2'}M_{k+1}^{\mu}B_{k+1}^{2})^{-1}$ in this special case.

6 Concluding Remarks

We derived an extension for the open-loop Stackelberg equilibrium solution of n-person discrete-time affine-quadratic dynamic games of prespecified fixed duration to an arbitrary number of followers, more general state and cost functions and the possibility of algorithmic implementation. Next steps for future research will consist in extending the numerical algorithm OPTCON (Behrens et al. 2003) to include the open-loop Stackelberg equilibrium solution derived here. Moreover, finding more intuitive conditions for the unique existence of the Stackelberg equilibrium solution in terms of matrices defining the affine-quadratic dynamic game is a task for future research. Some further extensions of our approach suggest themselves; for example, taking into account a scrap value at T can be easily implemented by modifying the terminal conditions for the costate variables of the leader and the followers, or the problem may be modified to a free-endpoint problem. Other extensions will be more involved. For instance, the open-loop information pattern for both players could be replaced by a feedback information pattern for either the leader (Cohen-Michel solution; Cohen and Michel 1988) or the followers, resulting in an asymmetry not only with respect to the roles of the players but also to the information on which they base their decisions. This would imply different solution concepts, as has been shown for the Cohen-Michel solution by Dockner and Neck (2008). Whether such solutions can serve as more "realistic" models of actual strategic dynamics is an open question; in any case, the solution methods used in the present paper can be applied to their open-loop part, too.

References

Başar, T., & Olsder, G. J. (1999). *Dynamic noncooperative game theory* (2nd ed.). Philadelphia: SIAM.

Behrens, D. A., Hager, M., & Neck, R. (2003). OPTGAME 1.0: a numerical algorithm to determine solutions for two-person difference games. In R. Neck (Ed.), *Modelling and control of economic systems 2002* (pp. 47–58). Oxford: Pergamon.

Cohen, D., & Michel, P. (1988). How should control theory be used to calculate a time-consistent government policy? *Review of Economic Studies, 55*, 263–274.

Dockner, E. J., & Neck, R. (2008). Time consistency, subgame perfectness, solution concepts and information patterns in dynamic models of stabilization policies. In R. Neck, C. Richter, P. Mooslechner (Eds.), *Advances in computational economics: Vol. 20. Quantitative economic policy* (pp. 51–101). Berlin: Springer.

Dockner, E. J., Jorgensen, S., Long, N. V., & Sorger, G. (2000). *Differential games in economics and management science*. Cambridge: Cambridge University Press.

Holly, S., & Hughes Hallet, A. (1989). *Optimal control, expectations and uncertainty*. Cambridge: Cambridge University Press.

Hungerländer, P., & Neck, R. (2009). *A generalization of the open-loop Stackelberg equilibrium solution for affine-quadratic dynamic games* (Research Report). Klagenfurt University.

Kydland, F. (1975). Noncooperative and dominant player solutions in discrete dynamic games. *International Economic Review 16*, 321–335.

Kydland, F. E., & Prescott, E. C. (1977). Rules rather than discretion: the inconsistency of optimal plans. *Journal of Political Economy 85*, 473–523.

Petit, M. L. (1990). *Control theory and dynamic games in economic policy analysis*. Cambridge: Cambridge University Press.

Simaan, M., & Cruz, J. B. (1973a). On the Stackelberg strategy in nonzero sum games. *Journal of Optimization Theory and Applications, 11*, 533–555.

Simaan, M., & Cruz, J. B. (1973b). Additional aspects of the Stackelberg strategy in nonzero sum games. *Journal of Optimization Theory and Applications, 11*, 613–626.

Kolibri 360 GmbH
Ferdinand-Jühlke-Straße 7
99095 Erfurt, Deutschland
produktsicherheit@kolibri360.de